Ch[...] Room

KT-476-026

Winchester.

How to Read Church History
Volume 1

WINCHESTER SCHOOL OF MISSION

08321

D44/11

Jean Comby

How to Read Church History

Volume 1

From the beginnings to the fifteenth century

SCM PRESS LTD

Translated by John Bowden and Margaret Lydamore from the French
Pour lire L'Histoire de L'Eglise Tome 1
published 1984 by Les Editions du Cerf,
29 bd Latour-Maubourg, Paris

© Les Editions du Cerf 1984

Translation © John Bowden and Margaret Lydamore 1985

All rights reserved. No part of this publication may be
reproduced, stored in a retrieval system, or transmitted,
in any form or by any means, electronic, mechanical, photocopying,
recording or otherwise, without the prior
permission of the publisher, SCM Press Ltd.

Drawings by Liliane Piorkowski

Maps by Stephen Bowden

Nihil obstat: Anton Cowan
Censor
Imprimatur: Rt Revd Mgr John Crowley, VG
Westminster
2 July 1985

The *Nihil obstat* and *Imprimatur* are a declaration that a book or
pamphlet is considered to be free from doctrinal or moral error. It is
not implied that those who have granted the *Nihil obstat* and
Imprimatur agree with the contents, opinions or statements
expressed.

British Library Cataloguing in Publication Data
Comby, Jean
  How to read church history.
  Vol. 1.
  1. Church history
  I. Title II. Pour lire l'Histoire de
l'eglise. *English*
  270   BR145.2

ISBN 0–334–02050–6

334 02050 6
First published in English 1985
by SCM Press Ltd, 26–30 Tottenham Road, London N1 4BZ

Typeset at The Spartan Press Ltd, Lymington, Hants
and printed in Great Britain by Fletcher & Son Ltd, Norwich

Contents

Ravenna. Mosaic from Sant' Apollinare Nuovo (sixth century):
Peter and Andrew follow Jesus

A Guide to Steer You through Church History

'Jesus Saves'

We have all been struck at one time or another by roadside slogans announcing 'Jesus saves!' or by car stickers proclaiming 'Jesus is alive!' or 'Jesus loves you!' We are always rather intrigued by the striking impact which God and Christ can make on someone's life: *God exists, I've met him* was the title of a work which at one time was quite a best-seller.

The church as the message about Jesus Christ

But how is it that we are able to talk about Jesus today? It is because his name has been handed down to us by the generations which came after him, over twenty centuries. And the handing on has not just been by means of a book which has been written and then printed. It has happened in the community of those who have heard the word of God proclaimed by Jesus which is itself the message of Jesus Christ. Nor do we meet Jesus by sticking rigidly to a creed which was formulated long ago, nor by jumping backwards over twenty centuries. We meet him in the fabric of our daily lives, in the form through which he has been embodied in the everyday living of those who went before us. The happenings and the people, rather than the formulas, have carried on the faith. And that is why these happenings and these people interest us today.

The gospel and civilizations

After twenty centuries, we may perhaps wonder what Jesus we shall uncover. The gospel message was proclaimed for the first time in the reign of the Emperor Tiberius in Palestine in a remote province of the Roman empire. Jesus and his disciples lived, worked and spoke against a background of biblical culture. Yet the message reached all the shores of the Mediterranean and then the whole world. All the time, it has had to be expressed in new languages, new cultures and new philosophies. Those who have received it have been farmers, townsfolk, nomads . . . In adapting to different cultures, has the message remained faithful to what it was in the beginning? Hasn't it been distorted, betrayed, as those 'traditionalists' imply who consider progress to be deviation, and maintain a fidelity to the past which other people call a fixation?

When the message has been expressed over a long period in any particular culture, what is it that the messengers are communicating? The gospel alone, or the message together with its cultural background? This 'Christian civilization' which since the sixteenth century has spread throughout the whole world has sometimes destroyed or pulled apart the ancient cultures of the nations which it has encountered. Sometimes the Christian message has been rejected as rocking the very foundations of a civilization. It is well known that the conquest of America by the Spanish and the preaching of Christianity in the New World coincided with the collapse of the ancient, pre-Columbian civilizations, for example those of the Aztecs and the Incas. The rejection of Christianity by Japan and China has been considered to be deliberate self-defence in the face of a destructive power.

Gospel and institution

The difficulties don't end there. The Christian life is not limited to the inner illumination of individuals. Witness comes first, but it necessarily entails education and the organization of an institution in order to be able to receive newcomers and teach them. Now every institution produces power, and all power is similar. The church which exists to hand on Jesus through his word and his sacraments is always tempted to organize itself like a political and social institution, and to take as its model the society by which it is surrounded. Christians then ask, 'Aren't we a long way from Jesus and his gospel? Shouldn't the church be purified?' In this way, down the centuries, movements are born which attempt to go back to the gospel, which have sometimes resulted in schisms in the church. In the Middle Ages, Waldo of Lyons and Francis of Assisi began by responding to this impulse. In the sixteenth century came the great split marked by the Reformation: Luther rebelled against Rome in the name of the gospel, and many others followed him.

Why study history?

In studying the twenty centuries of the church, we shall try to find answers to all these questions that we ask about the ways in which Jesus has come, right down to our own day.

People used to talk a lot about the 'lessons of history'; now we have come to be suspicious: so many atrocities have been justified in the name of alleged historical rights! History never begins all over again. 'One can never bathe twice in the same river,' said an ancient philosopher. We shall not find in church history a set of rules that we can apply directly. But church history is to some extent the treasure from which the scribe of the kingdom constantly draws out things old and new.

When several people have the same friend in common, each one recognizes something different in him, depending on his or her own character. Similarly, over the centuries Christians have experienced Jesus in different ways. Church history makes us share this experience and enlarges our own, which will always be limited. It helps us to discover the successive contributions of different eras to our own, present-day form of Christian living. Every heritage merits respect, but at the same time we receive it with certain qualifications.

The figures in the margin refer to the relevant boxes

The church, an old woman who regains her youth

Hermas, who is writing in the first part of the second century, is preoccupied with the problems of the church of his day, in particular with penitence. In a series of visions, an angel who takes the form of a young shepherd replies to his questions. That the church appears as an old woman primarily signifies its antiquity in the thought of God, but also the weakness and the sins of Christians who have made it lose its strength and its joy.

An old woman came, clothed in shining garments with a book in her hand. She sat down alone and greeted me, 'Good day, Hermas.' In my grief, and weeping, I said to her, 'Good day, Lady.'

'Who is she?' I asked the young man. 'The church,' he said. I said to him, 'Then why is she so old?' 'Because,' he said, 'she was created the first of all things. That is why she is so old, and for her sake the world was established.'

In the first vision I had seen her, very old and sitting in a chair. In the second vision her face was younger, but her body and hair were old; and she spoke with me standing; she was more joyful than in the first vision. In the third vision she was quite young and extremely beautiful, and only her hair was old; she was exceedingly joyful and sat on a couch.

'In the first vision,' asked the young man, 'why did she appear as old and sitting on a chair? Because your spirit was old and already fading away, and had no power through your weakness and double-mindedness.

In the second vision you saw her standing, and with a more youthful and more cheerful face than before, but with the body and hair of an old woman. The Lord had mercy on you and refreshed your spirit; you put aside your weakness and strength returned to you, and you were strengthened in the faith.

In the third vision you saw her younger, beautiful and joyful, and her appearance was beautiful. Those who have repented will completely regain their youth and be established.'

Shepherd of Hermas,
2.2; 8.1; 18.3f.; 20; 21.

Through history, we shall find out how the gospel judges Christian behaviour in the past and in the present. I can explain how the Inquisition came into being, and at the same time say that such an institution is contrary to the spirit of the gospel, even if I may not know how I would have behaved in the thirteenth century.

Each era of history has expressed the Christian message in its own language. We have to find one for our own time. The ancient languages have become part of our creed. Ought we to try to get rid of them? The situations in which we find ourselves are quite different from those of the past.

There is one question which we continually find ourselves asking: what does it mean to be a Christian? Knowing how Christians lived in the first centuries, in the Middle Ages and in the nineteenth century, can give us a partial answer. In this study we shall appreciate the heritage of the past at its true worth – and we shall sometimes assess ourselves in relationship to it. We shall see that some present-day crises are not new. We shall uncover unsuspected riches, and perhaps our imagination will be stimulated by them.

The content of a church history

Eusebius, Bishop of Caesarea in Palestine (born about 263, died about 340) is regarded as the 'father of church history'. In his *Ecclesiastical History* he has handed on to us a wealth of documents from the first centuries which without him would have been lost. Eusebius tells us his aims in writing his work. Would we have the same expectations of a church history today?

The succession from the holy apostles, together with the times that have elapsed from our Saviour's day down to our own; the important things that are said to have been accomplished in the history of the church; all those who took a prominent place in that history as leaders of the most famous communities; those who in each generation were ambassadors of the divine Word by word of mouth or by writings; the names, number and times of those who through love of innovation fell into the most grievous error, and have proclaimed themselves as introducers of knowledge falsely so called, like ravenous wolves cruelly ravaging the flock of Christ; moreover the disasters which befell the whole Jewish nation immediately after their plot against our Saviour; the nature, character and time of the wars waged by the heathens against the divine word; the great men who, when circumstances demanded, endured death and torture in the conflict on its behalf; the martyrdoms that have taken place in our own day, too, and the gracious and kindly aid of our Saviour to us all: these are the things I have undertaken to put down in writing.

I shall not begin other than with the beginning of the incarnation of our Saviour and Lord Jesus, the Christ of God.

However, the subject calls for lenience from the well disposed, and I confess that it is beyond my power to fulfil my promise completely and perfectly. I am in fact the first to attempt this work, to advance so to speak along a lonely and untrodden road.

Eusebius of Caesarea,
Church History I,i, ch. 1.

Reading and Work Plan

In this book, we are going to travel quickly through fifteen centuries of church history. Here, to start with, is the main outline of our trip through history and the plan we shall follow.

Church history is the history of people

We cannot separate church history from the general history of mankind. We must therefore describe the world in which Christians have lived, and remember the political, social and economic forces which influenced the life of the church. However, this short book does not set out to be a general history. Your own recollections of history learnt at primary and secondary school will be a great help, as will be your recollections of geography. It is a good thing to visualize the history you learned, the stages in the expansion of Christianity, to picture where towns, provinces, empires were, to work out distances in times when methods of transport were slow and dangerous. There are some maps in the book, but you should certainly consult an atlas as well.

Traces of the past

History makes the past come alive through the traces it has left us. As far as the history of religion is concerned, these can be buildings, churches, works of art, statues, frescoes. Archaeological excavations constantly have fresh surprises in store for us. We shall make use of these buildings, many of which our travels may have made us familiar with. There are countless illustrated books on art, buildings and religious sites.

Written evidence

But, however important archaeology and art may be, the historian's foremost tools are still the written sources, the texts. In the first two books in this series, you were invited to refer to the Bible, which contains all the texts of the Old and New Testaments. For church history, however, it is not a matter of consulting a single volume of historical texts, however large, even though there are a number of anthologies available. There just isn't time to look up a mass of writings. That is why this book gives just as important a place to the historical texts as it does to the narration of the events. It is not possible to include all the texts which throw light on a particular incident. One can only make a limited choice, and another guide might make a different one.

How to read and study a text

Look back at *How to Read the Old Testament*, pp. 11–15, since a biblical text is a historical text.

Here is a reminder of some of the basic rules. They do not give you a complete discussion of historical method, nor a rigid plan which has to be followed point by point with each text suggested here.

A part of the whole

A letter or an inscription may be a coherent whole. However, more generally, the text presented here will be an extract from a rather longer work. It does not necessarily give the true flavour of the whole content. The reference will make it possible for you to look up the complete work, and see what goes before and what follows. Don't hurl yourself frantically at quantities of text but, if the occasion demands, don't hesitate to stretch your curiosity a bit further.

Understanding

On a first reading, do your best to understand all the words of a text. Note the people involved and the places described. Of course on special points, written notes will make for accuracy.

Translation

An old saying has it that 'translators are traitors'; inevitably they cannot reproduce all the meaning of the original text. Very often, the texts you read will be in translation. You already know that several translations of the Bible exist, and that on some finer points there can be significant differences between one translator and another. As far as history is concerned, too, the words a translator chooses can be very important. For example, in the New Testament, the Greek words *episcopos* and *presbyteros* are usually either transliterated, or translated 'overseer' and 'presbyter'. In third-century works they are translated 'bishop' and 'priest', because what they denote would be to all intents and purposes what we mean today by those words. But when it comes to the second century, translators are hesitant, because while these ministries had evolved since the New Testament, they were not yet fixed in their later form.

Literary genres

It is important to give due consideration to the literary genre of a document. That enables us to understand properly any information it has to give us. A police report is not the same as a sermon, and a private letter is not the same as a legal document.

Incidental information

A text does not only give us the information which its author explicitly intends to pass on. Indirectly, it can give us other information which is even more valuable and more certain. In writing to Trajan, Pliny was primarily concerned with maintaining law and order and keeping in the Emperor's good books. But in doing this, he has given us the earliest information we have on the Christian communities in northern Asia Minor.

Where does the truth lie?

When faced with any kind of text, we ought to ask ourselves the questions: 'Is the author telling us the truth? Is he mistaken? Is he trying to mislead us?' It is obvious that in most cases we won't be able to answer with a straightforward yes or no. There are many factors to consider. We get our information about past happenings from historians who were not witnesses to them. How do they make use of sources which have now vanished? The persecutors of the Christians used to blacken their enemies' reputations. In self-defence, Christians would paint an idyllic picture of their own communities. Someone writing an autobiography reinterprets his own past. He is selective. He tries to justify himself. A historian does his best to sort out which of the evidence seems to him to be reliable.

Confronting the evidence

To obtain a balanced view of an important event, we find ourselves reading several papers with different political slants. We try to work out our own opinion. We do the same thing in respect of history when we are faced with different pieces of evidence. But it often happens, particularly for the earlier periods of history, that we have only one source of information on a particular occurrence. It is up to the historian whether or not he trusts this one source. That is why we are uncertain about some aspects of the early centuries: there are a lot of gaps in our documentation. Historians put forward hypotheses, produce harmonizations and make deductions. They sometimes set their imaginations to work overtime. Often they ought to admit their ignorance. Given all this, it is hardly surprising that we find quite different accounts produced from the same documents, so that it is always worth while reading different studies of the same period.

In reading this small book, you are not being asked to start critical work from scratch on the texts included here. This has already been done for you. But it is important to know what lies behind the historian's work, and just how tentative it sometimes is.

Letting our surroundings be changed

In the end of the day, though, things aren't quite as complicated as they seem to be. The important thing is to allow ourselves to be transported back into the past and its experience. We must not interpret the past by our own standards. We ought to know how to be surprised and how to wonder, and should not expect everything to be of immediate use. In due course, though, we shall certainly be asking how the events of the past still concern us today.

How to use this book

The book is in ten chapters of equal length. Each one consists partly of a continuous narrative describing events, institutions, etc., and partly of the documents which are the source of that particular story. These documents take the form of maps, charts, and above all texts on the period in question. The texts appear in a different type face, within numbered boxes.

The numbers in the margins beside the continuous narrative refer to the corresponding text documents in boxes.

→ This sign in front of particular paragraphs refers to New Testament passages or to other chapters of the book.

I have already outlined some aspects of historical method. It is important to go from the narrative to the document and back again, because they explain each other.

You can use the book by yourself, but it is just as suitable for group work. Given the limitations of its size, some people may feel that some periods have been passed over too quickly. So you will find below a list of books for further reading which the individual reader or the group leader might like to consult.

Working tools

Bibliographies generally have a way of discouraging readers: people think that they will never be able to read all that! But there is no need to read everything . . . It is just a matter of knowing where to find the information you want, by using the index if there is one.

The list which follows is only a short one, containing general works which throw light on the content of this book as a whole. Others will be mentioned at the end of each chapter. The books listed are not necessarily the most scholarly: they are the ones which are most likely to be found in a medium-sized library, or even in a bookshop.

For further reading

The books listed here only cover the period up to the Reformation. Some of the multi-volume series continue up to modern times; details of volumes on post-Reformation history will appear in *How to Read Church History*, Volume 2.

1. Multi-volume series

The Pelican History of the Church, Penguin Books
H. Chadwick, *The Early Church*, 1964
R. W. Southern, *Western Society and the Church in the Middle Ages*, 1970

The Christian Centuries, Darton, Longman and Todd and Paulist Press
1. Jean Daniélou and Henri Marrou, *The First Six Hundred Years*, 1964
David Knowles and Dimitri Obolevsky, *The Middle Ages*, 1969

A Handbook of Church History, ed. Hubert Jedin and John Dolan, Herder and Herder and Burns and Oates

1. *From the Apostolic Community to Constantine*, 1965
3. *The Church in the Ages of Feudalism*, 1969
4. *From the High Middle Ages to the Eve of the Reformation*, 1970
   (There is no volume 3)

2. Some important single-volume histories

K. Aland, *A History of Christianity*, Volume 1, *From the Beginnings to the Reformation*, Fortress Press 1985

W. H. C. Frend, *The Rise of Christianity*, Fortress Press and Darton, Longman and Todd 1984

J. Derek Holmes and Bernard W. Bickers, *A Short History of the Catholic Church*, Burns and Oates 1983

Paul Johnson, *A History of Christianity*, Penguin Books 1984

3. Histories of the Church in England

David L. Edwards, *Christian England*, Volume 1, *Its Story to the Reformation*, Fount Books 1982

J. R. H. Moorman, *A History of the Church in England*, A. & C. Black, third edition 1973

Translations of the most important doctrinal works of the church can be found in the following:

The Ante-Nicene Fathers
Nicene and Post-Nicene Fathers of the Christian Church, First and Second Series
These translations, made at the end of the last century, have recently been reissued by Eerdmans

Library of Christian Classics
A series of twenty-four volumes, published by SCM Press and Westminster Press in the 1960s

Some important Christian works from this period are also available as Penguin Classics.

The standard selected collections of historical and doctrinal documents are:

H. Bettenson, *Documents of the Christian Church*, Oxford University Press, second edition 1963

T. H. Bindley and F. W. Green, *The Oecumenical Documents of the Faith*, Methuen 1950

J. Stevenson, *Creeds, Councils and Controversies. Documents Illustrating the History of the Church, 337–461*, SPCK 1966

J. Stevenson, *A New Eusebius*, SPCK 1957

For further information about all the questions in this book the indispensable guide is F. L. Cross and E. A. Livingstone (eds.), *The Oxford Dictionary of the Christian Church*, Oxford University Press, second edition 1974

Geographical information and pictures relating to the early period are contained in F. van der Meer and Christine Mohrmann, *Atlas of the Early Christian World*, Nelson 1959

1

The Birth of the Church

Anastasis (Resurrection). St Saviour of Korah, Constantinople

I · The Apostolic Age

The church began in or around the year AD 30, in Jerusalem on the day of Pentecost. Twelve men announced the Good News to their countrymen. Jesus, who had been sent by God and crucified as a criminal, was alive. God had raised him up. He was the Saviour, the Messiah, awaited down the generations among the people of the Bible.

So church history begins with the events recounted in the New Testament; in the Acts of the Apostles, the letters of Paul, Revelation . . . The New Testament is accorded a privileged position, because it forms the title deeds of the church. However, as we are often told that revelation ceased with the death of the last apostle, we run the risk of making a radical division between the content of the scriptures and what happened later. One eternal, definitive and universal Word gave place to a changing history. Certainly the experience of the Twelve is unique: they are the witnesses to the life and

resurrection of Christ. But we ought also to consider the books of the New Testament as historical documents. At the beginning of the reading of the gospel during the liturgy we used to say, 'In those days'. That was a reference to a privileged time, but there was no break between it and what came next. This was also the period of the church to which we belong now: we are living in the twentieth century of this church.

You have doubtless already studied the New Testament, especially the Acts of the Apostles, so we only need to trace in broad outline the chronological and geographical stages of the church's development in the first century. The New Testament writings are our basic source, but traditions have been handed on to us in other ways. Eusebius of Caesarea collected some of them together. Then there are the writings which are attributed to an apostle or one of those around Jesus and which the Christian community did not recognize as inspired scripture. These are the apocryphal writings (etymologically, the word signifies a mysterious text, in the sense that its meaning was hidden, but eventually it came to imply an inauthentic text). These writings are often reminiscent of novels. They aim to satisfy our curiosity where scripture has nothing to tell us: about the family and childhood of Jesus, the lives of those apostles who are not covered by Acts, and so on. It is possible that some of these writings have elements of historical truth. In any case, they tell us a great deal about the religious mentality of the communities in which they originated. Many of them exercised a considerable influence on piety, worship, art and folklore.

1. Jesus' death and resurrection announced to the Jews

→ Acts 2–4

In about the year AD 30, in Jerusalem on the day of Pentecost, Peter made a proclamation to the Jewish pilgrims who were gathered together for the festival:

Jesus of Nazareth, a man attested to you by God with mighty works and wonders and signs which God did through him in your midst . . . this Jesus you crucified and killed by the hands of lawless men. But God raised him up . . . and of that we are all witnesses. Being therefore exalted at the right hand of God, and having received from the Father the promise of the Holy Spirit, he has poured out this which you see and hear . . . God has made him both Lord and Christ (Acts 2.22f.)

Those who heard him asked what they had to do:

Repent and be baptized every one of you in the name of Jesus Christ for the forgiveness of your sins; and you shall receive the gift of the Holy Spirit.

Three thousand were baptized. The church was born.

Like Jesus himself, these first church members were Jews. They spoke Aramaic, the Semitic language which was most widespread in the Near East. They went on living the life of pious Jews: they prayed at the temple, they observed the dietary prohibitions, they practised circumcision. In short, they seemed to be one new sect within Judaism among many others, Pharisees, Sadducees, Zealots, etc. They were the 'Nazareans'. Their distinguishing feature was their baptism in the name of Jesus, their diligent regard for the apostles' teaching, the breaking of bread (the eucharist) and their policy of having all things in common (Acts 2.31–37: 4.32–35).

2. The first expansion, the first break. The gospel message is not tied to Jerusalem

→ Acts 6–9

Soon Jews with an Aramaic background were joined in the community by others from a Greek background, Hellenists. Quarrels developed between the two cultural groups. So just as the Twelve were appointed to look after the 'Hebrew' community, seven men were designated to take responsibility for the Hellenists (Acts 6). Thus the community of believers was extended to include the Diaspora Jews, that is to say, those who lived outside the limits of Palestine.

Stephen, the chief of the Seven, launched an indictment against the Judaism of Jerusalem. He condemned the temple and its worship, since Jesus had been betrayed and killed by the Jews of Jerusalem. Jesus had spoken of worship in spirit and in truth which did not depend on a building. Stephen did not yet preach to the Gentiles; he did not all of a sudden propose a universal religion, but he did at least give a new direction to the community. For him, the gospel was a purified form of Judaism. Stephen's preaching caused him to be stoned as a blasphemer. He was the first to follow Jesus in his passion and death (Acts 7).

The persecuted Hellenists had to flee from Jerusalem to Samaria, the Mediterranean coast and Antioch (Acts 8; 11; 19). They became missionaries among the Jews who lived in these areas. Saul (Paul), who had been present at the stoning of Stephen, proved to be the fiercest persecutor of Jesus' disciples (Acts 8.20), but on the Damascus road he himself was taken hold of by Jesus (Acts 9) and soon went on to become the foremost proponent of the gospel.

3. The second expansion, the second disagreement. You need not be a Jew to be Jesus' disciple

→ Acts 10;11

A vision made Peter understand that the gospel was for all people. He saw the Holy Spirit come upon the centurion Cornelius, who was not a Jew. He welcomed him into the church through baptism, and agreed in principle that it was not necessary to become a Jew before embracing the faith.

→ Acts 13;14

In Antioch, where many of the Hellenists had taken refuge, the disciples of Christ were given the name of Christians. This was the title which from then on would be used to distinguish them from other religious groups. Antioch became the starting point for the evangelization of the Roman empire. In the course of his first missionary journey Paul, accompanied by Barnabas, first of all spoke to the Jews in the synagogues and then to the Gentiles, without imposing Jewish practices on them.

→ Acts 15

The community in Jerusalem thought it necessary to impose circumcision on new converts. In Antioch there were two communities: the Jewish Christians, who went on observing the laws of Judaism, and those who were Gentiles. Christians from different backgrounds faced a problem in eating meals together, because of the Jewish dietary prohibitions: a ban on pork, on blood, and on certain methods of preparing food, etc.

St Paul.
Amiens cathedral
(thirteenth century)

 Through the apocryphal Acts

A portrait of Paul (not guaranteed)

Onesiphorus followed the royal road which leads to Lystra and ceaselessly tried to discover Paul, studying the faces of the passers-by, according to the description which Titus had given him. And he saw Paul coming. He was a short man, with a bald head, bandy legged and sturdy; his eyebrows met in the middle and he had a slightly hooked nose. He was full of charm, for sometimes he had the appearance of a man and sometimes he had the face of an angel. When he saw Onesiphorus, Paul smiled; and Onesiphorus said, 'Hail, servant of the blessed God'; and he said, 'Grace be on you and on your house.'

Acts of Paul II–IV.

Were they able to celebrate the eucharist together, as was usually done at the end of a meal? Peter was evasive about this. In principle, he welcomed Gentiles into the church without reservations, but at the same time he was afraid of the people in Jerusalem. He no longer dared to eat with Gentile Christians (Gal. 2). This tension was resolved by a compromise which is often called the 'Council' of Jerusalem: on one side was James, the head of the community in Jerusalem, and on the other were Paul and Barnabas, who had returned there from their missionary journey. Peter acted as arbitrator in the middle. Paul's position was accepted: Jewish regulations were no longer to be enforced. However, James succeeded in imposing certain restrictions on Gentile Christians when they were in company with Jewish Christians: they had to abstain from eating blood . . . (Acts 15.29).

Thus the Christian faith was no longer tied to Judaism. No one had to be uprooted from their own culture to receive the gospel. The church became truly universal. Undoubtedly the two main parties, those of Paul and James, continued to exist in the church. A struggle for ascendancy went on, but Paul did his best to uphold unity among the groups by making a collection throughout the empire for the Christians in Jerusalem, who were in difficult circumstances (I Cor. 16.1–3; II Cor. 8;9; Rom. 15.26–28; Gal. 2.10; Acts 24.17).

4. The church expands with Paul

→ Acts 16–18

During his second journey across Asia Minor, at Troas Paul had a vision: 'A Macedonian stood

Rome. Via Appia

(4) **The dispersion of the apostles across the world**

It is said that this Mark travelled to Egypt and was the first to preach there the Gospel which he had written, and that he was the first to found churches in Alexandria itself.

Eusebius, *Church History* II, 16, 1

The holy apostles and disciples of our saviour were dispersed throughout the inhabited world. Thomas, according to tradition, was assigned the country of the Parthians (Matthew obtained Ethiopia, Bartholomew upper India), Andrew Scythia, John Asia where he lived: he died at Ephesus. Peter seems to have preached to the Jews of the Dispersion in Pontus, Galatia, Bithynia, Cappadocia and Asia; finally having come to Rome also, he was crucified head downwards, having himself asked that he might suffer in this way. What need we say of Paul who, from Jerusalem to Illyricum, fully proclaimed the gospel of Christ and finally bore witness at Rome under Nero? These are the express words which Origen uses in the third volume of his Commentaries on Genesis.

Eusebius, *Church History* III, 1.

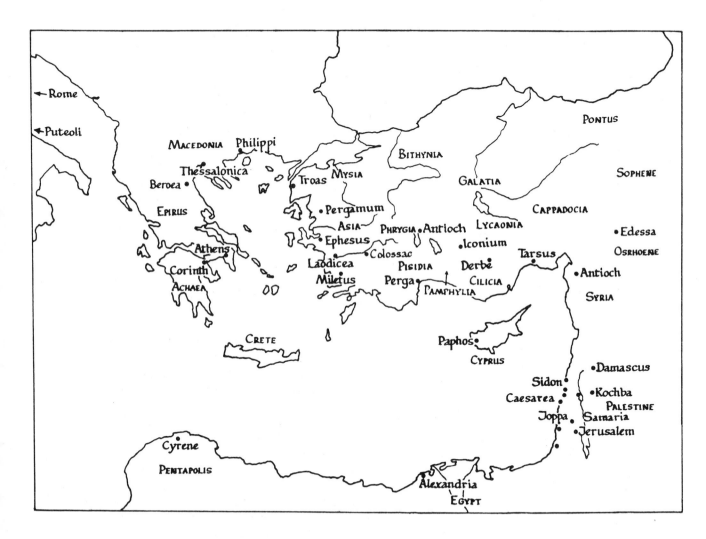

The Earliest Christian Communities

among the main ones mentioned in the documents from the first century

there appealing to him and saying, "Come across to Macedonia and help us'" (Acts 16.9). It was a major breakthrough. The gospel spread to Europe in about AD 50. Communities came into being at Philippi, Thessalonica, Corinth. Paul even found himself in the cultural centre, Athens. He tried to point out the parallels between Greek philosophy and the gospel. He even quoted a poet, but all in vain. 'We will listen to you another time' (Acts 17.16–33). He also preached in Corinth, where he was less concerned to please his audience and simply proclaimed: 'Jesus Christ and him crucified' (I Cor. 2.2.).

→ Acts 19–20

During a third journey, Paul again visited the communities of Asia and Europe. The difficulties had not eased, and Paul echoes them in his letters. He ran up against hostility from the Jews, who would not listen to his message about Jesus, and from the Gentiles, since he was endangering the trade which was tied up with pilgrimages and temples (Acts 19). Within the communities, particularly the community at Corinth, enthusiasm was often unbounded: all sorts of charismas became evident, the most spectacular of which was that of speaking in various incomprehensible tongues (I Cor. 14). But at the same time there were disputes among the various factions (I Cor. 3.3–9); possessions were not shared with the poor (I Cor. 11); some people abused their Christian liberty (I Cor. 5).

→ Acts 21–28

A fourth journey took Paul to Rome, but as a prisoner. He had come to Jerusalem to meet James and take him the collection. In order to demonstrate his loyalty to the Jewish traditions, he agreed to show himself in the temple. This action was seen as provocation. Paul became involved in a riot and was arrested. He spent two years in prison at Caesarea. Claiming his rights as a Roman citizen, he appealed to the Emperor through the procurator, who sent him as a

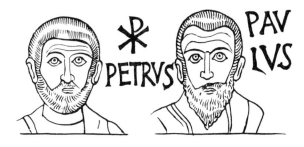

The apostles Peter and Paul (epitaph of Ansellus)

prisoner to Rome. After an eventful journey, he reached the capital of the empire. Two years of open arrest allowed him 'to preach the kingdom of God and teach about the Lord Jesus Christ quite openly and unhindered' (Acts 28.31). That is the last verse of Acts, and from then on we hear no more of Paul. It is about the year AD 63 . . .

5. Survey of the first century

The New Testament communities and others

→ Acts 2 and 3

A careful study of the information provided by the New Testament writings shows us where the Christian communities were, from Jerusalem to Rome: there were those which had been founded by the dynamic activity of the church in Antioch; those established by Paul in Greece; those mentioned in Revelation, under the influence of John; and the church in Rome, whose founder we do not know. Paul's letter to the Romans implies that there was an important and already long-established community in the capital of the empire. If Peter's coming to Rome is a traditionally accepted fact, the texts which tell us about it are late and uncertain. In any case, Paul's journey to Spain (Rom. 15.24) remains a conjecture.

5 Peter and Paul in Rome

Tradition associates Peter and Paul with the church in Rome. They were its pillars and foundation. Rome is said to have been the place of their martyrdom and it preserved their tombs. However, historical criticism, aware that the evidence that the two apostles were martyred in Rome goes back only to the last years of the second century, has subjected their deaths to closer scrutiny.

The role of the Pope in the universal church is based on the view that the Bishop of Rome is the successor of Peter. Protestants at the time of the Reformation pointed out that nowhere in scripture is it said that Peter came to Rome. We are told of Peter's crucifixion in a late apocryphal writing. Nevertheless, present-day historians think that the presence of Peter in Rome and his martyrdom there have a reasonable foundation on a network of circumstantial evidence: a detailed examination of a number of New Testament texts, the earliest Christian writings (Clement of Rome), liturgical texts and the result of archaeological excavations. One of the most telling arguments is thought to be the connection that has recently been established between the monument discovered under the basilica of St Peter and the trophy of Gaius referred to by Eusebius.

Acts states clearly that Paul arrived in Rome (Acts 28.16–31). Our uncertainties relate to the last years of Paul, the circumstances and date of his death. Paul indicated his desire to go to Spain after spending some time in Rome (Rom. 15.24–28). So it has been supposed that he was acquitted in 63, preached in Spain, and then once again in Asia Minor and Greece.

The letters to Timothy and Titus have been put into this framework. Paul is said to have been taken prisoner again (I Tim. 1) and then executed in 67. An allusion to this journey to Spain has been seen in the statement by Clement of Rome that Paul 'reached the limits of the West'. However, other historians interpret the silence at the end of Acts as an implicit indication of the death of Paul, who would thus have been executed in 63. The first attestation known to us of the beheading of Paul in Rome appears in Tertullian, writing at the end of the second century. The excavations made under the basilica of St Paul-without-the-Walls also suggest the discovery of indications of the trophy on the Via Ostia mentioned by Gaius.

6 The end of the apostles Peter and Paul according to Clement, Bishop of Rome (c. 95)

The 'Letter of the Church in Rome to the Church in Corinth' is probably the earliest text in Christian literature after the New Testament. Tradition is unanimous in attributing it to Clement, leader of the church in Rome about 95. Clement wants to restore peace in the community of Corinth, which is disturbed by a group which has dismissed the presbyters. He says that the cause of this is the jealousy already provoked by the deaths of Peter and Paul. This allusion is an obscure one for us, but it is the earliest evidence of the death of the two apostles.

But leaving aside examples from olden times, let us come to those who contended in recent days: let us take the noble examples of our own generation. Through jealousy and envy the greatest and most righteous pillars of the church were persecuted and contended to their deaths. Let us set before our eyes the good apostles:

Peter, who because of unjust jealousy suffered not one or two but many trials, and having thus given his testimony went to the glorious place which was his due.

Through jealousy and strife Paul showed the way to the prize of endurance: seven times he was in bonds, he was exiled, he was stoned, he was a herald both in the East and in the West, he gained the noble fame of his faith. Having taught righteousness to all the world, when he had reached the limits of the West he gave his testimony before rulers, and thus passed from the world, and was taken up into the holy place – the greatest example of endurance.

Clement of Rome, *Letter to the Corinthians, 5.*

7 The tombs of Peter and Paul in Rome

They say that in the reign of Nero Paul was beheaded at Rome itself, and that Peter likewise was crucified, and this story is confirmed by the association of the names of Peter and Paul with the cemeteries there, which has lasted to this day. That is also affirmed by a churchman called Gaius who lived in the time of Zephyrinus (199–217), Bishop of the Romans. When discoursing in writing with Proclus, the head of the sect of the Phrygians, Gaius in fact said this of the places where the sacred tabernacles of the said apostles were laid: 'But I myself can point out the trophies of the apostles. For if it is your will to go to the Vatican or to the Ostian way, you will find the trophies of those who founded this church.'

Eusebius of Caesarea,
Church History, II, 25, 5–7.

Other sources give us more information, but of a rather limited kind. Eusebius imagined that the world was divided up among the apostles to evangelize. The land of the Parthians corresponded to present-day Iran, Scythia to the areas to the north of the Black Sea. The apocryphal writings provide us with information which it is difficult to check. The Acts of Thomas, which is really an adventure story, perhaps includes some historical facts about the spread of the gospel in the East. But the difficulty of relations with these countries as a result of the permanent hostility between the Parthian (and then the Persian) empire and the Roman empire explains both the limits of evangelization and those of our information.

Two decisive events

According to tradition, Nero's persecution in AD 64 saw the end of the apostles Peter and Paul. However, the historians do not agree over the precise date: Peter died in 64, Paul in 63 according to some but not until 67 according to others.

The destruction of Jerusalem in AD 70 marked a still greater division in the life of the infant church. The Jews, who wanted to establish an independent nation which would honour God according to the laws of their ancestors, were in revolt against the Romans. Bitter warfare resulted in the destruction of the city and the temple. At the outset of the revolt, the Christian community in Jerusalem had fled the city and taken refuge on the other side of the Jordan. The destruction of the temple succeeded in breaking Christians of Jewish customs. God had showed by his action that the old law had passed away. The event stressed the universality of the gospel.

Deprived of the temple, Judaism reorganized itself at Jamnia (south of Tel-Aviv) and its hostility to Christians was strong. Among the latter, those who still remained faithful to Jewish practices from then on were no more than small groups more or less assimilated to sects (see *How to Read the New Testament*, p.31).

The formation of the Christian scriptures

This obscure period of the last decades of the first century saw the gradual formation of the Christian writings, what we now call the New Testament. Paul's letters were collected. The Gospels assumed their final form. But a great deal of time was to elapse before the communities agreed on which books they considered to be their rule of faith.

At the end of this first century, Christianity was firmly turned towards the West, making use of the structures offered by the Roman empire.

II · The Roman Empire

1. The Roman empire a 'preparation for the gospel'

Melito, Bishop of Sardis in Asia Minor during the second century, wrote a letter to the Emperor Marcus Aurelius, who was known as a philosopher, i.e. reputed for his wisdom. In defence of the persecuted Christians, Melito presented their doctrine as a way of life, a 'philosophy', and he pointed out the providential coincidence between the beginning of the empire and the appearance of Christianity: Jesus was born in the reign of Augustus and taught during the reign of Tiberius. The church and the empire blossomed together, and that was a bond between them. This theme of the empire, the providential setting for the preaching of the gospel, was often to be repeated. Pascal and Péguy are witnesses to this.

We are less amenable today to this reading of history. However, Christianity is not a timeless doctrine. After developing in the Semitic world of the Bible, it rooted itself firmly in the Roman world, which, ever since Paul heard the Macedonian's call (Acts 16.9), had become the most important area of evangelization. Soon enough, Persia and perhaps India were evangelized, but the political and military barrier formed by the Persian empire put many obstacles in the way of this preaching. On the other hand, on the Western flank the Roman empire had unified the Mediterranean basin. There was no obstacle to the free movement of people, goods or ideas.

Those who preached the gospel made use not only of the geographical and material possibilities afforded them by the empire, but also of the means of expression and ways of thinking which have characterized Christianity up to our own times. That was to cause certain problems when this Mediterranean Christianity was spread to the four corners of the earth after the end of the fifteenth century, at the time of the great discoveries.

A short history of Rome

One Italian city, Rome, founded in 753 BC, conquered the Mediterranean basin during the first century BC. Pompey took Jerusalem in 63 BC, Julius Caesar completed the conquest of Gaul in about 50 BC and Octavius (Augustus) annexed Egypt in 30 BC. To begin with, the Roman republic was only a small municipality. Its institutions were unsuitable for the administration of such a large area. Octavian, who had assumed the name of Augustus, instituted a new regime without actually making that fact clear. This was the empire, which came into being in 27 BC. At its head, the chief citizen (*princeps*) kept and handed down the titles of emperor (*imperator*, victorious general) and Caesar (his adoptive father). There was an end to civil war. The 'Roman peace' was established. It has often been stressed that Jesus was born at a time when there was peace in the world. From then on, the Mediterranean basin formed a political and administrative unity. Anyone travelling today between, say, London and Jerusalem has to pass through a great many frontiers, which often present some difficulties. In the first century, everyone lived in the same state. The empire was divided into provinces, whose governors were appointed in Rome by the emperor or by the Senate: these were the proconsuls, the legates, the prefects or the procurators. In some remote areas, a few kings continued to rule, but with very limited powers. They were quickly replaced by an imperial official when they showed the slightest tendency towards independence. All these figures appear often in the New Testament: Luke 3.1–3; Acts 13.6f.; 18.12; 23.26; 24.27, etc. The garrisons established everywhere maintained the Roman rule, while the law made for a kind of legislative unity.

There were some problems over the succession of emperors, because there were no fixed rules. Although we need not accept absolutely all the gossip of the historians, it does seem that there were some depraved characters among Augustus' successors, including Caligula and Nero. Vespasian and Titus were the best emperors. The dynasty of the Antonines in the second century (from Trajan to Marcus Aurelius) brought the empire to its peak.

The 'cities' of the empire

It does not do, however, to imagine the empire as a state which was strictly centralized in all its aspects. The basic unit in the countries of the Mediterranean may be said still to have been the city. Undoubtedly, the time of the Greek cities in Greece itself, Asia Minor or Sicily, now lay long in the past. The cities had lost their independence a

The Roman empire. Preparation for the gospel

For our philosophy at first flourished among barbarians; but after it had appeared among your peoples during the mighty principate of your ancestor Augustus, it became an auspicious benefit, especially to your empire. For from that time on the power of the Romans increased in a great and splendid way: you have become the successor to this whom the people desired and will continue to be so, along with your son, if you protect the philosophy which was nursed in the cradle of the empire and saw the light along with Augustus, which also your ancestors honoured, as they did other religions. And this is the greatest proof of its excellence, that our doctrine has flourished at the same time as the happy beginnings of the empire and that from the time of the principate of Augustus no evil has befallen it, but, on the contrary, all things have been splendid and glorious in accordance with the prayers of all . . .

Letter of Melito, Bishop of Sardis,
to the Emperor Marcus Aurelius, c.170,
quoted in Eusebius,
Church History IV, 26, 7–8.

⑨

How fine it is to see, with the eyes of faith, Darius and Cyprus, Alexander, the Romans, Pompey and Herod working, without knowing it, for the glory of the Gospel!

Pascal, *Pensées* 700.

The Emperor Augustus

⑨

And the boots of Caesar marched for him,
from the depths of Gaul to the banks of Memphis.
Every man found his way to the feet of the divine Son.
He had come like a thief in the night . . .

He had come to inherit the Stoic school.
He had come to inherit the heritage of Rome.
He had come to inherit the hero's laurel wreath.
He had come to inherit all human effort.

He had come to inherit a world already made,
and yet he had come to make it completely . . .
He had come to inherit a world already made,
and yet he had come to make it young again.

Charles Péguy, *Eve.*

long time ago with the formation of the empires of Alexander and his successors and then of the Roman empire. But they still had a large measure of autonomy in their internal administration. A city was not confined to an urban area, but also included the surrounding countryside. However, everything was defined in terms of the city. Early Christianity was an urban religion. The church was first and foremost a local community: 'The church of God founded in Corinth' (I Cor. 1.2); 'Paul, Silvanus and Timothy to the church in Thessalonica' (I Thess. 1.1).

The Pont du Gard

Well-organized communications

→ Acts 27 and 28

People and goods travelled from one end of the empire to the other by land as well as by sea. The routes used by goods and people were the very ones along which religious teachings and the gospel travelled. It seems that the Syrian merchant whose epitaph has been found in Lyons was both a businessman and a preacher. Paul's journeys were alternately by land and sea. Acts 27 and 28 are among the most splendid pages in the history of navigation in the ancient world. Travelling conditions played an important part in the difficulties and trials of Paul's ministry.

Three times I have been shipwrecked; a night and a day I have been adrift at sea; on frequent journeys, in danger from rivers, danger from robbers, danger from my own people, danger from Gentiles, danger in the city, danger in the wilderness, danger at sea, danger from false brethren; in toil and hardship, through many a sleepless night, in hunger and thirst, often without food, in cold and exposure (II Cor. 11.25–27).

And so we can see how the gospel came to be preached first of all in the ports, along the major lines of communications, both roads and valleys. In Gaul, travel by sea ended at Arles, where it gave way to navigable river routes up the Rhône and the Saône: from there it was possible to travel as far as Germany. People travelled about on business, to study (they went to Athens to study philosophy and to Pergamon to study medicine, and so on) and as tourists (to see the Seven Wonders of the World). Officials and soldiers went back to their homes, and slaves were carried far away from theirs. Those who preached the gospel were able to do so at all the major stopping places.

→ Acts 13.13f.; 14.1f.; 15.21; 17.1ff.; 28.17f.

The precarious nature of these journeys and their length explain the importance of the hospitality which is constantly commended in the New Testament writings and in the period which followed. Each person could find fellow-countrymen living together in an area of a large town such as Alexandria, Antioch and particularly Rome, in the same way that people from Greece, Turkey, Italy, China or Poland may congregate in British or American towns. The Jews were dispersed throughout the empire, and often the preaching of the Christian gospel began in the local synagogue. However, one of the oldest Christian documents, the Didache (or Teaching of the Lord) calls for mistrust of these parasites, even though they claim the preaching of the gospel as their authority: 'Welcome every apostle on arriving as if he were the Lord. But he must not stay beyond one day. In case of necessity, however, the next day too. If he stays three days, he is a false prophet' (11.4f.).

The postal service was used only for administrative purposes, letters being entrusted to travellers. A letter could take a couple of months to go from Lyons to Ephesus.

Cultural unity

The empire was a conglomeration of various nations, each of which retained its own customs, language and culture. The first Palestinian Christians spoke in Aramaic, the language which Jesus used. Others spoke the related semitic languages, like Syriac. There were Celtic speakers in Gaul, Berbers in Africa. However, two languages became dominant throughout the empire.

Greek, at first the language spoken in some cities, became the common language of the East as a result of Alexander's conquests. This Greek, which replaced the many dialects, was actually called *koine*, that is to say, 'common language'. It was not only the language of culture and philosophy but also the international language used by merchants. It was for the most part familiar in Rome and in the large towns of the East. There are many Greek inscriptions even in the French city of Lyons. It was a little like English is today. In addition, Greek was the main language of the church. Christians used the Greek version of the Jewish Bible known as the Septuagint. The New Testament was written in Greek, as were Christ-

Communications in the Roman empire

The network of roads

Almost all the network of roads in Italy dates from the time of the republic. The present railway network largely reflects it. Usually the roads bore the name of the magistrate who created them. The emperors were mainly responsible for developing the network of roads in the provinces.

Some of the best known roads are:

From Rome to Brindisi: the *Via Appia*;

From Rome to Genoa: the *Via Aurelia*;

From Italy to Spain via Narbonian Gaul: the *Via Domitia*;

From Durazzo to Byzantium: the *Via Egnatia*.

The weight of carriages was limited by the inadequacy of harnesses. No vehicle was more than 500 kg. Vehicles transporting goods covered about eighteen miles a day. Private postal services did not cover more than thirty-six miles a day. The imperial post managed ninety miles a day, but only by travelling round the clock. So news moved slowly.

Sea voyages

Sea voyages were often preferred to land routes. Even quite insignificant ships could carry several hundred tons. Some vessels transporting grain could carry more than a thousand tons. As to passengers, we know that Paul's ship was carrying 276 passengers (Acts 27.37), and that of Josephus 600 (*Vita*, 15). However, sailing was at a standstill between November and March. Seafarers were at the mercy of storms, prolonged calms, and pirates. So the duration of voyages varied considerably. We know the record times:

Nine days from Pozzuoli (near Naples) to Alexandria;

Six days from Sicily to Alexandria;

Seven days from Cadiz to Ostia;

Two days from Africa to Ostia;

Three days from the Narbonnaise to Ostia.

However, most of the time voyages were much longer. Sometimes it was necessary to winter for long months before continuing the voyage (cf. Paul's voyage).

While navigation on the Mediter-ranean was the most important, ships also sailed on the Red Sea in the direction of India. The sailors used the monsoons. They could travel out and return between July and February.

Public carriage. Bas relief. Belgrade

Ship at the port of Ostia depicted in a Roman mosaic

---

ian documents and liturgical texts, even in Rome, up until the third century.

Latin, the language of Rome and then of the West, was from the outset less widespread than Greek, but throughout the empire it was the language of law and order. In the church it was used as the normal language, first of all in Africa from the end of the second century, then in Rome, and then, during the course of the third century, throughout the Christian West.

→ Chs. 4, 5 and 6

To the degree that Christians made use of these languages, they brought with them into the church a particular way of thinking. Greek philosophy provided the basis for the development of a first theology. Through Latin, the Roman law provided a legal framework for the communities of the West. Once the respective spheres of Latin and Greek had been marked out in a rigid way, during the fourth century, the two cultural spheres of the church continued to develop differently right up to the time when they separated.

2. Religious unease favoured the acceptance of the gospel

Within the empire, Christian preaching came up against very varied religious systems. These religions could be opposed to the message of the gospel, but they were also capable of being stepping stones towards the Christian revelation. Simplifying things a bit, we might group this religious life of antiquity under three headings.

Traditional religions

Artemis of Ephesus

Among these we can distinguish a religion of the countryside from a religion of the cities. Rural religion continued to flourish. It consisted largely of nature cults revering supernatural forces in order to ensure the fertility of nature, the land and the animals: there were gods to protect the harvests, the flocks and the water supplies. At the time when the country areas became largely Christian (in the fifth century), traces of these old religions were absorbed into Christianity and nourished folklore.

→ Acts 14.12f.; 19.23–40

Each city, whether Greek or Latin, had its own (12) gods. With the conquests, these gods of Greece and Rome had been adopted more or less everywhere. Parallels were established: Zeus-Jupiter, Hermes-Mercury, Poseidon-Neptune. Since the cities had lost their independence, the religions were losing their vitality. Often formalities, they were a matter of *do ut des*, 'I give to you so you give to me'; they no longer satisfied enlightened spirits and real religious needs. However, even if people's hearts were no longer in such religions, they stayed loyal, because it was a matter of a 'custom inherited from ancestors'. Augustus tried to revive them somewhat, because he saw them as a social cement. Participating in the city's cult was a civic act, even if one was (13) completely sceptical about it.

Emperor worship

This originated in the East where the Greek sovereigns, Alexander's successors, had developed it. But in the West it appeared as a novelty when the Roman emperors tried to make (14) it universal throughout the empire. It was a political religion, comparable, all things being equal, to those which have become familiar in

---

(11)

Merchant and Preacher

If you want to know which mortal lies here, with no secrets, only his works, this inscription will tell you everything.

Euteknios is his surname, Iulianos his name, Laodicea his home, a splendid adornment to Syria. There was renown on his father's side, and his mother was of equal rank; at the service of all

and giving them their due, and in return receiving the affection of all.

When he spoke to the Celts, persuasion dropped from his lips. He travelled among many nations. He knew numerous people and showed the strength of his spirit among them. Ceaselessly exposed to waves and to the sea, he brought to the Celts and the land of the

West all that God had determined should be borne by the land of the East, in all its fertility, because he loved it, man that he was.

He moved the three tribes of the Celts towards the degrees . . .

Greek inscription (beginning of the third century?) found in Lyons in 1972.

recent years in connection with Stalin, Mao and several others. But the emperors did not employ the same methods as today's dictators. And if some of them showed their megalomania, many of them proved moderate. In the Eastern provinces the emperors were divinized during their lifetimes; but in Rome only after their death.

Joining in the worship of Rome and of Augustus was an act of political loyalty, but emperor worship did not become compulsory until the third century. In the meantime only magistrates and soldiers had to participate in it. When attempts were made to force Christians to pay homage to the emperor, they refused to give him the title of Lord (Kyrios). This they kept for God and Christ.

Sacrifice of animals. Louvre museum

Traditional religion

Tacitus (c.55– c.120), writer and Roman politician, wrote the history of his time from Augustus to Domitian in the *Histories* and the *Annals*. This text conjures up many features of Roman religion: the Capitol, the temple of the three guardian deities of Rome: Jupiter, Juno and Minerva; the celebrants: the praetor, the vestal virgins, the pontiff, the haruspices who examined the liver of the victims; the discovery of favourable features and the niggling ritual . . .

The consecration of the rebuilt Capitol in AD 70

On the twenty-first of June (AD 70), under a cloudless sky, the area that was dedicated to the temple was surrounded by fillets and garlands; soldiers, who had auspicious names, entered the enclosure carrying boughs of good omen; then the vestals, accompanied by boys and girls whose fathers and mothers were living, sprinkled the area with water drawn from fountains and streams. Next Helvidius Priscus, the praetor, guided by the pontifex Plautius Aelianus, purified the area with the sacrifice of the souvetaurilia *(a boar, a ram and a bull) and placed the vitals of the victims on an altar of turf; and then, after he had prayed to Jupiter, Juno, Minerva and to the gods who protect the empire to prosper this undertaking and by their divine assistance to raise again their home which man's piety had begun, he touched the fillets with which the foundation stone was wound and the ropes entwined; at the same time the rest of the magistrates, the priests, senators, knights and a great part of the people, putting forth their strength together in one enthusiastic and joyful effort, dragged the huge stone to its place. A shower of gold and silver and of virgin ores, never smelted in any furnace, but in their natural state, was thrown everywhere against the foundations: the haruspices had warned against the profanation of the work by the use of stone or gold intended for any other purpose. The temple was given greater height than the old: this was the only change that religious scruples allowed, and the only feature that was that wanting in the magnificence of the old structure.*

Tacitus, *Histories* IV 53.

Epitaph of an unbeliever

Traveller, do not neglect this epigram; stop, listen and learn before going further. In Hades there is no boat, no ferryman Charon, no Ajax guarding the keys and no hound Cerberus. All of us below, the dead, have become bone and ash and nothing else. I have told you true: go on, traveller, lest I seem too garrulous for the dead.

There is no point in sending or offering perfumes and garlands; there is a stone. And do not light fires; that is a useless expense. In my lifetime, if you have anything, share it with me, but by pouring drink on ashes you will make mud, and the dead do not drink. That is what I shall be, and as you pile up the earth there, you will say: I have become again what I was when I was not.

Greek inscription from the first century.

The 'second form of religion'

This was the title given to a group of spiritual currents which made themselves felt at the beginning of the Christian era. Many of the empire's peoples had been uprooted: slaves, soldiers, officials. For this huge population the gods of the city and of nature had ceased to hold any interest. Some people gave way to utter scepticism, while others seached for a deity who could bring consolation to the believer.

Philosophy

→ Acts 17.27

The most philosophical types progressed slowly towards monotheism, towards a unique and transcendent God, towards a religion which called for duty to be done and which provided support in adversity. Such was Stoicism, which demanded submission to the order of the universe. The Stoics reinterpreted the ancient religions and the old polytheism in a psychological and individualistic way. After all, the various gods were only different ways of speaking of the deity. While still remaining faithful to ritual, the Stoics put the accent on moral purity.

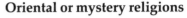

Oriental or mystery religions

This other current excited more and more interest in all the most densely populated areas. Transplanted slaves, soldiers and officials carried the religions of Asia Minor and Egypt to Rome and to the whole of the West. These cults were a response to the existential anguish of men and women, distressed and unhappy. Their ritual, which shows the best and the worst of them – processions, resonant chanting and intoxicating music – is a far cry from the formality of the ancient cults. These religions offered to the chosen few a mysterious initiation in which they personally encountered the deity. Purified by various trials and tribulations, the faithful had the feeling of being saved and of belonging to a privileged group. The country religions celebrated the death and resurrection of the natural world. In the mysteries, it was the faithful themselves who died and were born again to new life.

The most widespread of the oriental religions were the Egyptian cult of Isis, the Persian cult of Mithras and the cult of Cybele-Attis which originated in Phrygia (Asia Minor). 'The sewers of the Orontes flow into the Tiber,' wrote a satirical Roman poet, with irony. But nothing

Mithras, the mysterious god

could halt the progression of these new religions.

Some pointers show that these differing religious currents were moving towards a great unity, towards a fusion of their various elements into a universal religion. It was at this time that Christianity appeared, itself also a religion capable of gratifying people's need of moral elevation and of salvation. Yet the gospel allowed no concessions. It did not merge with other religious doctrines. Christianity took for itself quite a different position in the religious firmament of the early centuries.

3. The empire and the gospel

A co-operative of goodwill

That term has been used by one historian to describe the Graeco-Roman civilization of the first three centuries. It remained a solid edifice, but the goodwill which it offered only benefited a minority of privileged people. Among them were distinguished aristocrats whose pursuits were noble and refined: philosophy, literature, art and friendship. Seneca and Pliny were cases in point. But there were also common plutocrats, racketeers who had made their money in big business and who found their pleasures in overeating, sexual orgies and thermal baths, like the heroes of Petronius' *Satyricon*.

A society hard on the weak

The economy of antiquity was based on slavery. Manual work, the occupation of slaves, was despised. That explains the lack of technical progress, although Greek science had made important discoveries. In some towns two-thirds of the inhabitants were slaves. A slave had no rights. He could neither marry nor have possessions. Even under Nero, a master had the right of life and death over his slaves. Stoicism encouraged its adherents to see each slave as a human being and act accordingly, but it is a far cry from seeing to doing. Only a few slaves escaped their lot by being freed. Even free men were by no means on a par with one another. In the provinces, a distinction was made between those who could call on the protection of the Roman law and the others. Theoretically Roman citizens could appeal to the Emperor for justice – Paul provides examples (Acts 25.12; 26.32). Others had little hope of justice being done. A Roman citizen's status was not always recognized. And

The imperial cult

. . . And let the magistrate place on the first stand the statue of the god Augustus, father of Caesar; on the second, to the right, that of Julia Augusta (Livia, spouse of Augustus) and on the third that of Tiberius Caesar, son of Augustus, the city providing the statues for the magistrate. And in addition let him place a table in the middle of the theatre and an incense burner, and before the arrival of the artists let the members of the council and all the colleges of magistrates burn incense for the safety of the princes . . .

Greek inscription from AD 14–15, the beginning of the reign of Tiberius.

Stoicism

Man is made to sing to God

Epictetus (c.50–c.125), who came from Phrygia, was brought to Rome as a slave. Freed there, he opened a school of Stoic philosophy in Rome and then withdrew to Greece, to Nicopolis. He was lame as a result of tortures which he suffered when he was a slave. One of his disciples, Arrian, set down his teachings in writing.

Since most of you have become blind, ought there not to be someone to fulfil this office for you and sing the hymn of praise to God on behalf of you all? Why, what else can I, a lame old man, do but sing hymns to God? If I were a nightin-gale, I should be singing like a nightingale; if I were a swan, I should be singing like a swan. But as it is, I am a rational being. Therefore I must be singing hymns of praise to God. This is my task. I do it, and will not desert this post, as long as it may be given me to fill it; and I exhort you to join me in this same song.

Epictetus, *Discourses*, I, 16, 19–21.

The creed of a stoic

Marcus Aurelius, born in Rome in 121, was emperor from 161 to 180. He died of the plague in Vienna during a war against the barbarians. In spite of his lofty thought, Marcus Aurelius did not think much of the Christians. For him, the martyrs merely testified to 'a simple spirit of opposition'.

Every hour make up your mind gravely, as a Roman and a man, to do what you have in hand with scrupulous and unaffected dignity, with love, independence and justice; and to say good-bye to all other thoughts. You will give yourselves this if you perform every action in your life as though it were your last . . .
All things are mutually intertwined and the one time is sacred, and scarcely anything is alien the one to the other. For all things have been ranged side by side, and together help to order one ordered universe. For there is only one universe, made up of all things, and one God immanent in all things, and one substance, one law, one reason common to all intelligent creatures, and one truth . . .

Marcus Aurelius,
Meditations II, 5; VII, 9.

17

The mystery religions

Plutarch (c.50 – 125), who wrote in Greek, was born and lived in Greece, but travelled a good deal. A moralist and philosopher, he was particularly interested in religious problems: he belonged to the priestly college at Delphi.

At the moment of death, the soul has the same experience as those who are initiated into the great mysteries . . . These are primarily random wanderings, painful detours, endless disconcerting journeys through the darkness. Then, before the end, the terror reaches its climax: shuddering, trembling, cold sweat, fright. However, at that point a marvellous light dawns, and we pass on to the pure atmosphere of verdant meadows, over which songs and dances resound; sacred words and divine visions inspire a religious veneration.
Thenceforward the initiate, in a state of perfection, becomes free and moves freely, celebrating the mysteries with a crown on his head. He lives with pure and holy men. He sees on earth the mass of those who are not initiated and purified; they batter and crush one another in the mire and the darkness, and in fear of death, persevere in evil doing for fear of what lies beyond.

Plutarch (46–127),
Treatise on the Soul.

citizens came to be divided into two classes, *humiliores* and *honestiores* (lower class and nobility) according to their wealth and social status, entailing two scales of justice. In Rome, many of the citizens were poor and only survived through free distributions of corn. They were allowed circus games in the amphitheatre: *panem et circenses* – bread and circuses.

Women and children

Graeco-Roman civilization was predominantly masculine. Women were looked upon as inferiors. Emancipation was certainly talked about in the empire. One poet wrote satirically of those women who married in order to get divorced, and who got divorced in order to marry. But this freedom was only accorded those women who had money of their own which enabled them to be independent. Poor women who had to leave their husbands were forced to become prostitutes. The collapse of moral standards rebounded on women who had already been brought low. The children were in a still worse state, since a father could refuse to accept a newly born infant, which would then be either killed outright or left to die of exposure. Those children which survived this treatment were brought up and sold as slaves. Education was very rough and ready, the 'pedagogue' being merely a slave entrusted with bringing up the children.

Rome,
Trajan's column.
Roman soldiers

---

(18)

Slaves in Rome in the first century

How they should be treated

Seneca (4 BC to AD 65) exercised political functions. He was tutor to Nero, but when Nero became emperor, he forced Seneca to commit suicide. A Stoic moralist, Seneca did not always act in accordance with his principles.

I am glad to learn, through those who came from you, that you live on friendly terms with your slaves. That befits a sensible and well-educated man like yourself. 'They are slaves?' people declare. No, rather, they are men. 'Slaves?' No, but comrades. 'Slaves?' No, they are unpretentious friends. 'Slaves?' No, they are our fellow slaves, if one reflects that Fortune has equal rights over slaves and free men alike . . .

He whom you call your slave sprang from the same stock, was smiled upon by the same skies . . . It is just as possible for you to see in *him a freeborn man as for him to see in you a slave.*

Seneca, *To Lucilius*, Letter 47.

(19) **How they were treated**

Shortly afterwards (AD 61), the city prefect, Pedanius Secundus, was murdered by one of his own slaves; either because he had been refused emancipation after Pedanius had agreed to the price, or because he had contracted a passion for a catamite, and declined to tolerate the rivalry of his owner. Be that as it may, when the whole of the domestics who had been resident under the same roof ought, in accordance with *the old custom, to have been led to execution, the rapid assembly of the populace, bent on protecting so many innocent lives, brought matters to the point of sedition, and the senate house was besieged. Even within its walls there was a party which protested against excessive harshness, though most members held that no change was advisable . . .*

The party advocating execution prevailed; but the decision could not be implemented, because a threatening crowd gathered, having taken up stones and firebrands. The Caesar then reprimanded the populace by edict, and lined the whole length of the road, by which the condemned were being marched to punishment, with detachments of soldiers.

Tacitus, *Annals* XIV, 42–45.

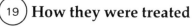

27

The empire meets the dynamism of the gospel

Because of the way in which it was organized, the Roman empire facilitated the rapid spread of the gospel in the countries of the Mediterranean basin. Such a thing would have been impossible a few centuries earlier. Besides, the gospel met a deep need in the men and women of the first centuries of our era. Without encouraging a social revolution, the Christian community welcomed everyone because they were equal in the sight of God, and Christ had died to save them all. In a world which was hostile to them, slaves, the poor, women and children were particularly receptive.

The fact that Christianity went against certain features of the time did not hinder it. It rejected a religion reserved for a small number of privileged people. The moral demands of the gospel were set against any kind of contempt of life, sexual laxity, a taste for luxury living and wealth, all of which were hallmarks of the imperial society. The Christian message refused to be treated as just another religion and be numbered among the other cults; nor would it accept the divinization of the state.

This explains the ensuing conflict over several centuries between the empire and Christianity – and yet also the continuing attraction which the gospel had for the inhabitants of the same empire.

For further reading

In addition to the general works mentioned above see:

Etienne Charpentier, *How to Read the New Testament*, SCM Press and Crossroad Publishing Company 1982

J. D. G. Dunn, *Unity and Diversity in the New Testament*, SCM Press and Westminster Press 1977

Lucas Grollenberg, *Jesus*, SCM Press and Westminster Press 1978

Lucas Grollenberg, *Paul*, SCM Press and Westminster Press 1978

Eduard Lohse, *The New Testament Environment*, SCM Press and Abingdon Press 1976

2

Christians in a Hostile World

First to Third Centuries

The Coliseum. Roman amphitheatre built in AD 80

The number of Christians was increasing, and they could be distinguished from the Jews. The latter, who enjoyed a special status in the empire, found it difficult to understand that the Christians were no longer their kind. From the time when they formed a significant minority, Christ's followers presented a problem. The secrecy with which they surrounded their worship made people fear the worst. Something of crowd psychology is evident here. Christianity came from the East, and the Christians were to some extent immigrants whose customs were unfamiliar. They formed a sect, and everyone knew what that meant! That is why the Roman world regarded Christians rather unfavourably. Christian writers, the apologists, tried to defend their community against public opinion and the authorities, but they could not stop persecution hounding Christians.

I · The Views of Others

A few anti-Christian writings have come down to us, often handed on by Christians themselves as they sought to refute them. The accusations ranged from the crudest slanders to intellectual objections, which still have not lost their point.

1. Common slanders

There were three main accusations against the Christians.

– They were *atheists*. Because they did not take part in traditional or imperial worship, or even in Eastern religions, it was assumed that they had no religion. This was unheard-of to the ancient mind. It threatened the stability of the city. It was thought that the rejected gods would take their revenge by sending disasters such as floods, earthquakes, plagues and invasions by hostile tribes. Christians were supposed to take part in another worship they could not admit – the worship of a donkey, or of a crucified thief . . .

– Christians practised *incest*. When they got together for their evening meals, it was only to indulge in orgies, the worst kinds of wickednesses between 'brothers' and 'sisters'.

– They were *cannibals*. The flesh and blood which they consumed was that of a child victim of ritual murder.

Although these slanderous stories were widespread, they were not accepted by everyone as true; still, for many years Christians were generally misunderstood. Pliny, the writer and governor, wrote of an 'unreasonable and limitless superstition'; the historian Suetonius, who wrote about AD 120, recorded a 'new and dangerous superstition'; the historian Tacitus a 'detest-

Rumour

About AD 200, Minucius Felix, a Roman lawyer, wrote a dialogue in which he reported a discussion between a Christian, Octavius, and a pagan. The pagan echoed the horrible rumours which were circulating about the Christians. The passage which follows gives some indication of what they were. Octavius goes on to show the pagan calmly and persuasively what Christians really are.

I hear that, persuaded by some absurd conviction, they adore the head of an ass, the basest of creatures . . . The story about the initiation of new recruits is as detestable as it is well known. An infant, covered with flour, in order to deceive the unwary, is placed before the one who is to be initiated into the mysteries. Deceived by this floury mass, which makes him believe that his blows are harmless, the neophyte kills the infant . . . They avidly lick up the blood of this infant and argue over how to share out its limbs. By this victim they are pledged together, and it is because of their complicity in this crime that they keep mutual silence . . . !

Everyone knows about their banquets, and these are talked of everywhere . . . On festivals they assemble for a feast with all their children, their sisters, their mothers, people of both sexes and every age. After eating their fill, when the excitement of the feast is at its height and their drunken ardour has inflamed incestuous passions, they provoke a dog which has been tied to a lampstand to leap, throwing it a piece of meat beyond the length of the cord which holds it. The light which could have betrayed them having thus been extinguished, they then embrace one another, quite at random. If this does not happen in fact, it does so in their minds, since that is their desire.

Minucius Felix, *Octavius* 9,6.

Christians, naive and credulous people

Lucian (c.125–192) was an original Greek writer from Samosata in Syria. He travelled a good deal and wrote a number of short works which are often dialogues. He paints an amusing picture of the society of his time, ridiculing established philosophical and religious values. In *The Death of Peregrinus* he tells the life-story of a boastful swindler who at one stage exploits the credulity of Christians. This gives the author the opportunity to show that Christians are naive.

The poor wretches have convinced themselves, first and foremost, that they are going to be immortal and live for all time, in consequence of which they despise death and even willingly give themselves into custody, most of them. Furthermore, their first lawgiver persuaded them that they are all brothers of one another after they have transgressed once for all by denying the Greek gods and by worshipping that crucified Sophist himself and living under his laws. Therefore they despise all this indiscriminately and consider them common property . . . So if any charlatan and trickster, able to profit by occasions, comes among them, he quickly acquires sudden wealth by imposing upon simple folk.

Lucian, *De morte Peregrini*, 13.

able superstition'. The Emperor Marcus Aurelius, himself a sage, thought Christians were headstrong. The satirical writer Lucian saw them only as naive people laying themselves open to exploitation.

2. Objections from philosophers and politicians

Those who spread gossip about Christians did not know them well. Gradually, however, intelligent people investigated Christians more closely, read the scriptures and undertook a vigorous refutation of Christianity. Two of the best-known writers, Celsus in the second century and Porphyry in the third, launched their attacks in three directions.

Ignorant and pretentious poor

Christians did their recruiting from the socially inferior classes, from among the despised manual workers, weavers, shoemakers and tanners. They concentrated on women, children and slaves, taking advantage of their credulity. Christianity called into question the values of Roman civilization which afforded pride of place to the comfortably off wise man who did not soil himself with servile and material tasks. In making out that women and children could know more about things than their husbands and fathers, Christians sapped both marital and parental authority.

Bad citizens

Christians took part in neither the city's nor the empire's worship. They did not recognize 'ancestral custom'. Moreover, they rejected the magistracy and military service. They were therefore not interested in political affairs or in the welfare of the empire. In fact, Celsus was writing at the time when Marcus Aurelius was fighting the Germans on the banks of the Danube. If all the citizens behaved like the Christians, that would soon have meant the end of the empire.

Christian doctrine was unreasonable

Some of the objections of Celsus and Porphyry have survived the centuries and are still met with today. The incarnation is nonsense. God, who is

The objections of a wise man

About 170, a well-educated pagan, Celsus, who had made a thorough investigation of Christianity, launched a systematic attack on the doctrine and behaviour of Christians in a Greek work, *The True Doctrine*. Would Celsus' objections find an echo today?

There is a new race of men born yesterday, with neither homeland nor traditions, allied against all religious and civil institutions, pursued by justice, universally notorious for their infamy, but glorying in common execration: these are Christians . . .

Their injunctions are like this. 'Let no one educated, no one wise, no one sensible draw near. For these abilities are thought by us to be evils. But as for anyone ignorant, anyone stupid, anyone uneducated, anyone who is a child, let him come boldly.' By the fact that they themselves admit that these people are worthy of their God, they show that they want and are able to convince only the foolish, dishonourable and stupid, and only slaves, women and little children . . . (III, 44)

The assertion that some God or son of God has come down to the earth as judge of mankind is most shameful, and no lengthy argument is required to refute it. What is the purpose of such a descent on the part of God? Was it in order to learn what was going on among men? Does not he know everything? If then he does know, why does he not correct men, and why can he not do this by divine power, without sending some one specially endowed for the purpose . . . (IV, 2f.)

Is it that God wants to give us knowledge of himself for our salvation, in order that those who accept it may become good and be saved, but that those who do not accept it may be proved to be wicked and punished? But is it only now after such a long age that God has remembered to judge the life of men? Did he not care before . . . God is good and beautiful and happy, and exists in the most beautiful state. If then he comes down to men, he must undergo change, a change from good to bad, from beautiful to shameful, from happiness to misfortune, and from what is best to what is most wicked. Who would choose a change like this? God could not be capable of undergoing this change (IV 7,14).

If Christians refuse to worship in the proper way the lords in charge of them, then they ought neither to come to marriageable age nor to marry a wife, nor to beget children, nor to do anything else in life. But they should depart from this world leaving no descendants at all behind them, so that such a race would entirely cease to exist upon earth. But if they are going to marry wives, and beget children, and taste of the fruits, and partake of the joys of this life, and endure the appointed evils, then they ought to render the due honours to the beings who have been entrusted with these things . . . (VIII, 54)

If everyone were to do the same as you, there would be nothing to prevent the emperor from being abandoned, alone and deserted, while earthly things would come into the power of the most lawless and savage barbarians, and nothing more would be heard among men either of your worship or of the true wisdom . . . (VIII, 68).

Help the emperor with all your power, and co-operate with him in what is right, and fight for him, and be fellow-soldiers if he presses for this, and fellow generals with him. Accept public office in your country if it is necessary to do this for the sake of the preservation of the laws and of piety . . . (VIII 73,75).

Altar of Rome and Augustus at Lyons

Extracts contained in Origen, *Contra Celsum*, a third-century work; the translations here come from the version edited by H. Chadwick.

perfect, unchangeable, would not lower himself to become a tiny baby. Besides, why had the incarnation happened so late in time? Jesus was only a poor man, incapable of dying, like Socrates, a wise man's death. His teaching was nothing but a bad copy of the oldest Egyptian and Greek teaching. The bodily resurrection was nothing but a monstrous lie. Porphyry saw the Old and New Testaments as a fabric of crude stories of an anthropomorphic kind. The peaceful God of the Gospels contradicted the warlike God of the Old Testament. The four accounts of the Passion contradicted one another. Christian ceremonies were immoral. Baptism encouraged vice when a drop of water pardoned all sin at a stroke. Even if interpreted allegorically, the eucharist was still a cannibalist ritual. And finally, wise people in our day have commented on the division of Christians into sects which anathematize one another.

3. The Christians' reply to their detractors

In the face of these attacks, Christians wanted to enlighten public opinion and defend themselves. In their writings they tried to give a clear presentation of their beliefs and practices in order to put paid to misunderstandings. These writings were called 'apologies', a term indicating defence or justification. Their authors are known as 'apologists'.

The apologists

They wrote for those who did not share their faith – the emperor, magistrates, the intelligentsia, public opinion. They had to work out a language intelligible to those for whom they were writing, that is to say, in terms of Graeco-Latin culture. In this way, Christianity broke free from its cultural isolation. The apologists Helle-

---

Christianity is absurd

Porphyry (234–305), a Hellenized Jew who came from Tyre, was a pupil of the philosopher Plotinus. He was a philosopher who adopted a lofty moral position and was interested in the occult sciences. He wrote a treatise *Against the Christians*, in which he noted the inconsistencies in the Gospels and the absurdity of Christian dogmas, in particular of the incarnation and resurrection.

Even supposing that some Greeks were stupid enough to think that gods dwell in statues, this would be a purer conception than to accept that the divine had descended into the womb of the Virgin Mary, that he had become an embryo, that after his birth he had been wrapped in swaddling clothes, stained with blood, bile and worse . . .

Why, when he was taken before the high priest and governor, did not the Christ say anything worthy of a divine man . . . ? He allowed himself to be struck, spat upon on the face, crowned with thorns . . . Even if he had to suffer by order of God, he should have accepted the punishment but should not have endured his passion without some bold

speech, some vigorous and wise word addressed to Pilate his judge, instead of allowing himself to be insulted like one of the rabble from off the streets.

A remarkable lie (a reference to the description of the resurrection in I Thess. 4.14)! If you sang that to mindless beasts which can do nothing but make a noise in response you would make them bellow and cheep with a deafening din at the idea of men of flesh flying through the air like birds, or carried on a cloud . . .

Porphyry.

nized Christianity and Christianized Hellenism. In this way they worked out a first theology.

Many of these apologists are no more than names, and a few extracts handed down by Eusebius of Caesarea. However, some important works have survived. Justin who, between the years AD 140 and 150, had a school of Christian philosophy in Rome, defended the Christian faith against Gentiles and Jews. One of the most famous passages by an unknown author, addressed to Diognetus, portrays Christians as the soul of the world. Just as the soul, according to Greek anthropology, gives life to the body, so Christians make the world alive and give it a meaning. That is the way in which this author answers the big question: what is it that makes Christians different from other people?

However, undoubtedly the best known of all Christian defences is the *Apology* in which Tertullian of Carthage puts to work all his talents and his lawyer's ardour, about AD 197.

All the apologists pointed out the injustice of the accusations against the Christians, the judgments and condemnations at the time of the persecutions. They demolished one by one the charges made against them.

No secrets among us

'We can describe all our celebrations to you,' they declared. That has resulted in our knowing the principal Christian ceremonies performed in the second century from Justin's accounts, and how the community lived from Tertullian's. You accuse us of hiding ourselves like rats, they said.

Christians in the world

We do not know who wrote the work addressed to Diognetus. It seems to have been composed in Alexandria about 200. The author gives a deeply felt defence of Christianity to his pagan audience.

For Christians cannot be distinguished from the rest of the human race by country or language or customs. They do not live in cities of their own; they do not use a peculiar form of speech; they do not follow an eccentric manner of life. This doctrine of theirs has not been discovered by the ingenuity or deep thought of inquisitive men, nor do they put forward a merely human teaching, as some people do. Yet although they live in Greek and barbarian cities alike, as each man's lot has been cast, and follow the customs of the country in clothing and food and other matters of daily living, at the same time they give proof of the remarkable and admittedly

extraordinary constitution of their own commonwealth. They live in their own countries, but only as aliens. They have a share in everything as citizens, and endure everything as foreigners. Every foreign land is their fatherland, and yet for them every fatherland is a foreign land. They marry, like everyone else, and they beget children, but they do not cast out their offspring. They share their board with each other, but not their marriage bed.

It is true that they are 'in the flesh', but they do not live 'according to the flesh'. They busy themselves on earth, but their citizenship is in heaven. They obey the established laws, but in their

own lives they go far beyond what the laws require. They love all men, and by all men are persecuted . . . They are defamed, and are vindicated. They are reviled, and yet they bless . . .

To put it simply: what the soul is in the body, that Christians are in the world. The soul is dispersed through all the members of the body, and Christians are scattered through all the cities of the world. The soul dwells in the body, but does not belong to the body, and Christians dwell in the world, but do not belong to the world . . . The soul, when faring badly as to food and drink, grows better; so too Christians, when punished, day by day increase more and more. It is to no less a post than this that God has ordered them, and they must not try to evade it.

Letter to Diognetus, 5,6.

The earliest Christian prayer for the authorities

See the introduction to 6. The Letter of Clement ends with a long 'universal prayer' for Christians and all men.

Give us, O Master, peace and concord even as you did to our forefathers when they called devoutly upon you in faith and truth; and make us obedient to your own almighty and all holy name and to all who have the rule and governance over us upon earth.

For it is you, Lord, who in your supreme and ineffable might has given them their sovereign authority; to the intent that we, acknowledging the glory and honour you have bestowed upon them, should show them all submission. Grant to them health and peace, harmony and security, that they may exercise without offence the sovereignty which you have given them.

Clement of Rome, *To the Corinthians*, 60f.

Now we go everywhere freely. We carry on the same activities as you, eat the same food, wear the same clothes. We only refuse to go to the temples and the presentations at the amphitheatre.

You are the ones with despicable customs

Roman society practised infanticide and abortion, things which were forbidden among Christians. Again, Christians said, 'It is you who exalt sexuality, who tell stories of the gods' amorous adventures, who accept wife-swapping . . . ' Tertullian, in his turn, yielded to exaggerations which hardly endeared him to important Romans.

Christianity is a reasonable belief

By linking Christian doctrine with the Old Testament, the apologists intended to show that Christianity was older than Greek philosophy. Moses had lived before the Greek thinkers, who had done no more than plagiarize him. A lot of talking between deaf men! Celsus affirmed that Moses had borrowed from the Egyptians. It was left to the apologists to defend Christianity by attacking heathen religions without too much psychology. Pagan gods were evil, without morals. 'We are atheists as far as your make-believe gods are concerned,' maintained Justin.

Christians are good citizens

→ Acts 17 and 18

In the early centuries the state had two faces as far as Christians were concerned. The climate of thought represented by the Revelation of St John and those who commented on it saw the state of Rome as Babylon, or the Beast, because the state was idolatrous and persecuted the church. It was doomed to destruction, like the colossus with feet of clay. It was equally certain that Christians who were awaiting Christ's imminent return (the *parousia*) were uninterested in worldly affairs. However, following the example of Romans 13.1–7 and I Peter 1.13, the apologists never stopped proclaiming their loyalty. 'We do not look upon the emperor as a god, but we obey him and pray for him. We are the first to pay our taxes.'

Christians in the administrative system and in the army

In his *Apology*, Tertullian affirms that Christians are to be found everywhere, even in the army. A decade later, in his treatise *De Corona*, 'On the Soldier's Garland', he thought that a Christian could not be a soldier. This negative point of view can be explained by Tertullian's move over to the sect known as the Montanists, fanatics

Tertullian describes the Christian community for the benefit of the magistrates

Tertullian of Carthage (c. 155–222) used his talents as an advocate in the service of Christians whose courage had converted him. His work, the most important in Latin Christian literature after that of Augustine, is primarily polemic. To defend Christianity he presses its virtues home and goes over to the attack.

We are but of yesterday, and we have filled every place among you – cities, islands, fortresses, towns, market-places, even the camps, tribes, companies, palace, senate, forum – we have left nothing to you but the temples of your gods.

I shall go on to demonstrate the peculiarities of the Christian society, so that, having refuted the evil accusations against it, I may point out its positive good. We are a body knit together by the sense of one belief, united in discipline, bound together by a common hope. We form an alliance and a congregation to assail God with our prayer, like a battalion drawn up for combat. This violence God delights in. We pray, too,

for the emperors, for their ministers and all in authority, for the welfare of the world, for the prevalence of peace, for the delay of the final consummation . . .

But it is mainly the deeds of a love so noble that lead many to put a brand of infamy on us. 'See how they love one another', they say, for they themselves are animated by mutual hatred. And they are angry with us, too, because we call one another brother; for no other reason, as I think, than because among themselves names of affinity are assumed only in a mere pretence of affection. But we are your brothers as well, by the law of our common mother nature, though you are hardly human,

because you are such bad brothers. But with how much more reason does one call and treat as brothers those who recognize a same god as father, who have drunk in one spirit of holiness, who from the same womb of a common ignorance have made their painful way into the same light of truth.

We live with you, eat the same food, wear the same clothing, have the same way of life as you; we are subject to the same needs of existence. We are not Indian Brahmins or fakirs living in woods and exiling themselves from ordinary life . . . We live in the same world as you: we go to your forum, your market, your baths, your shops, your workshops, your inns, your fairs and the other places of trade. We sail with you, we serve as soldiers with you, and till the ground and engage in trade . . .

Tertullian, *Apology*, chs. 37,39,42,
written about 200.

who advocated a complete break from a world whose end was near. But other texts of the period show profound reluctance for Christians to be involved in the army and in official positions. Certain requirements in respect of candidates for baptism confirm this.

There are two reasons for the hesitation shown by the *Apostolic Tradition*. The activities of magistrates and soldiers could be in contravention of

the gospel because the one would sooner or later be forced to take part in idolatrous religious ceremonies and the other to use violence: magistrates gave death sentences and soldiers killed others in battle. And were not those who had the power of the sword called on to renounce it? For a soldier, the situation was more complicated. A Christian could be told not to join the army, since it only consisted of volunteers anyway, but anyone who had already signed up, usually for twenty years, could not escape. Then church discipline required that from then on he should refuse either to kill or to take the oath, since that was a form of idolatry. It was not easy.

Military service was not compulsory. Christians could avoid the army with no danger of being despised for it. As long as they were few in number, it did not matter a great deal. However, when the numbers of Christians increased and there was trouble on the frontiers, their abstention began to be a problem. Hence Celsus' reproach. With the peace of the church in 313, Christian reluctance disappeared, since the risk of idolatry had gone. One embarrassment remained, however, as purification was required of a soldier who had shed blood.

27

A Christian cannot be a soldier

By forbidding Christian soldiers to wear the crown during religious ceremonies, Tertullian concludes that it is impossible for Christians to remain in the army.

Shall it be held lawful to make an occupation of the sword, when the Lord proclaims that he who uses the sword shall perish by the sword? And shall the son of peace take part in the battle when it does not become him even to sue at law? And shall he apply the chain, and the prison, and the torture, and punishment, who is not the avenger even of his own wrongs? And shall he keep guard before the temples which he has renounced? And shall he take a meal where the apostle has forbidden him? And shall he diligently protect by night those who in the day time he has put to flight by his exorcisms, leaning and resting on the spear the while with which Christ's side was pierced? Shall he carry a flag, too, hostile to Christ?

Tertullian, *De corona* ch. 11, about AD 210.

28

Occupations forbidden to candidates for baptism

Hippolytus, a priest in Rome at the beginning of the third century, suggests models for liturgical prayer in his *Apostolic Tradition* and indicates the conditions needed for baptism and ministry.

If a man be a priest of idols or a keeper of idols either let him desist or let him be rejected.

A soldier of the government must be told not to execute men; if he should be ordered to do it, he shall not do it. He must be told not to take the military oath. If he will not agree, let him be rejected.

A military governor or a magistrate of a city who wears the purple, either let him desist or let him be rejected.

If a catechumen or a baptized Christian wishes to become a soldier, let him be cast out. For he has despised God.

Hippolytus, *Apostolic Tradition*, II, xvi, 16–19.

II · The Persecutions

The apologists did not convince their audience. When people looked for the cause of misfortunes in this period, calumnies provoked riots against the Christians. In order to calm the fury of the common people, the authorities then announced their intention of condemning those who were supposedly to blame. This was the origin of the persecutions.

1. Persecution and martyrdom

For many people today the words 'persecution' and 'martyrdom' conjure up pictures of blood, torture and Christians going underground in catacombs to worship together. But although there is some foundation for this, the terms 'persecuted church', 'church of the martyrs' and even 'church of the catacombs' are too generalized.

The many meanings of 'persecution'

In the first place, Christians were not persecuted continually for three centuries. Besides, the idea of persecution is less well-defined than it might seem. At the time of the anti-clerical laws at the beginning of the twentieth century, French Catholics used to speak of persecution. In our own time we know that Christians are being persecuted behind the Iron Curtain. But are we talking about the same thing when we think of Poland, of Hungary and of Russia? In the same way, in antiquity persecution took various

---

Under Nero (64)

But neither human help, nor imperial munificence, nor all the modes of placating heaven, could stifle scandal or dispel

The Emperor Nero (54–68)

the belief that the fire had taken place by order. Therefore, to scotch the rumour, Nero substituted as culprits, and punished with the utmost refinements of cruelty, a class of men, loathed for their vices, whom the crowd style Christians. Christus, the founder of the name, had undergone the death penalty in the reign of Tiberius, by sentence of the procurator Pontius Pilate, and the pernicious supersition was checked for a moment, only to break out once more, not merely in Judaea, the home of the disease, but in the capital itself, where all things horrible or shameful in the world collect and find a vogue. First, then, the confessed members of the sect were arrested; next, on their disclosures, vast numbers were convicted, not

so much on the count of arson as for hatred of the human race. And derision accompanied their end: they were covered with wild beasts' skins and torn to death by dogs; or they were fastened on crosses, and, when daylight failed, were burned to serve as lamps by night. Nero had offered his gardens for the spectacle, and gave an exhibition in his circus, mixing with the crowd in the habit of a charioteer, or mounted on his car. Hence, in spite of a guilt which had earned the most exemplary punishment, there arose a sentiment of pity, due to the impression that they were being sacrificed not for the welfare of the state but to the ferocity of a single man.

Tacitus, *Annals* XV, 44
(published about 115).

forms. Nero's persecution was an open affair limited to the city of Rome: Diocletian's persecution extended to the whole of the empire. Finally, Christians did not spend three centuries worshipping in the catacombs. They did not acquire these underground burial grounds until the beginning of the third century. The catacombs could not be a place of refuge, since they were plots marked on the land registry. Let's say that, for the first three centuries, Christians lived in relative insecurity, but all the same they enjoyed long periods of religious peace.

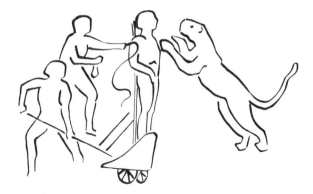

Games in the amphitheatre. Libyan mosaic

What is a martyr?

'Martyr' calls to mind someone who dies under a sophisticated form of torture. However, we must recall that the Greek word means 'witness'. A martyr witnesses to his faith in Jeşus who is the only Lord to the exclusion of all others, including the emperor. A Christian does not set out to be a martyr, though he might sometimes be required to become one. He avoids persecution. But when he is arrested, he remains a witness until the end, following Jesus in his passion and death. In this way the martyr identifies himself with Jesus. Pothinus is Jesus in the Garden of Gethsemane; Blandina is Jesus on the cross; and Sanctus is the suffering Jesus. And so the martyr is resurrected with his master.

Stories of unequal value

We know about the persecutions through various sources: from the accounts of non-Christian historians such as Tacitus and Pliny, from the minutes of trials – those which are known as the Acts of the Martyrs, like the condemnation of Cyprian of Carthage. Eye-witnesses have left us accounts written near to the events, like the Christians ·of Lyons in 177. All these sources are trustworthy. However, after the peace of the church in 313, martyrs were so highly esteemed that many communities claimed the patronage of some rather doubtful

ones. Some accounts were composed at that time which were more legend than anything else.

2. The persecutions of the first two centuries

The first two centuries were free of general persecution, nor was there any definite law concerning Christians. Persecutions remained local ones, and were of very limited duration. Only the most well known will be mentioned here.

Nero, the first imperial persecutor

The historian Tacitus tells us of the persecution of Christians by Nero. This was a result of the burning of Rome in 64. Christian authors allude to it, but only vaguely. Tacitus accepts the bad reputation attached to Christians, but without believing that they were to blame for the fire. Nero forced Christians to suffer punishment as fire-raisers. This persecution does not seem to have gone beyond Rome. According to tradition, Peter and Paul are thought to have been the victims of Nero.

The age of Trajan (98–117)

A letter from Pliny the Younger, governor of Bithynia in the north of Asia Minor, to the

Letter from Pliny to the Emperor Trajan (c. AD 111–12)

Pliny the Younger (61–114), nephew and adopted son of the encyclopaedist Pliny the Elder, was an advocate, orator and politician. Trajan appointed him legate for Bithynia. An honest and educated man, Pliny published his correspondence; this includes his letter to Trajan on the subject of Christians and the emperor's reply.

In investigations of Christians I have never taken part; hence I do not know what is the crime usually punished or investigated, or what allowances are made . . . whether punishment attaches to the mere name apart from secret crimes, or to the secret crimes connected with the name.

Meantime, this is the course I have taken with those who were accused before me as Christians. I asked them whether they were Christians, and if they confessed, I asked them a second and third time with threats of punishment. If they kept to it, I ordered them for execution; for I held no question that whatever it was that they admitted, in any case obstinacy and unbending perversity deserve to be punished. There were others of like insanity: but as these were Roman citizens, I noted them down to be sent to Rome . . . Several distinct cases arose.

As to those who said that they neither were nor ever had been Christians, I thought it right to let them go, since they recited a prayer to the gods at my dictation, made supplication with incense and wine to your statue, which I had ordered to be brought into court for the purpose together with the images of the gods, and moreover cursed Christ – things which (so it is said) those who are really Christians cannot be made to do.

Others said that they had ceased to be Christians, some three years ago, some a good many years, and a few even twenty. All these too both worshipped your statue and the images of the gods, and cursed Christ.

They maintained, however, that the amount of their fault or error had been this, that it was their habit on a fixed day to assemble before daylight and recite by turns a form of words to Christ as a god; and that they bound themselves with an oath, not for any crime, but not to commit theft or robbery or adultery, nor to break their word, and not to deny a deposit when demanded.

After this was done, their custom was to depart, and to meet again to take food, but ordinary and harmless food; and even this (they said) they had given up doing after the issue of my edict, by which in accordance with your commands I had forbidden the existence of clubs. On this I considered it the more necessary to find out from two maidservants who were called deaconesses, and that by torments, how far this was true; but I discovered nothing else than a perverse and extravagant superstition.

I therefore adjourned the case and hastened to consult you. The matter seemed to me worth deliberation, especially on account of the number of those in danger; for many of all ages and every rank, and also of both sexes are brought into present or future danger. The contagion of that superstition has penetrated not the cities only, but the villages and the country; yet it seems possible to stop it and set it right. At any rate it is certain enough that the almost deserted temples begin to be resorted to, that long disused ceremonies of religion are restored . . .

Pliny the Younger,
Letters 10, 96.

Emperor Trajan tells us about the pursuit and execution of Christians in his province. The governor does not think much of Christians, but his investigation has not discovered anything serious. What should he do? Sentence them just because they call themselves Christians, or when they are proved to be criminals? Trajan's reply is disconcerting: 'One cannot lay down a general rule to give a fixed method of procedure.' It is unnecessary either to pursue enquiries about Christians or to believe anonymous denunciations of them. But those who persist in calling themselves Christians must be sentenced . . . In addition to what it tells us about a governor's uncertainties, Pliny's letter gives us exact details about the life of a very early Christian commun-

The martyrs of Lyons (177)

To every question Sanctus replied in Latin: 'I am a Christian.' This he confessed again and again, instead of name and city and race and all else, and no other word did the heathen hear from his lips . . . When nothing else was left to inflict upon him they applied red-hot brazen plates to the most tender parts of his body. And though these were burning, Sanctus himself remained unbending and unyielding, and firm in his confession: for he was bedewed and strengthened by the heavenly fountain of the water of life which issues from the side of Christ. His poor body was a witness to what he had undergone – one whole wound and bruise, contracted, having lost the outward form of a man – in which body Christ suffered and accomplished mighty wonders, bringing the adversary to nought and showing for the example of those that remained that nothing is to be feared where the love of the Father is, nothing is painful where there is the glory of Christ . . .

Now the blessed Pothinus, to whom had been committed the ministry of the episcopate at Lyons, was above ninety years of age, and very frail in body. He breathed with difficulty because of the bodily weakness which was laid upon him, but the earnest desire for martyrdom filled him with that renewed strength which a willing spirit supplies. He too was taken off to the tribunal, and though his body was weakened both by age and disease, his life was preserved within him, that through it Christ might triumph. He was conveyed to the tribunal by the soldiers, escorted by the city authorities and the whole multitude, who gave utterance to all sorts of cries, as if he were Christ himself; and so he gave the good witness. Being examined by the governor as to who the God of the Christians was, he replied, 'If you are worthy, you will know.'

Blandina, suspended on a stake, was exposed as food to wild beasts which were let loose against her. Even to look on her, as she hung cross-wise in earnest prayer, fortified those who were also contending, for in their conflict they beheld with their outward eyes, through their sister, him who was crucified for them, that he might persuade those who believe in him that all who suffer for the glory of Christ have unbroken fellowship with the living God . . .

The blessed Blandina, last of all, having, like a highborn mother, exhorted her children and sent them forth victorious to the King, travelled herself along the same path of conflicts as they did, and hastened to them, rejoicing and exulting at her departure, like one bidden to a marriage supper, rather than cast to the wild beasts. And after the scourging, after the wild beasts, after the frying pan, she was at last thrown into a basket and presented to a bull. For a time the animal tossed her, but she had now lost all perception of what was happening, thanks to the hope she cherished, the grasp of the objects of her faith, and her converse with Christ. Then she too was sacrificed and even the heathen themselves acknowledged that never in their experience had a woman endured so many and terrible sufferings.

Letter from the Christians of Lyons and Vienne, preserved in Eusebius, *Church History* V, 1.

ity. Tradition dates another famous martyr to the time of Trajan: Ignatius, Bishop of Antioch. We still have the letters he wrote at the time of his transfer to Rome, but we do not know the circumstances of his maryrdom.

The age of Marcus Aurelius (161–180)

In the reign of the philosopher-emperor, the apologist Justin was sentenced in Rome, and Bishop Polycarp, a disciple of John and the 'cathechist' of Irenaeus, the future Bishop of Lyons, in Smyrna. With Polycarp we have the first evidence of the cult of the relics of martyrs. On the day of the anniversary of their death, their true 'birth', Christians met at their tombs.

A letter from the Christians of Lyons to their brothers in Asia, handed down by Eusebius of Caesarea, has preserved for us a moving account of the persecution in Lyons in 177. A popular riot, the cause of which we do not know, led to

Gallery in the catacomb of St Callixtus

(32) Felicity, martyred at Carthage in 203

Felicity was a slave, who was a companion to the noble lady Perpetua in her imprisonment and martyrdom. This passage from the long account of their arrest and execution is often quoted; it evokes the presence of Christ in those who die for their faith.

Felicity obtained great grace from the Lord. She was eight months pregnant at the time of her arrest. When the day of the games approached, she was saddened by the thought that they would put off her martyrdom because of her state, since the law prohibited the execution of pregnant women. She was also afraid that she would later have to shed her pure and spotless blood among a horde of criminals. Her companions in martyrdom were saddened by the thought of leaving such a good companion alone, a friend who was journeying with them towards the same hope.

So three days before the games, all together in common supplication, they *addressed their prayers to the Lord. Hardly had they ended their request than Felicity was racked with labour pains. By reasons of the natural difficulties of a delivery in the eighth month, she suffered much and groaned. One of the gaolers said to her, 'If you groan like that now, what will you do when you are handed over to the wild animals which you have braved by refusing to sacrifice?' Felicity said to him, 'Now it is I who am suffering what I am suffering. But there another will be in me who will suffer for me, because it is for him that I shall be suffering.'*

Felicity brought a girl into the world, whom a Christian woman adopted as her child.

the arrest and execution of about fifty Christians. Among them, Pothinus, the old nonagenarian bishop, the deacon Sanctus, and Blandina, the weak slave who was the last to succumb, have specially been remembered. Apart from anything else, this letter is the oldest proof we have of the presence of Christianity in Gaul.

Under which law?

It is not easy to see the legal basis for the investigations against Christians during the first two centuries. There was a distinction in the empire between lawful and unlawful religions. Judaism was lawful, but by contrast Christianity fell into the category of the un-lawful. However, the Romans were very tolerant. Up until the third century, imperial worship was not obligatory for all the peoples of the empire. Nero does not appear to have set up definite legislation against Christians, but his attitude created a precedent. The most probable explanation is that Christians came within the scope of the existing laws of order, and the governors interpreted these as they chose. When a riot broke out against Christians, the authorities made them shoulder responsibility for the break-up of order: they were seen as fire-raisers, murderers . . . And justice in that age knew no mercy. Condemnations tended to lower the tension caused by ill-will and provided participants for sport in the amphitheatre.

3. Third-century persecutions; decrees against Christians

From the end of the second century, the sound construction of the empire was beginning to crack: civil war, danger from barbarians on the frontiers, inflation, a decrease in the population . . . The emperors wanted to get rid of the causes of division and draw the links binding the peoples of the empire closer together by the expedient of emperor worship. While not ceasing to declare their loyalty, Christians refused to have anything to do with this. In addition, the emperors wanted to work out in many new ways anti-Christian legislation, for the sake of the unity of the empire.

A law of Septimus Severus (193–211)

This emperor tried to stop the growth of marginal religious groups by forbidding conversion to Judaism or Christianity on pain of severe punishment. In other words, the catechumenate was illegal, and Christians were rounded up by the police (202). That is undoubtedly the reason for the martyrdom of Felicity and Perpetua – the story about them tells us that they were catechumens and were baptized in prison (203).

It was also to weaken the church that the Emperor Maximian had numbers of its leaders put to death (235).

From Decius (249–251) to Valerian (253–260)

In an empire whose frontiers were threatened, the Emperor Decius wanted to be certain that the citizens remained loyally behind him. They all had to sacrifice to the gods of the empire and obtain a certificate (250). That was the beginning of the first general persecution of Christians. And if many of them underwent martyrdom, there were also a good many who performed the sacrifices, since the persecution came as a surprise after a long period of calm. Cyprian, Bishop of Carthage, has given us an account of those who surrendered and deeply troubled the life of the community in Africa. When calm was restored, the communities were divided on how they should behave towards those who had offered sacrifices and now wanted to be received back into the church.

Valerian tried to unite the empire against the Persians. Christians seemed to him to be an alien body. In 257 the emperor took measures against the clergy, and prohibited worship and meetings in the cemeteries. In 258, those who refused to offer sacrifices were put to death. Cyprian of Carthage, Sixtus, the Bishop of Rome, and his deacon Laurence suffered martyrdom.

Calm after the storm

Christians saw Valerian's capture and tragic death among the Persians as divine punishment. In 261, the Emperor Gallienus issued an edict of tolerance. For forty years the church enjoyed a kind of universal peace, still disturbed by some local riots. Numbers of Christians increased rapidly, particularly in Asia Minor, and many churches were built.

4. The last persecution in the Roman empire

The later empire, a totalitarian regime

When he came to power in 285, Diocletian undertook the complete restoration of the imperial administration. He divided the empire into four, with two emperors in the East, himself and

The Emperors Decius (249–251) and Gallienus (253–268)

43

Martyrdom of Cyprian, Bishop of Carthage, in 258

The proconsul Galerius Maximus ordered Cyprian to be brought to him . . .

GM Are you Thascius Cyprianus?

C I am.

GM Do you appear as the pope[1] of these impious men?

C I do.

GM The most sacred emperors have commanded you to conform to the Roman rites.

C I refuse.

GM Take heed for youself.

C Do as you are bid; in so clear a case I may not take heed.

Galerius, after briefly conferring with his judicial council, with much reluctance pronounced the following sentence. 'You have long lived an irreligious life, and have drawn together a number of men bound by an unlawful association, and professed yourself an open enemy to the gods and the religion of Rome; and the most pious, most sacred and august Emperors, Valerian and Gallienus, and the most noble Caesar Valerian, have endeavoured in vain to bring you back to conformity with their religious observances; – whereas, therefore, you have been apprehended as principal and ringleader in these infamous crimes, you shall be made an example to those whom you have wickedly associated with you; the authority of law shallbe ratified in your blood.'

He then read the sentence of the court from a written tablet: 'It is the sentence of this court that Thascius Cyprianus be executed with the sword.'

C Thanks to be God.

From the *Acta proconsularia* of St Cyprian, in *A New Eusebius*, 261f.

[1] The word 'pope' was used of all bishops down to the fifth century: it means father.

Galerian, and two in the West, Maximian and Constantius Chlorus, forming a tetrarchy. The ninety-six provinces were grouped into twelve dioceses. An implacable taxation system closed in on the citizens, because of the need to finance a sizeable army and huge buildings. The government behaved as if were controlling a totalitarian police state. Justice proved increasingly severe. Emperor worship reached its peak: the emperor wore a diadem and carried a sceptre, and every loyal citizen was expected to 'adore' him. So this was a twofold restoration, both political and religious: it was wicked to question what had been established of old. Religious dissidents were hunted down: first the Manichaeans (297) and then the Christians.

Doing away with the Christians

The refusal of some Christian soldiers to take part in the ceremonial of emperor worship upset Diocletian. For Galerian, Diocletian's colleague in the East, Christianity endangered old and traditional society. This is the explanation for the last and most terrible of the persecutions. From February 303 until February 304 the edicts came one after the other, each more severe than the last: destruction of sacred books, of places of worship, legal confiscation of the property of Christians, general sacrifice, banishment to the mines or sentence of death . . . How these edicts were applied varied greatly from one region to another. In Gaul, the Emperor Constantius Chlorus contented himself with demolishing a few churches. In Italy, Spain and Africa the persecution was violent but short (303–305). In the East, in the areas under Galerian, it was very severe and very long – almost continuous from 303 to 313. The number of Christians had already grown to almost fifty per cent of the population. Galerian spread apocryphal stories against the Christians, and the judges showed unprecedented sadism.

A turning point

From 306, Diocletian's political system began to break down. Instead of four, there were as many as seven emperors, all waging war on one another. Constantine, the son of Constantius Chlorus and the Christian Helena, eliminated his rivals in the West one by one. His victory in 312 over Maxentius at the Milvian Bridge over the Tiber put an end to civil war. Afterwards, the Christian writers Lactantius and Eusebius explained that this victory was due to miraculous intervention. Constantine had seen a glowing cross in the sky bearing the words, 'In this sign you will conquer.' Thus converted, he had Christ's monogram inscribed on the *labarum*, the imperial banner, and so ensured his success.

General peace for the church (313)

The persecutions in the West had been over for several years. In the East, Galerian, who was on the point of dying from a dreadful disease, had signed an edict of tolerance in 311, though his successor had not stood by it. Licinius, the new master of the East, in his turn decreed a religious peace. In 313 the two emperors, Constantine and Licinius, agreed together on a common religious policy which they described in a letter to the governor of Bithynia: this is what is traditionally known as 'the Edict of Milan'. The letter recognized complete freedom of worship for all the citizens of the empire, of whatever religion. The buildings confiscated from the Christians had to be returned to them. All the religions of the empire seemed to be put on an equal footing, but this equilibrium was soon to be shattered again, this time in favour of Christianity. In 313 a new era began for the church and for the empire. From now on people were to speak of 'The Church of Constantine' and 'The Christian Empire'.

(34)

The number of martyrs

How many martyrs were there? People used to speak in terms of hundreds of thousands, even

---

(34)

Letter to the Governor of Bithynia, traditionally called the Edict of Milan, 313

When we, Constantine and Licinius, emperors, had an interview at Milan and conferred together with respect to the good and security of the commonwealth, it seemed to us that, among those things that are profitable to mankind in general, the reverence paid to the divinity merited our first and chief attention, and that it was proper that the Christians and all others should have liberty to follow that mode of religion which to each of them appeared best; so that God, who is seated in heaven, might be benign and propitious to us and to every one under our government. And therefore we judged it a salutary measure, and one highly consonant to right reason, that no man should be denied leave of attaching himself to the rites of the Christians, or to whatever other religion his mind directed him, that thus the supreme divinity, to whose worship we freely devote ourselves, might continue to vouchsafe his favour and beneficence to us. And accordingly we wish you to know that, without regard to any provisos in our former orders to you concerning the Christians, all who choose that religion are to be permitted, freely and absolutely, to remain in it, and not to be disturbed or molested in any way.

Handed down by Lactantius,
How the Persecutors Died, 48.

of millions, of victims. These figures are altogether exaggerated. One cannot compare the persecutions with modern mass exterminations. So in reaction, modern historians tend only to count the martyrs of whose names and manner of death we have a record. This considerably reduces the numbers: less than three thousand for the last persecution. No doubt the truth lies somewhere in between these two extremes, if we take account of the terrifying memories left by Diocletian's persecution.

Witnesses to freedom of conscience

It it a more important and interesting exercise to consider the meaning of the word martyr, and of this witness in which our church has its roots. The martyrs were witnesses to Jesus, but we cannot separate them from all the other witnesses who mark out the centuries down to our own day. Together they are witnesses to a freedom of conscience maintained until death in the face of a totalitarian power.

For further reading

Jean Daniélou, *Gospel Message and Hellenistic Culture*, Darton, Longman and Todd and Westminster Press 1973

E. R. Dodds, *Pagan and Christian in an Age of Anxiety*, Cambridge University Press 1965

W. H. C. Frend, *Martyrdom and Persecution in the Early Church*, Blackwell and New York University Press 1965

Adolf von Harnack, *The Mission and Expansion of Christianity in the First Three Centuries* (1904), reissued Harper and Row 1962

A. D. Nock, *Conversion*, Oxford University Press 1933

Joseph Trigg, *Origen*, John Knox Press 1984 and SCM Press 1985

R. L. Wilken, *The Christians as the Romans Saw Them*, Yale University Press 1984

Games in the amphitheatre. Libyan mosaic

3

Being a Christian in the Early Centuries

First to Third Centuries

The Good Shepherd: Catacombs of Domitilla

To be a Christian is to accept the good news of Jesus and let your life be transformed by it. The word can be spread everywhere. Baptism can be given on a river bank. But a Christian is not an isolated individual. He or she belongs to a community, to a new people of God, the church. Jesus did not work out the rules of a society point by point, nor did the apostles on the day after Pentecost. But a group of people who wanted to live and go on living gradually brought to Christianity the organization it needed to function in the world in which they lived. Meeting places were needed; future Christians had to be prepared to receive this gift of Jesus. At regular intervals, Christians met together to celebrate the eucharist: the rules of how this was done emerged gradually. In this chapter we shall try to see how the internal life of these Christians was organized: the entry into the church through baptism, the celebration of the eucharist and prayer, the responsibilities of communities, and the bonds and the tensions which existed between Christians spread across the empire.

I · Liturgy and Prayer

1. From private houses to places of worship

In the early days of the church, Christians met in one another's homes, which indicates that there were at least some better-off Christians whose houses were big enough. In the East, Christians used the room high up under the roof, which was quietest and most tucked away (see Acts 20.7–11). In the West the meeting place was probably the dining room in the Roman house of a comfortably off Christian. The bathroom or *piscina* was used for baptisms. To start with, the word 'baptistry' denoted a pool and 'baptism' immersion. Before too long, Christians were able to meet in an enclosed place in the open air, in a garden or cemetery. From the end of the second century, Christians donated houses which were used solely as places of worship. Actual churches were built from the middle of the third century. The oldest known Christian building is the house-church of Dura Europus on the Euphrates (about 250). Buildings dedicated to the Christian religion were already numerous in the time of Diocletian, who ordered their destruction at the outset of the persecution.

2. Christian initiation

It must be understood that the term 'Christian initiation' covers what we know today as baptism, confirmation and first communion, together with a time of preparation.

For Christian initiation, Jesus' disciples used a bath of water, a practice inherited from Judaism. They added new significance to the traditional meaning of conversion and purification: uniquely and definitively, baptism brought about rebirth through the Spirit. Christians had to experience the death and resurrection of Christ (Rom. 6.2–11; Gal. 3.27; Col. 2.11–13). Anyone who wanted to become a Christian had to repent of his or her sins, observe the commandments, receive the good news and proclaim his or her faith in Christ the Saviour. This implies a preparation which nevertheless could be quite short at the outset.

In a church which was not centrally organized as it is today, the preparation and rituals varied according to time and place. Thanks to Hippolytus' *Apostolic Tradition*, we have a good knowledge of the rituals which took place in Rome at the end of the third century. At this period, the

(36

---

(35)

Baptism in the second century

The *Didache* (Teaching of the Lord handed on to the nations by the twelve apostles) is a kind of missionary manual composed at the beginning of the second century in Syria. The work includes a moral catechesis on the theme of the two ways (one of life and one of death) along with liturgical and pastoral regulations.

The procedure for baptizing is as follows. After rehearsing all the preliminaries, immerse in running water, 'In the Name of the Father, and of the Son, and of the Holy Spirit.' If no running water is available, immerse in ordinary water. This should be cold, if possible; otherwise warm. If neither is practicable, then sprinkle water three times on the head, 'In the name of the Father, and of the Son, and of the Holy Spirit.' Both baptizer and baptized ought to fast before the baptism, as well as any others who can do so; but the candidate himself should be told to keep a fast for a day or two beforehand.

Didache 7.

Baptism in the third century

Hippolytus, a Roman priest at the beginning of the third century, on several occasions expressed his opposition to the bishops of Rome and formed a rival community. He died a martyr in 235. He has left us works against heresies, commentaries on scripture, and the *Apostolic Tradition*, which describes the liturgical customs of the Roman community.

And at the hour when the cock crows they shall first pray over the water . . . The candidates shall put off their clothes. And they shall baptize the little children first. And if they can answer for themselves, let them answer. But if they cannot, let their parents answer or someone from their family. And next they shall baptize the grown men and last the women, who shall have loosed their hair and laid aside their gold ornaments. Let no one go down to the water having any alien object with them.

And at the time determined for baptizing, the bishop shall give thanks over the oil and put it into a vessel, and it is called the Oil of Thanksgiving. And he shall take other oil and exorcize over it, and it is called the Oil of Exorcism. And let a deacon carry the Oil of Exorcism and stand on the left hand of the presbyter. And another deacon shall take the Oil of Thanksgiving and stand on the right hand.

And when the presbyter takes hold of each one of those who are to be baptized, let him bid him renounce, saying, 'I renounce you, Satan, and all your service and all your works.'

And when he has said this let him anoint him with the Oil of Exorcism, saying: 'Let all evil spirits depart far from you.' In this way he shall hand him over to the presbyter who stands by the water to baptize.

A deacon shall descend with him in this way. And when the one who is baptized has descended into the water, he who baptizes him shall lay hand on him and say:

Do you believe in God the Father Almighty?

And he who is being baptized shall say, 'I believe.' Let him forthwith baptize him, once, having his hand laid upon his head.

And after this let him say:

Do you believe in Christ Jesus the Son of God,
Who was born of the Holy Spirit and the Virgin Mary,
Who was crucified in the days of Pontius Pilate,
And died,
And rose the third day living from the dead
And ascended into the heavens
And sat down at the right hand of the Father,
And will come to judge the living and the dead?

And when he says 'I believe', let him baptize him the second time.

And again let him say,
Do you believe in the Holy Spirit in the Holy Church, and the resurrection of the flesh?

And he who is being baptized shall say, 'I believe.' And so let him baptize him a third time.

And afterwards when he comes up he shall be anointed by the presbyter with the Oil of Thanksgiving, saying, 'I anoint you with holy oil in the name of Jesus Christ.' And so, each one drying himself, they shall now put on their clothes, and after this let them be together in the assembly.

And the bishop shall lay his hand upon them invoking and saying,

'Lord God, you did count these worthy of deserving the forgiveness of sins by the bath of regeneration; make them worthy to be filled with your Holy Spirit and send upon them your grace, that they may serve you according to your will; for to you is the glory, to the Father and to the Son with the Holy Spirit in the holy church, both now and ever and world without end.'

After this, pouring the consecrated oil and laying his hand on his head, he shall say:

'I anoint you with holy oil in God the Father Almighty, and Christ Jesus and the Holy Spirit.'

And sealing him on the forehead he shall give him the kiss and say, 'The Lord be with you.' And he who has been sealed shall say, 'And with your spirit.' And so he shall do to each one. Then they shall pray henceforth together with all the people . . .

Hippolytus of Rome,
Apostolic Tradition III, xxi, 1–xxii, 6.

preparation, or catechumenate, could last for three years. The candidate for baptism had to be presented by Christians who would stand sponsor for him and guarantee his good behaviour (godparents). Certain trades connected with idolatry or immoral behaviour had to be renounced.

28

Preparation for baptism comprised a period of teaching on doctrine and morality, which was given the name catechesis (meaning 'to help to remember'). This was designed to reveal the content of the faith to those who had been aroused by the preaching (kerygma) of the gospel (for example, the speeches of Peter and Paul in Acts). Hippolytus tells us that this catechism was given by a 'doctor', who could be either clerical or lay. Each period of instruction was followed by prayer together and the laying on of hands by the doctor. At the end of the catechumenate, a candidate would be examined on his or her progress.

On the Friday before their baptism, the catechumens, together with others of the community, would fast. In a last preparatory meeting, on the Saturday, the bishop would lay his hands on the candidates, absolve them, breathe on their faces and make the sign of the cross on their foreheads, ears and nostrils. The catechumens stayed awake throughout the night, from Saturday to Sunday, listening to lectures and being instructed.

The eucharist in the middle of the second century

To reply to the attacks of those who suspected Christian worship of immorality, Justin, in the middle of the second century, wrote an apology, i.e. a defence of the Christians, to the Emperor Antoninus Pius. There is nothing secret about us, he says; this is how we celebrate our worship. And in this way he introduces us to baptism and the eucharist in the second century.

It is easy to identify in this text the structures of the celebration of the eucharist which are still to be found in our eucharist today: Bible readings, homelies, prayers for the world, eucharistic prayer and communion.

And on the day called Sunday there is a meeting in one place of those who live in cities or the country, and the memoirs of the apostles or the writings of the prophets are read as long as time permits. When the reader has finished, the president in a discourse urges and invites us to the imitation of these noble things. Then we all stand up together and offer prayers. And, as said before, when we have finished the prayer, bread is brought, and wine and water, and the president similarly sends up prayers and thanksgivings to the best of his ability, and the congregation assents, saying the Amen; the distribution, and

reception of the consecrated elements by each one, takes place and they are sent to the absent by the deacons. Those who prosper, and who so wish, contribute, each one as much as he chooses to. What is collected is deposited with the president, and he takes care of orphans and widows, and those who are in want on account of sickness or any other cause; and those who are in bonds, and the strangers who are sojourners among us, and briefly, he is the protector of all those in need. We all hold this common gathering on Sunday, since it is the first day, on which God transforming darkness and matter made the universe, and

Christ Jesus our Saviour rose from the dead on the same day . . .

Shortly before, Justin specified the conditions for taking part in a eucharist which is not an ordinary meal.

This food we call eucharist, of which no one is allowed to partake except one who believes that the things we teach are true, and has received the washing for forgiveness of sins and for rebirth, and who lives as Christ handed down to us. For we do not receive these things as common bread or common drink; but as Jesus Christ our Saviour being incarnate by God's word took flesh and blood for our salvation, so also we have been taught that the food consecrated by the word of prayer which comes from him, from which our flesh and blood are nourished by transformation, is the flesh and blood of that incarnate Jesus.

Justin, *Apology* I, 67, 66.

Afterwards, at the end of the paschal night, came the rites of baptism itself. There was a final laying on of hands and a final unction from the bishop, after the baptized had dressed again. This is what gave rise to confirmation. Immediately afterwards, the newly baptized took part in the eucharist, which concluded Christian initiation. It was quite usual to wear white garments in the days following baptism. In some churches, the baptized person wore a garland of leaves and consumed milk and honey, because he had just entered the Promised Land of the church.

The baptismal rites primarily involved adults, but children could be baptized at any age, at the same time as their parents, or later, if their parents were already Christians. However, many were opposed to the baptism of children. Tertullian, the polemical lawyer from Carthage, wrote: 'One is not born a Christian, one becomes one.'

3. The eucharist, or the celebration of the Lord's resurrection

Christians celebrated the Lord's resurrection every Sunday. It was the first day of the week, whereas the sabbath was the last. Christ made creation anew, the work of the first day. But Sunday was also the 'eighth' day, the fulfilment of time and the sign of Christ's second coming.

Easter Day

But if there was one day when the resurrection was celebrated more solemnly than any other, it was Easter Day. Possibly the festival of Easter was only celebrated at first by Christians in the East, those in the West being satisfied with Sunday. At all events, by the end of the second century all Christians celebrated Easter, but they were not agreed on the precise date. In some Eastern provinces, Christians retained the Jewish date for Easter. Everywhere else, they chose the Sunday following the Jewish festival. After a

Vase + bread = eucharist; peacock = immortality; dolphin + anchor = hope

few controversies, in which Irenaeus, Bishop of Lyons, tried to calm hot tempers down (about 190), the latter view prevailed.

The eucharist

At the heart of the Christian Sunday and even more solemnly on Easter Day, the celebration of the Last Supper, to which Christians gave the name eucharist (meaning to give thanks), allowed them to share in the death and resurrection of Jesus. The New Testament tells us little about the development of this ceremony of 'breaking bread' (Acts 2.42; 20.7–11; 27.35; I Cor. 10.16; 11.17–33). This meal which Christians held had already attracted the attention of Governor Pliny in his investigation. The Didache required those who took part to confess their sins before doing so. It is easy to identify from Justin's text the structures of the celebration of the eucharist which are still to be found in our eucharist. The homily was a new form of teaching given to Christians: it backed up their original catechesis. It established a link between the Old Testament and the person of Jesus and at the same time delivered a moral exhortation. Hippolytus suggested a framework of eucharistic prayer which allowed for free improvization.

30 37 38

The communicants received the consecrated bread in the palms of their hands. To each the bishop said, 'The bread of heaven, Jesus Christ,' and each replied, 'Amen!' That is a custom which has been restored today. Christians reserved the sacrament in their homes, and partook of it before a meal. They considered that it had healing powers.

A eucharistic prayer from the beginning of the third century

This text preserved by Hippolytus inspired the second eucharistic prayer in the Roman Catholic liturgy. You might like to compare the two. The Sanctus was introduced into the eucharistic prayer after the fourth century and is general by the middle of the fifth century.

Let the deacons bring the oblation and the bishop with all the presbyters laying his hand on the oblation say, giving thanks, 'The Lord be with you.' And the people shall say: 'And with your spirit.' 'Lift up your hearts.' 'We have them with the Lord.' 'Let us give thanks unto the Lord.' 'It is meet and right.'

And then he shall continue thus:

'We give you thanks, O God, through your beloved child Jesus Christ, whom in the last times you did send to us a saviour and redeemer and messenger of your counsel, who is your word inseparable through whom you made all things and in whom you were well pleased, whom you did send from heaven into the Virgin's womb and who, conceived within her, was made flesh and demonstrated to be your Son, being born of Holy Spirit and a Virgin.

Who, fulfilling your will and preparing for you a holy people, stretched forth his hands for suffering, that he might release from sufferings those who have believed in you.

Who when he was betrayed to voluntary suffering that he might abolish death and rend the bonds of the devil and tread down hell and enlighten the righteous and establish the ordinance and demonstrate the resurrection, taking bread and making eucharist to you said, "Take, eat, this is my body which is broken for you." Likewise also the cup, saying, "this is my blood which is shed for you. When you do this you make memory of me."

Therefore making memory of his death and resurrection, we offer you the bread and the cup, making eucharist to you because you have bidden us to stand before you and minister as priests to you. And we pray you to grant to all your saints who partake to be united to you that they may be fulfilled with your Holy Spirit for the confirmation of their faith in truth, that we may praise and glorify you through your child Jesus Christ, through whom glory and honour be to you with the Holy Spirit in your holy church now and for ever, and world without end.'

And the bishop shall give thanks according to this model. It is not altogether necessary for him to recite the very same words which we gave before as though studying to say them by heart in his thanksgiving to God; but let each one pray according to his own ability. If indeed he is able to pray suitably with a grand and elevated prayer this is a good thing. But if on the other hand he should pray and recite a prayer according to a fixed form, no one shall prevent him. Only let his prayer be correct and right in doctrine.

Hippolytus, *Apostolic Tradition*, I, iv, 4–13; x, 4–5.

4. Penance

In the New Testament it is primarily through baptism that God forgives sins (Acts 2.38). But in a wider way, Jesus gave the Twelve and the church community the power to remit sins and to exclude sinners (John 20.22–23; Matt. 16.18–19; 18.15–18). Paul called for the expulsion from the community in Corinth of an incestuous man (I Cor. 5). Could all sins be pardoned? Some obscure texts were given different interpretations in different situations (Matt. 12. 31–32; I John 5.16f.; Heb. 6.4–7; 10.26–31). In the second century, the Didache (4.14; 14.1) invited Christians to 'confess their sins' before praying and celebrating the eucharist. This related to shortcomings in everyday life; it had already been called for by the Letter of James (5.6). A baptized person ought not to commit a serious sin.

The Christian should no longer sin

Remind yourself of the text in Box 1. Hermas is speaking with the angel of penitence, otherwise called the Pastor.

Hermas *I have heard from some teachers that there is no second repentance beyond the one given when we went down into the water and received remission of our former sins.*
The Pastor *You have heard correctly, for that is so. For he who has received remission of sin ought never to sin again, but to live in purity. But the Lord, who knows the heart and knows all things beforehand, knew the weakness of man and the subtlety of the* devil . . . *Being merciful, therefore, he had mercy on his creation and established this repentance, and to me was the control of this repentance given. And I tell you, after that great and holy calling if a man be tempted by the devil and sin, he has one repentance, but if he sin and repent repeatedly it is unprofitable for such a man, for he shall hardly live.*

Shepherd of Hermas, Mandates 4, 3,1–6.

The Good Shepherd. Crypt of Lucinus

A painful trial

In the passage which follows, Tertullian admits the possibility of penance for serious sins, once in a lifetime. A little later, he entered a sect and thought that some sins, like adultery, could never be pardoned.

The narrower, then, the sphere of action of this second and only repentance, the more laborious is it to undertake. It does not just consist in inner attitudes, but has to be translated into action. This action . . . is the avowal by which we confess our sin to God . . . This discipline is for man's prostration and humiliation, calling for a demeanour calculated in win mercy. As to dress and food, it commands the penitent to lie in sackcloth and ashes, to cover his body in mourning, *to lay his spirit low in sorrows, to make amends by severe treatment for the sins that he has committed . . . The penitent will usually feed his prayers on fastings, groan, weep and make outcries to the Lord his God; he will bow before the feet of the presbyters and kneel to God's dear ones, bidding all his brothers join in his supplications.*

Tertullian, *On Repentance*, 9.

However . . . during the second century it was generally admitted with reluctance that serious offences (such as apostasy, murder, adultery) could only be forgiven once, by assimilation to baptism, which was renewed by penitence. That was Tertullian's first view, but he subsequently changed his mind. For him, adultery was an unforgivable sin. The Decian persecution (250) led to an argument on the subject of whether apostates could be reconciled. Those who were inclined to be indulgent came into conflict with those who were not, in Carthage and in Rome. This resulted in schisms and the setting up of dissenting communities. The development of penance during the first three centuries is not very well known.

Praying figure. Catacomb of Priscilla

5. Some other aspects of prayer and worship

Several authors suggest a prayer which extends throughout the day. On rising, the Christian is invited to pray in the direction of the East 'whence comes the true light'. He or she prays at nine o'clock, at midday, at three in the afternoon, at sunset and when the lamp is blessed. Christians usually prayed standing, with arms uplifted and palms opened outwards. That was the attitude of the suppliant. The hands were not joined together.

Prayer marked out the important stages of life, from birth to death. That does not necessarily mean that there was a special ritual for each of

---

Christian marriage according to Tertullian

Tertullian here writes to his wife to say what she is to do when he is dead. Having asked her not to remarry, he nevertheless accepts that she may do so if her next husband is a Christian. Tertullian is thus led on to describe Christian marriage. Some scholars have regarded this text as an indication of a Christian ceremony of marriage from the second century on. Today the majority think that Tertullian simply wants to say, with reference to St Paul, that faith transforms the marriage of Christians.

Where can I find the words to describe adequately the happiness of that marriage which the church cements, which the oblation confirms and the blessing seals? The angels proclaim it and the heavenly Father ratifies it . . .

What kind of yoke is that of two Christians, united in one hope, one desire, one discipline and one service? Both are children of the same Father, servants of the same Master; nothing separates them, either in the spirit or in the flesh; on the contrary, they are truly two in one flesh. Where the flesh is one, so is the spirit. Together they pray, together they prostrate themselves, together they observe the fasts; they teach each other, exhort each other, encourage each other. They are both equal in the church of God, equal at the banquet of God, equal in trials, persecutions, consolations . . .

‑ Tertullian, *To His Wife II*, 8, 6–8.

these stages. For instance, there does not seem to have been a Christian marriage ceremony in the first centuries.

'Christians marry in the same way as everyone else,' says the letter to Diognetus. But, unlike everyone else, Christians endowed marriage with a new meaning. They retained traditional customs while refusing or modifying everything that could be seen as pagan. They condemned certain practices of the age like abortion or the abandoning of children to die of exposure. Pauline texts (Eph. 5) provided a spirituality of marriage for husbands and wives. The indissolubility of marriage was a Christian innovation. The most important thing for married Christians was that they should share the same faith. Quite early on there seems to have been a prayer for married couples, but it was not properly speaking a marriage ceremony.

The leaders of the community were encouraged to visit the sick and anoint them with consecrated oil. It also seems likely that this oil was used as a remedy in the hope of a cure.

In common with all their contemporaries, Christians venerated their dead, and among these martyrs, had a privileged place. The anniversaries of their deaths, which were looked upon as their births, were celebrated on their tombs. Originally Christians were buried amongst the other dead, but from the third century onwards they were allocated their own burial grounds like other identifiable groups. In Rome these were the catacombs.

Christian art

These burial grounds gave rise to Christian art, in the form of paintings of scenes from the Gospels and the Bible, or Christian symbols such as an anchor, or a fish (the letters of the Greek word for fish, *ichthys*, correspond to the initials in Greek of Jesus Christ, Son of God, Saviour = *Iesous Christos Theou Uios Soter*). The oldest Christian funerary inscriptions date from the end of the second and the beginning of the third century, for instance the epitaph of Abercius.

II · Setting up Ministries

Ministries took several centuries to become fixed. Their development is often obscure. The terms used are very varied and the same term does not always have the same meaning, depending on the place and the period. At all events, we do not find in the New Testament all the organization of our church today.

1. The Palestinian community

The primitive community had a twofold organization. The group of Twelve which dated back to the earthly life of Jesus (Mark 3.16–19) and whose number was made up after the death of Judas (Acts 1.15–26) administered the Hebrew-speaking (Aramaic-speaking) Palestinian community. The group of the Seven, inspired by Stephen (Acts 6.1–6), looked after the community which had emerged from Hellenistic Judaism and which spoke Greek.

2. The beginnings of mission

The persecution which followed the martyrdom of Stephen resulted in the dispersal of the Hellenistic Jews, who became missionaries.

From this time on, different organizations came into being depending on the origin of the communities.

The community in Jerusalem and others derived from Judaism modelled themselves on the Jewish community. At their head was a college of elders or presbyters (from the Greek *presbyteros*, older). In Jerusalem, James was the head of the college of elders. The Twelve founded several communities along these lines.

A missionary church with a double organization came into being from Antioch:

Travelling missionaries (suggested by I Cor. 12.28) practised a charismatic ministry which seems to have been their whole life. These were the apostles who were not necessarily part of the Twelve, for example Paul and Barnabas. As those responsible for evangelizing, they travelled about all the time. Then there were the prophets, who expounded the word of God in the congregations, and finally the doctors, a kind of Christian rabbi, who specialized in the scriptures.

In the course of their travels the missionaries founded local communities and appointed responsible people at the head of each: these were *episkopoi* (overseers) and deacons (those who ministered or served, Phil. 1.1). The author of the Letter to Titus also gives *episkopoi* the title presbyters (Titus; I Tim. 3.13). They preached, baptized and presided at the eucharist. All ministers were appointed by the laying on of hands, accompanied by prayer and fasting (Acts 6.6; 13.3; I Tim. 5.22). The New Testament is not very clear about all this. Yet other categories of ministries appeared elsewhere, like those mentioned in Eph. 4.11: apostles, prophets, evangelists, pastors and teachers.

42   Ministry at the end of the first century

Remind yourself of the text in Box 6. Clement is recalling to the Corinthians the origin of ministries in the church in order to reproach them for having dismissed their own ministers without reason. The vocabulary does not yet seem to be fixed: Clement uses presbyter and episcopos at random.

Now, the gospel was given to the apostles for us by the Lord Jesus Christ; and Jesus the Christ was sent from God. That is to say, Christ received his commission from God, and the apostles theirs from Christ. The order of these two events was in accordance with the will of God. So thereafter, when the apostles had been given their instructions, and all their doubts had been set at rest by the resurrection of our Lord Jesus Christ from the dead, they set out in the full assurance of the Holy Spirit to proclaim the coming of God's kingdom.

And as they went through the territories and townships preaching, they appointed their first converts – after testing them by the Spirit – to be bishops and deacons for the believers of the future . . .

Similarly, our apostles knew, through our Lord Jesus Christ, that there would be dissensions over the title of bishop. In their full foreknowledge of this, therefore, they proceeded to appoint the minsiters I spoke of, and they went on to add an instruction that if these should fall asleep, other accredited persons should succeed them in their office.

In view of this, we cannot think it right for these men now to be ejected from their ministry when, after being commissioned by the apostles with the full consent of the church, they have since been serving Christ's flock in a humble, peaceable and disinterested way, and earning everybody's approval over so long a period of time . . . .

How happy those presbyters must be who have already passed away, with a lifetime of faithfulness behind them; they at least need fear no eviction from the security they are now enjoying.

Clement of Rome,
To the Corinthians 42,44.

3. Development in the second and third centuries

The rather vague language of the New Testament continues among the writers of the late first and the early second centuries. Clement of Rome and the Didache spoke of the communities having presbyter *episkopoi* and deacons. Gradually a president emerged from the college of presbyter *episkopoi* and before long he alone was given the title *episkopos* and became completely separated from the college of presbyters. The deacon – minister, subordinate – was attached to the person of the *episkopos*. This led to the three orders of ministry which we know today: bishop, priest and deacon. Ignatius of Antioch is the first to testify to this in his letters. The situation from then on is described as a 'monarchical episcopate', the bishop being clearly separated from the priests.

The itinerant ministers gradually disappeared. The apostles (successors of the Twelve Apostles) stayed put and became amalgamated with the bishops who, from then on, seemed to all intents and purposes to be the successors of the original apostles.

In addition there were other ministries which were thought to be inferior. They varied according to churches and periods. About 250, the Bishop of Rome introduced his church in this way: 'There are forty-six priests, seven deacons, seven sub-deacons, forty-two acolytes, fifty- two exorcists, readers and doorkeepers, more than fifteen hundred widows and beggars, all of whom are supported by the grace and love of the Lord' (Eusebius, *Church History*, VI, 43, 11).

Early in this period, only the bishop presided at the eucharist, preached, baptized and gave absolution. Priests did no more than help the bishop. When Christians grew in number, the episcopal sees increased in particular areas, such as Africa; but in some large towns like Rome and Alexandria, several centres of worship were created to which priests were appointed who in this way achieved a certain responsibility of their own.

The clergy and the people took part in the appointment of ministers in various ways. The essential element in ordination was the laying on

Lamp with monogram of Christ, from Carthage

---

(43)

Itinerant ministers and ministers of local communities

The apostles, prophets and teachers mentioned in this passage are to be understood as those in I Cor. 12.28f. This text could be very close to the apostolic period.

Now about the apostles and prophets: Act in line with the gospel precept. Welcome every apostle on arriving as if he were the Lord. But he must not stay beyond one day. In case of necessity, however, the next day too. If he stays three days, he is a false prophet. On departing, an apostle must not accept *anything but sufficient food to carry him till his next lodging. If he asks for money, he is a false prophet . . .*

Every genuine prophet who wants to settle with you 'has a right to his support' (Matt. 10.10). Similarly, a genuine teacher himself, just like a 'workman, has a right to his support' . . .

You must choose for yourselves overseers and deacons who are worthy of the Lord: men who are gentle, generous, faithful, and well tried. For their ministry to you is identical with that of the prophets and teachers. You must not, therefore, despise them, for along with the prophets and teachers they enjoy a place of honour among you.

Didache 11, 13, 15.

The three degrees of ministry

Ignatius, who was in charge of the church in Antioch, was taken to Rome (c.110?) to be martyred there. He wrote to several churches in Asia Minor to encourage them and exhort them to be united in the faith. He bears witness clearly to the existence of a threefold hierarchical ministry, plainly distinguishing the episcopate from presbyters and deacons. So one could translate the words he uses as bishop, priest and deacon in the modern sense. However, the vocabulary is still fluid with Irenaeus, at the end of the second century.

Follow your bishop, every one of you, as obediently as Jesus Christ followed the Father. Obey the presbyters (the college of presbyters) as you would the apostles; give your deacons the same reverence that you would a command from God. Make sure that no step affecting the church is ever taken by anyone without the bishop's sanction. The sole eucharist you should consider valid is one that is celebrated by the bishop himself, or by some person authorized by him. Where the bishop is to be seen, there let all his people be; just as wherever Jesus Christ is present, we have the catholic church. Nor is it permissible to conduct baptisms or agapes (a meal of support and fellowship with a religious significance but different from the eucharist) without the bishop. On the other hand, whatever does have his sanction can be sure of God's approval.

Ignatius, *To the Smyrnaeans*, 8.

It is for the rest of you to hold the deacons in as great respect as Jesus Christ; just as you should also look upon the bishop as a type of the Father and the clergy as the apostolic circle forming his council; for without these three orders no church has any right to the name.

Ignatius, *To the Trallians*, 3.

of hands. For the ordination of a bishop, the other bishops laid on hands; for priests, it was the bishop and other priests; and for a deacon, the bishop alone. In the case of other ministers such as readers, they were just given the article through which they would serve: say, a book.

Ministry and priesthood

In the New Testament writings, ministers of communities concentrated on preaching the gospel (I Cor. 17) while still presiding at prayer, celebrating the breaking of bread and conducting the affairs of the community. They were unlike the priests of Judaism or of pagan religions. All Christian people were priestly (I Peter 2.9), and Jesus was their great high priest. Gradually, however, under the influence of reading the Old Testament and also in comparison with other religions, in the case of Christian ministers the emphasis came to be put on their liturgical role, like that of other religions. So Hippolytus uses a priestly language when speaking of Christian leaders. This explains the ambiguity of the word *priest*, which etymologically means 'elder' and in fact denotes someone charged with a sacred function in worship.

Some bishops, like Cyprian, chose to remain celibate, but this was not obligatory for the ministers of the church.

4. The ministry of women

In the New Testament, there were women followers of Jesus (Luke 8.1–3) who then took part in proclaiming the gospel and in prophecy (Rom. 16.1–3; Phil. 3.2–3; Cor. 11.4–5; Acts 21.9), but it is difficult to find exact parallels with male ministers. It is important to note the reservations over the active role of women in congregations (I Cor. 14.34f.; I Tim. 2.11–14). An order of widows emerged in the communities (I Tim. 5.3–16). These were dedicated to prayer and to various services in connection with women, such as visiting the sick.

Deaconesses are attested quite clearly in Syria in the third century. They were the equivalent of deacons in the ministry of women and received the laying on of hands. Virgins often formed a distinct group in the community; we cannot speak of them in connection with the ministry in the strict sense, but there was a certain overlap in the roles of widows, deaconesses and virgins.

Deaconesses in Syria in the third century

Establish for yourself, bishop, administrators of justice as helpers who can join with you in the work of salvation. Choose those who please you from among all the people and appoint them deacons, a man for the execution of the many things that are necessary, and a woman to serve among women. For there are houses where you cannot send a deacon to women because of the pagans, but you can send a deaconess. And also because the office of a woman deacon is necessary in many other things. In the first place, when the women go down into the water they must be anointed with the oil of anointing by a deaconess . . . But a man should pronounce the names of the invocation of the deity over them in the water. And when the woman who is baptized comes out of the water, let the deaconess welcome her, and let her take her and teach her how the seal of baptism must be kept intact in purity and sanctity.

Didascalia Apostolorum.

III · Division and Unity between the Churches

1. The church spread throughout the world

A common factor can be discerned in the writings of Abercius, Origen and Irenaeus. From the end of the second century, Christians became aware that the universality of the church was something real: there were Christians throughout the world, that is to say in practice throughout the Roman empire. Christians were most numerous in the East (in Asia Minor, Syria and Palestine), particularly in the countryside. At the time of the last persecution, some areas had a majority of Christians.

In the West, evangelization progressed unequally. There was a high concentration of Christians in central Italy, in southern Spain and in Africa (the equivalent of the modern Morocco, Algeria and Tunisia). They were less numerous in Illyricum (present-day Yugoslavia), in northern Italy and in Gaul, In this last area, with the exception of Lyons and perhaps a few other places, the major churches were not founded until the middle of the third century (Toulouse, Paris, Rheims, Trier).

Beyond the frontiers of the Roman empire, the kingdom of Edessa (present-day Urfa and Turkey) was converted about 200. In the Persian empire, Christians were most numerous in upper Mesopotamia. During his campaigns against Antioch, King Chapur I (240–272) deported the Christians and their bishops to the interior of his empire, where they were soon subject to persecution. Armenia became Christian around 300 (through Gregory the Illuminator and King Tiridates).

46

The church spread to the ends of the earth

In a poetic language understandable to believers, the author of this epitaph proclaims his faith in Jesus, the church and the eucharist. He already bears witness to the 'catholicity' (universality) of the church. The fish (in Greek *ichthys*) symbolizes Christ, since the letters of the Greek word have the initials of Jesus Christ, Son of God, Saviour.

My name is Abercius. I am a disciple of a holy pastor who fed his flocks of sheep on the mountains and in the plains; who has keen eyes that can see everywhere. He taught me the scriptures which are worthy of faith. It was he who sent me to Rome to contemplate the sovereign majesty and to see a queen with garments and shoes of gold. I saw there a people marked with a radiant sign. I also saw the plain of Syria and all the cities, Nisibis on the other side of the Euphrates. I met Christians everywhere. Everywhere faith was my guide. Everywhere it provided for me as food a fish from the source, very great, very pure, caught by a holy virgin. She gave it constantly as food to eat with friends; she had a delicious wine which she offered with the bread. I, Abercius, have written these things at the age of seventy-two. May the brother who understands them pray for Abercius . . .

Funerary inscription of Abercius,
Bishop of Hierapolis in Syria,
end of the second century.

2. The church threatened by unrest and division

The unity of this church, which was the same throughout the world, was nevertheless intermittently threatened. There were arguments on liturgical procedures, or others arising over the forgiveness of apostates at the time of the persecutions, not to mention the personal rivalries for episcopal office.

Some were more serious. During the second century, the Christian message was faced, even within the church itself, with a great many doctrines which gave rise to rival groups. Were these groups still part of the church? How could the true faith be measured? Such were the problems of a church which seemed to be threatened with an explosion. We must confine ourselves here to a few examples.

The Jewish Christians wanted to preserve at all costs their own special rituals and theologies. They were loyal in the matter of circumcision and food restrictions. Anxious to safeguard biblical monotheism, they saw Jesus as no more than a man whom God had adopted on the day of his baptism. They were forced to retreat within themselves and were soon regarded as heretics by the other communities.

The diversification of groups and sects

Those Christians who were influenced by Greek dualism, which drew a marked contrast between matter and spirit (body and soul), and obsessed with the problem of evil, reinterpreted the Old Testament and the New Testament in a radically different way. They denied the incarnation and appealed to a knowledge (gnosis) mysteriously handed down through small groups. This knowledge brought salvation. These forms of knowledge brought together elements taken from Christianity, Judaism, Hellenism and even from some Iranian religions. Christian writers looked on them as Christian heresies, but historians wonder whether they were not connected with alien religions which had absorbed some Christian elements.

Marcion, about whom Irenaeus speaks, eliminated from the Bible everything which indicated a creator God and the incarnation, because he believed that matter and the body are evil. Other writers launched out into complicated speculations.

Mani (216–277), who came from Mesopotamia, professed an absolute dualism which brought together doctrines from Iran and Christianity. The history of the world was an enormous

---

The gospel proclaimed to all social groups

For Origen see chapter 3. Origen, who came from Alexandria, travelled a good deal in the empire and throughout the East. He himself proclaimed the gospel, and his *De Principiis*, on First Principles, is the earliest manual of dogmatic theology (first half of the third century).

If we observe how powerful the gospel has become in a very few years, despite the persecution and the torture, the *death and the confiscation, despite the small number of preachers, the word has been proclaimed throughout the earth.* *Greeks and barbarians, wise and foolish, have joined the religion of Jesus. We cannot doubt that this goes beyond human powers, for Jesus taught with authority and the persuasion necessary for the word to be established.*

Origen, *De principiis*, IV, 1,2.

The unity of the church threatened by the teaching of Marcion

The diversification of doctrines, groups and sects was a threat to the Christian message and to the universal church. So Irenaeus wanted to unmask these pseudo-revelations put forward by charismatic leaders. Marcion is perhaps the best known of these. His teaching had the advantage of simplicity and strict logic, which made it dangerous. By distinguishing the God of the Old Testament, an evil creator God, from the God of love revealed by Jesus, and denying that Jesus had a real human nature, Marcion opposed the view that human beings were saved wholly, body and spirit.

After him came Marcion of Pontus, who developed his teaching, shamelessly blaspheming the God whom the Law and the Prophets proclaimed, describing him as the author of evils, desirous of wars, changing his opinions and contradicting himself. But Jesus was from the Father who is above the God that formed the world, and came into Judaea in the time of Pontius Pilate, who was procurator of Tiberius Caesar; manifest in human form to those who were in Judaea, he abolished the Prophets and the Law, and all the works of that God who made the world, whom he calls the World Ruler. In addition to this he mutilated the Gospel according to Luke, removing everything about the birth of the Lord, and much of the teaching of the words of the Lord, in which the Lord is recorded as clearly confessing the creator of this universe as his Father. He persuaded his disciples that he was more veracious than the apostles who handed down the gospel, giving them not a gospel but a mere fragment of a gospel. He also similarly cut up the Epistles of Paul, removing whatever the apostle said clearly about the God who made the world, that he is the Father of our Lord Jesus Christ, and whatever the apostle teaches by referring to the prophetic writings that predict the coming of the Lord.

According to Marcion, only the souls of those who have learned his teaching will come to salvation; the body, since it is taken from the earth, cannot be saved.

Irenaeus of Lyons,
Against the Heresies, I, 27, 2f.

The Good Shepherd. Kirchen Museum

battle between the God of Goodness, or Light, and the God of Evil, or Darkness. Humankind was made up of fragments of light enclosed in evil matter. These fragments of light had to join up with the kingdom of Goodness again after many purifying actions or reincarnations. Jesus showed the way. Mani was his apostle, the new Paraclete.

These doctrines met with success because they answered the deep anguish of human beings. Some of the Gnostics were engaged in a true religious search. Those from whom we hear of them were often their opponents: they happened to be badly disposed towards them and simply gathered together a hotch-potch of un-verified rumours. But could the church accept this uncontrolled growth without risk when Christians were in danger of losing ground?

3. The rule of faith

In his work *Against the Heresies*, written at the end of the second century, Irenaeus, Bishop of Lyons described a certain number of doctrines which he deemed to be in error. He followed this up by pointing out where the true church, and therefore true doctrine, could be found. Christians must refer back to the tradition of the apostles, and this has been handed down to us in the churches where it is possible to trace the line back to the apostles through the succession of bishops or presbyters. That is why Irenaeus was

The characteristics of the true church

Having discussed the false doctrines, Irenaeus indicates the features by which the true church may be recognized.

(49) The church proclaims an identical message throughout the world

So having received this preaching and this faith, the church, though dispersed throughout the whole world, guards it with care, as though it lived only in a single dwelling. It believes there in an identical way, as though it had but one soul and one heart, and it preaches them, teaches them and hands them down with a unanimous voice, as though it had but one mouth.

Though languages may differ throughout the world, the content of the tradition is one and the same. The churches established in Germany do not have another faith or another tradition, nor do those among the Iberians (Spain) nor those among the Celts, nor those in the East, in Egypt, in Libya, nor those which are established at the centre of the world (Rome). Rather, like the sun, this creature of God is one and the same throughout the world, and likewise this light which is the preaching of the truth shines everywhere and illuminates all men who want 'to arrive at the knowledge of the truth' (I Tim. 2.4).

(50) The church transmits the tradition of the apostles in the succession of bishops

The tradition of the apostles, manifested throughout the world, can be clearly seen in every church by those who wish to behold the truth. We can enumerate those who were established by the apostles as bishops in the churches, and their successors down to our time . . . They certainly wished those whom they were leaving as their successors, handing over to them their own teaching position, to be perfect and irreproachable, since their sound conduct would be a great benefit . . . But since it would be very long in such a volume as this to enumerate the successions of all the churches, I can by pointing out the tradition which that very great, oldest, and well-known church, founded and established at Rome by those two most glorious apostles Peter and Paul, received from the apostles, and its faith known among men, which comes down to us through the successions of bishops, put to shame all of those who in any way, either through wicked self-conceit, or through vainglory, or through blind and evil opinion, gather as they should not. For every church must be in harmony with this church because of its outstanding pre-eminence, that is, the faithful from everywhere, since the apostolic tradition is preserved in it by those from everywhere.

Irenaeus of Lyons,
Against the Heresies, III, 3, 1–2.

at pains to list the bishops who had succeeded one another in Rome since Peter and Paul. In the churches of Smyrna and Ephesus, too, the succession of bishops could be traced back to the apostles. In a letter to a friend, Irenaeus recalls with some emotion that he had once heard Polycarp, Bishop of Smyrna, speak to him of John who had seen the Lord. And so, through Polycarp, Irenaeus himself is linked back to Jesus.

(51)

The Christian scriptures

Irenaeus decreed that no heed be paid to the scriptures which were handed down outside the apostolic succession. But it was not easy to tell which these were. Until the beginning of the second century, Christians had not stressed writings which might be special. For them, as for the Jews, scripture was what we call the Old Testament, the Bible, the inspired book. But Christians read the Bible in a different way from the Jews. They saw it as the prophetic book which foretold Christ's coming. They sought Jesus from it rather than the history of the Hebrew people. This assumes that they knew something about Jesus.

In speaking of Jesus, people referred to the witness of the apostles and those who were with them; this testimony was originally oral. When the apostles were gone or scattered, it was necessary to refer to their writings. In order to give a text authority it was attributed to an apostle. Each small group had its own Gospel, be it of Thomas, James, Paul or Peter. Some made their own choice, like Marcion or others.

In the face of such an abundance, the communities looked for criteria by which to choose. Apostolicity was one, because it was synonymous with antiquity, but forgeries were not unknown. The most important were pinpointed during the second century. As far as Irenaeus was concerned, four Gospels were universally recognized and no more. Directly or indirectly they were the work of one of the four great apostles, as were the other books he recognized: Matthew (Gospel), Peter (Epistle, Gospel of Mark), Paul (Epistles, Gospel of Luke and Acts); John (Gospel, Revelation, Epistles). Another writing from the middle of the century, the Muratorian fragment, named after the person who discovered it in the eighteenth century, gives very similar information. There was sometimes hesitation over some books (Revelation, Jude). On the other hand, certain Christians were tempted to consider the *Didache* or the *Shepherd of Hermas* among the inspired books.

---

(51)

From Irenaeus to Jesus

Round about 190, Irenaeus wrote to his friend Florinus, who had entered a heretical group. He reminded him that when they had been children, they had both heard Polycarp. Polycarp was the link in the chain which, through John, bound Irenaeus and his friend to Christ.

I can describe the place where blessed Polycarp sat and talked, his goings out and comings in, the character of his life, his personal appearance, his addresses to crowded congregations. I remember how he spoke of his intercourse with John and with the others who had seen the Lord; how he repeated their words from memory; and how the things that he had heard them say about the Lord, his miracles and his teaching, things that he had heard direct from the eyewitnesses of the Word of life, were proclaimed by Polycarp in complete harmony with scripture. To these things I listened eagerly at that time, by the mercy of God shown to me, not committing them to writing but learning them by heart. By God's grace, I constantly and conscientiously ruminate on them, and I can bear witness before God that if any such suggestion had come to the ears of that blessed and apostolic presbyter he would have cried out and stopped his ears . . .

Reported by Eusebius of Caesarea,
Church History, V, 20, 6f.

At the end of the second century the church drew up its canon (criterion) of the scriptures of the New Testament.

4. The birth of theology

Faced with this burgeoning of doctrines, the leaders of the communities tried to enlighten Christians as to what was the true faith of the church. They expounded the accepted writings, showing how Christ was the fulfilment of the bibilical revelation. They explained this orally at celebrations of the eucharist and in catechisms to those who were to be baptized. Several of these bishops, priests, and others turned writer and gave birth to the first theologies.

In the seven letters of his that we have, Ignatius, Bishop of Antioch at the beginning of the second century, tried to safeguard the doctrinal unity of the communities of Asia Minor. Whereas many people spoke of Jesus as one who had taken on the likeness of a man, Ignatius vehemently defended the reality of the incarnation: Jesus was a real historical person, truly a man. Christians encountered this Jesus in a unified community in the eucharist: 'Only take part in one eucharist, because there is only one flesh of our Lord Jesus Christ, and only one cup to unite us in his blood . . . as there is one bishop . . .'

Irenaeus, whom we have already seen as a peacemaker in the argument over the date of Easter and opposing the pseudo-revelations, put forward a theology in his *Against the Heresies* and *Demonstration of the Apostolic Preaching*, which is a biblical catechism. Irenaeus constructs all his theological thinking around the theme of 're-capitulation' put forward in Paul (Eph. 1.10). The life of humanity is a slow process of moving forward under the guidance of the Word of God. The Word incarnate in Jesus summed up all mankind and the whole history of the world. It is impossible to forget his famous saying, 'The glory of God is living mankind, and the life of man is the

vision of God.'

Coming originally from Alexandria in Egypt, Origen (185–253) dedicated his life to teaching and preaching. The bishop entrusted him with a catechetical school which seems to have been the first of its kind. Origen travelled a lot. At Caesarea in Palestine he became a priest and founded a great Christian library. He died as a result of tortures suffered during the Decian persecution. Origen spent his life commenting on or preaching the scriptures. The greater part of his immense output of work has been lost, because of the accusations of heresy lodged against him two centuries later . . . For Origen, Christ is present in the whole of the scripture. The people and events of the Old Testament foretold Christ, the sacraments and the church. Just as human beings consist of a body, soul (the vital principle) and spirit according to Greek anthropology, so scripture has three interpretations: a literal one (historical), a moral one and a mystical, or spiritual one. Origen thus launches out on an allegorical interpretation which is sometimes quite bewildering.

We have already met Tertullian and one or other of his famous phrases: 'The blood of martyrs is the seed of Christians,' he said, because it was the courage of Christians which converted him. Violent by temperament, at the end of his life he joined a sectarian group and fought against the mainstream communities of Carthage and Rome. His talent as a polemicist must not make us forget that he was also a theologian. He provided Christian thought with a Latin vocabulary, employing the terms 'Trinity' and 'Person' for the first time in connection with God.

Cyprian (200–258), who was born a pagan, found moral liberation in Christianity. He became a priest, and then Bishop of Carthage. He was caught up in the turmoil of the Decian persecution, and then in coping with the effects of a plague. At one time he had a tense relationship with the Bishop of Rome: the two men

Origen (185–253)

52 Scripture always has a spiritual sense, but it does not always have a literal sense

Jericho collapsed at the sound of the priests' trumpets. I said before that Jericho is a figure of this world, the power and defences of which are destroyed, as we see, by the priests' trumpets. The world's power and defences, the walls it relied on, were the worship of idols . . . The son of Nun, Joshua (Greek Jesus) foreshadowed the coming of Christ. When Christ came, he sent out his apostles, as Joshua had sent out the priests, and like the priests they carried resonant trumpets, namely the gospel . . . and all the devices of idolatry and the dogmas of the philosophers have been razed to the ground . . .

Origen, *Homily on Joshua*, 7

53 The Good Samaritan (Luke 10.30–37)

'A man went down from Jerusalem to Jericho.' We see in this man Adam, man and his true destiny, the fall which followed disobedience. Jerusalem is paradise or the heavenly Jerusalem; Jericho is the world; the robbers represent the hostile powers, the demons or those false doctrines which came before Christ; the wounds are disobedience and sin; the theft of clothing symbolizes the stripping off of incorruptibility and immorality, along with all the virtues; the man left half-dazed represents the present state of our nature which has become semi-mortal (in fact the soul is immortal); the priest is the Law; the Levite the Prophets; the Samaritan the Christ who took flesh in Mary's womb; the beast of burden is the body of Christ; the wine is the word of his teaching (which cures through reconciliation); the oil is the word of goodwill to men and merciful compassion; the inn is the church; the innkeeper represents the apostles and their successors, the bishops and teachers of the church . . . ; the return of the Samaritan is the second manifestation of Christ.

Origen, *Homily on Luke*, II, 120f.

33

were not in agreement over the theology of baptism. In Carthage, repentant heretics were baptized again; in Rome their first baptism was considered to be valid. Cyprian ended his life as a martyr. A pastor, in his work he touched on the various aspects of the Christian life: prayer, alms, clothing . . . In many writings he tried to safeguard the unity of the church after the upsets of the persecution. The unity of the church is a sign that it has encountered the authentic Christ; this unity lies in the agreement of the bishops amongst themselves. In his letters Cyprian evokes a multitude of people and events.

For further reading

H. F. von Campenhausen, *The Formation of the Christian Bible*, A. & C. Black and Fortress Press 1977

Gregory Dix, *The Shape of the Liturgy*, Dacre Press 1945

Joachim Jeremias, *Infant Baptism in the First Four Centuries*, SCM Press and Westminster Press 1962

Joseph Martos, *Doors to the Sacred. A Historical Introduction to Sacraments in the Christian Church*, SCM Press and Doubleday 1981

W. Rordorf, *Sunday*, SCM Press and Westminster Press 1968

Edward Schillebeeckx, *The Church with a Human Face. A New and Expanded Theology of Ministry*, SCM Press and Crossroad Publishing Company 1985

4

The Church in the Christian Empire

Fourth and Fifth Centuries

The Emperor Constantine

The church of Constantine . . .

The peace of the church in 313 marked the beginning of the 'church of Constantine'. This term implies a new kind of relationship between church and society: the church was integrated into a state which considered itself Christian. Many inferences follow from this. The state intervened in the life of the church and expected ideological support from it. The emperor tried to smooth over doctrinal conflicts which upset law and order, and took the initiative in convoking councils. At the same time the church obtained certain financial, material and legal advantages from the state. It relied on the emperor to fight against heresy and paganism. Talk of the church of Constantine has often had pejorative connotations. From that time on, the church was to be imprisoned in a political and cultural framework

which dulled for ever the fervour of the gospel. For some people, this church of Constantine only came to an end with the Second Vatican Council, which at last accepted that the spheres had become separated and distanced itself from civil powers.

. . . or of Theodosius?

If we look more closely, things are not so simple. Developments began before Constantine and continued long afterwards. From the end of the third century, some of the bishops had adopted a style of power which was close to that of the Roman governors. Besides, Christianity did not become the state religion until the time of Theodosius (380).

Rather than definite goodwill on the part of religious and political leaders, it was more a question of a slow absorption of the church into the cultural and legal milieu which surrounded it.

This chapter describes the transformation of the church in a state which from that time was well disposed towards it, and also the transformations in society itself which came about once the church had become an important and omnipresent institution.

I · From Religious Freedom to State Religion

1. The religion of Constantine

Constantine, who was born in 280 in Nis (in Mesia, present-day Yugoslavia), the son of the tolerant emperor Constantius Chlorus and Helena, a Christian, espoused Christianity in 312. The circumstances of this 'conversion', like the nature of his faith, are uncertain. The tendency in his family was towards a solar syncretism, that is to say towards a kind of monotheism. The edifying legend of the battle at the Milvian Bridge (see chapter 2, p.45) allows us to say that something happened there and that the emperor thought of himself as a Christian from that time on. He only indicated the credibility of those Christians who told him that it was Christ who had granted him the victory. In spite of Eusebius' praises, Constantine was never a model Christian. He was baptized on his death bed (337), and his many crimes are witness to morals that were far from being Christian. He played the executioner to his own family, ordering the death of his father-in-law, three brothers-in-law, a son and his wife. A good example of faith without morals!

Constantine, sole emperor

In 313, Constantine was ruler in the West and Licinius in the East. The two emperors soon clashed, and Licinius took it out on the Christians. In taking up arms against him, Constantine gave the impression of waging a religious war to defend the church. With Licinius defeated and assassinated, Constantine was left in 324 as the sole emperor. We may take this date as the real starting point of the 'Christian empire.'

The foundation of Constantinople

Constantine decided to stay in the East and to found a new capital for the empire. He chose the small town of Byzantium on the Bosphorus and gave it the name Constantinople (Constantine's town). The choice of site had been revealed to him by God in a dream. The solemn consecration took place on 11 May 330, during a ceremony which was at the same time pagan and Christian. This switch of capitals had important consequences for the empire and for the state. The empire's centre of gravity shifted towards the East, and the emperors became less interested in the West. Moreover, within the church Constantinople sought to be a 'second Rome' and attracted Christians of Greek culture. The foundation of the new capital had within it the germ of the future division of the church.

2. The Christian emperors

The emperors retained the title *pontifex maximus* (great pontiff), i.e. head of traditional religion, but as Christians they played a similar role in the church. Christian symbols (a Christ monogram) appeared on the coinage from 315, and so the coinage also became an instrument of universal propaganda. The emperor looked on himself as the 'equal of the apostles' or as an 'outside bishop', which explains his interference. For Eusebius and most Christians, this change of heart after the persecutions was unheard of and beyond all hopes. The kingdom of God had come down to earth. Christians now accepted the sacred nature of the emperor, whom they naturally enough looked on as the head of the Christian people: a new Moses, a new David. It was under this title that he convened the councils.

Imperial favours

Christians were mindful of his favours. He gave them official buildings (basilicas) and palaces to put to religious use. He had beautiful places of worship built, such as the basilicas of St Peter of the Vatican, the Holy Sepulchre, Bethlehem, and all the churches of Constantinople, and he gave rich presents to the bishops. The Christian communities were allowed to receive bequests, and so the church came to inherit an enormous legacy. The clergy obtained legal privileges; the episcopal tribunals had a civil jurisdiction, and the bishops were considered to be on an equal footing with governors.

Policing worship

No emperor could dissociate himself from religious affairs, above all when they threatened

---

54

The empire of Constantine, the kingdom of God on earth?

Thus all men living were free from oppression by the tyrants; and released from their former miseries, they all in their various ways acknowledged as the only true God the Defender of the godly. Above all for us who had fixed our hopes on the Christ of God there was unspeakable happiness, and a divine joy blossomed in all hearts as we saw that every place which a little while before had been reduced to dust by the tyrants' wickedness was now, as if from a prolonged and deadly stranglehold, coming back to life; and that cathedrals were again rising from their foundations high into the air, and far surpassing in magnificence those previously destroyed by the enemy.

Emperors too, the most exalted (Constantine and Licinius) by a succession of ordinances in favour of the Christians, confirmed still further and more surely the blessings that God showered upon us; and a stream of personal letters from the emperor reached the bishops, accompanied by honours and gifts of money.

On this medal, dating from the time of Constantius II, the son of Constantine, you can see the Labarum or standard with the arms of Christ which Constantine had placed at the head of his legions

Old troubles were forgotten, and all irreligion passed into oblivion; good things present were enjoyed, those yet to come eagerly awaited. In every city the victorious emperor published decrees full of humanity and laws that gave proof of munificence and true piety. Thus all tyranny had been purged away, and the kingdom that was theirs was preserved securely and without question for Constantine and his sons alone. They, having made it their first task to wipe the world clean from hatred of God, rejoiced in the blessings that he had conferred upon them, and, by the things they did for all men to see, displayed love of virtue and love of God, devotion and thankfulness to the Almighty. Eusebius of Caesarea, *Church History*, X, 2, 10.

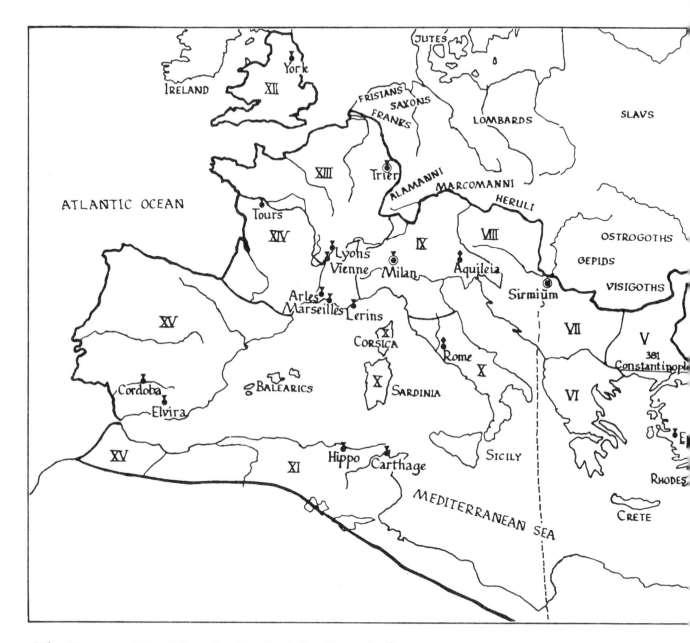

The Roman World at the End of the Fourth Century

The dioceses are rearrangements of provinces

I Egypt	III Pontus	V Thracia	VII Dacia	IX Italia annonaria	XI Africa
II East	IV Asia	VI Macedonia	VIII Pannonia	X Italia suburbcaria	XII Britannia

70

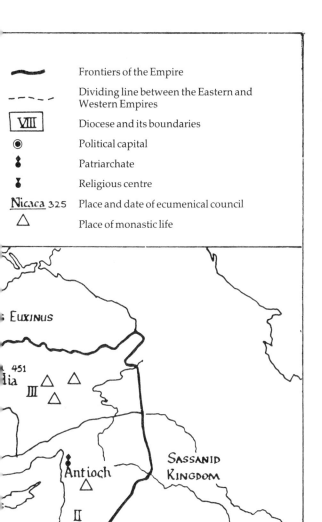

Euxinus

451

dia III △ △
      △

Antioch
△

SASSANID
KINGDOM

II

DEAD SEA

dria △

XIII Gallia
XIV The Seven Provinces   XV Hispania

stability within the empire. Besides, Christians appealed to the emperor to arbitrate in their quarrels. The following chapter will consider at length the imperial interventions in the Arian crisis from 325 onwards, but before that we must look at an earlier crisis. From 313 on, Christians in Africa had been asking for the emperor's help over the Donatist affair, which poisoned the life of the church in Africa throughout the fourth century. In 312, the election of Caecilian as Bishop of Carthage was contested. Those who consecrated him were said to have been guilty of apostasy during the Diocletian persecution. Another bishop, Donatus, was appointed. The conflict spread throughout all of Roman Africa. In many cities, two rival bishops set up against each other. The emperor only granted money to legitimate bishops, in this case Caecilian and his friends, but the Donatists appealed to Constantine to recognize the justice of their cause. He put the problem to the bishops of Italy and then of France (in Arles, in 314), they condemned Donatus. His followers revolted, and Constantine sent troops to dislodge them from the churches which they were occupying. Since no peace was achieved, Constantine granted freedom of worship to all and gave money to the Catholics to rebuild other churches.

3. The slow elimination of paganism

In 313, Constantine had granted freedom of conscience and freedom of worship to all religions. Although lacking their former strength, the old faiths were still alive. The East apart, most of the regions of the empire were not even half Christian. The traditional religion was still deeply entrenched at both ends of the social scale. The milieu of Roman senators and intellectuals remained loyal to the cultural and political tradition, with its religious dimension. Country people kept up the rites which assured the fertility of the land and the livestock. The word paganism comes from *paganus*, country-dweller.

71

Constantine, benefactor of bishops and clergy and defender of sound doctrine

These two letters date from 313. Caecilian was the bishop whose election had been contested by the supporters of Donatus at the beginning of the Donatist schism. This is the 'unstable thought' of which the emperor speaks.

55 Constantine to Caecilian, Bishop of Carthage

Inasmuch as I have resolved that in all provinces, namely, Africa, Numidia and Mauretania, certain named ministers of the lawful and most holy catholic religion should receive some contribution towards expenses, I have sent a letter to Ursus, the Eminent Finance Officer of Africa, informing him that he must arrange the transfer to Your Steadfastness of three thousand folles in cash (sum uncertain, but a very large amount of money).

And whereas I have learnt that certain persons with unstable thought desire to lead astray the laity of the most holy Catholic church by disreputable enticements, this is to inform you that

I have given full instructions to Anulinus the Proconsul and also to Patricius the Prefect's Vicarius in person, that in all matters, and particularly in this, they are to make the appropriate arrangements and are on no account to overlook such incidents. If therefore you observe any such persons persisting in this insane conduct, you must without hesitation apply to the aforementioned judges and refer the matter to them, so that, as I have instructed them in person, they may bring pressure to bear.

Eusebius of Caesarea,
Ecclesiastical History, X, 6.

56 From Constantine to Anulinus, Proconsul of Africa at Carthage

So in the province entrusted to you, in the catholic church over which Caecilian presides, I desire those who give their services to these sacred observances – the people commonly known as clergymen – once and for all to be kept entirely free from all public duties. This will ensure that by no error or sacrilegious fall from grace will they be drawn away from the worship owed to the Godhead; rather will they be completely free to serve their own law at all times. In thus rendering wholehearted service to the Deity, it is evident that they will be making an immense contribution to the welfare of the community.

Eusebius of Caesarea,
Ecclesiastical History, X, 7.

The first basilica of St Peter of the Vatican (following a reconstruction by K. J. Conant) had a wide atrium at its entrance

Slow elimination of paganism

However, during the fourth century, legislation became increasingly favourable towards the old religion. On their own initiative and often under pressure from Christians, the emperors gradually forbade the pagan cults. A few laws taken from the Codes will serve as illustrations. Constantine prohibited certain practices: magic and divination (consulting the entrails of animals). Then the prohibitions increased and became more and more severe. Constantine forbade sacrifices, closed the temples and decreed the death sentence for those who disobeyed (356).

57

But the law was not applied rigorously, and there was resistance to it, which should be noted.

Julian and the 'return' of paganism

Paganism enjoyed a revival under the Emperor Julian (361–3) whom Christians surnamed 'The

---

(57)

From religious liberty to state religion

The imperial decisions were collected at several stages in Codes. The most important are the Theodosian Code (which takes its name from the Emperor Theodisius II, in 438, and the Justinian Code (from the name of the Emperor Justinian, in 529). The names of the authors of the laws have been kept. From 392 onwards the term religion was synonymous with Christianity.

The Emperor Constantine in 319

Theodosian Code IX, 16,2

We prohibit soothsayers and priests and those persons who are accustomed to minister to such ceremonies to approach a private home or to cross the threshold of another person under the pretext of friendship. We have provided punishment against them if they should disregard this statute. But you who think that this art is advantageous to you, go to the public altars and shrines and celebrate the rites of your custom; for We do not prohibit the ceremonies of a bygone perversion to be conducted openly.

The Emperor Constantius in 356

Theodosian Code XVI, 10,6

If any persons should be proved to devote their attention to sacrifice or to worship images, We command that they shall be subjected to capital punishment.

The Emperor Theodosius, Edict of Thessalonica in 380

Theodosian Code XVI, 1, 2

It is Our will that all the peoples who are ruled by the administration of Our Clemency shall practise that religion which the divine Peter the Apostle transmitted to the Romans, as the religion which he introduced makes clear even unto this day. It is evident that this is the religion that is followed by the Pontiff Damasus and by Peter, Bishop of Alexandria . . . We command that those persons who follow this rule shall embrace the name of Catholic Christians. The rest, however, whom We adjudge demented and insane, shall sustain the infamy of heretical dogmas, their meeting places shall not receive the name of churches, and they shall be smitten first by divine vengeance and secondly by the retribution of Our own initiative, which we shall assume in accordance with the divine judgment.

The Emperors Theodosius, Arcadius and Honorius in 392

Theodosian Code XVI 10, 2

But if any person should venerate, by placing incense before them, images made by the work of mortals . . . or should bind a tree with fillets, or should erect an altar of turf that he has dug up . . . this is a complete outrage against religion. Such person, as one guilty of the violation of religion, shall be punished by the forfeiture of that house or landholding in which it is proved that he served a pagan superstition.

Translations from *The Theodosian Code*, ed. Clyde Pharr, Corpus of Roman Law I, Princeton 1952.

The Emperor Theodosius (378–395)

Apostate'. A nephew of Constantine, he had escaped the massacre of his entire family by Constantine's heirs, and so had some reason to doubt the value of Christianity. Brought up as a Christian, he shook off Christianity when he became emperor. He was infatuated with classical literature and did his best to revive the traditional religion and denounce Christianity in his work *Against the Galileans*. In spite of his undoubted qualities, Julian was not popular, and his death in battle was considered to be divine punishment. The momentum of Christianity could not be halted.

Outlawed paganism

With Julian dead, his successors increased their measures against paganism and against Christian heretics. In 379 Gratian rejected the title of

---

St Augustine: from persuasion to repression

Augustine, Bishop of Hippo from 396, encountered the rivalry and opposition of a Donatist bishop. The Donatist schism often led to violence, because it drew on social conflicts. Augustine primarily used persuasion and sweetness to convince his adversaries. Gradually, worn down by the violence of the Donatists, he moved from persuasion to 'good coercion' and finally to repression organized by the authorities. The reference to the words *compelle intrare* ('force them to come in') in Luke 14.23 will often be taken up in the Middle Ages.

I do not propose to compel men to embrace the communion of any party, but desire the truth to be made known to persons who, in their search for it, are free from disquieting apprehensions. On our side there shall be no appeal to men's fear of the civil power; on your side let there be no intimidation by a mob of Circumcelliones.[1] Let us attend to the real matter in debate, and let our arguments appeal to reason and to the authoritative teaching of the divine scriptures, dispassionately and calmly, so far as we are able; let us ask, seek, and knock, that we may receive and find, and that to us the door may be opened.

Letter 23, 7 (392).

You must not consider just the mere fact of the coercion, but the nature of that to which one is coerced, whether it be good or bad: not that anyone can become good in spite of his own will, but that, through fear of suffering what he does not desire, he either renounces his hostile prejudices or is compelled to examine the truth of which he had been contentedly ignorant, and under the influence of this fear repudiates the error he was wont to defend, or seeks the truth of which he formerly knew nothing, and now willingly holds what he formerly rejected . . .

I have therefore yielded to the evidence afforded by these instances which my colleagues have laid before me. For originally my opinion was that no one should be coerced into the unity of Christ, that we must act only by words, fight only by arguments, and prevail by force of reason, lest we should have those whom we knew as avowed heretics feigning themselves to be Catholics. But *this opinion of mine was overcome not by the words of those who controverted it, but by the conclusive instance to which they could point.*

Letter 93, 16,17 (408).

There is a persecution of unrighteousness, which the impious inflict upon the church of Christ; and there is a righteous persecution, which the church of Christ inflicts upon the impious . . . Moreover she persecutes in the spirit of love, they in the spirit of wrath . . . Wherefore, if the power which the church has received by divine appointment in its due season, through the religious character and the faith of kings, be the instrument by which those who are found in the highways and hedges – that is, in heresies and schisms – are compelled to come in, then let them not find fault with being compelled, but consider whether they be so compelled. The supper of the Lord is the unity of the body of Christ . . .

Letter 185,11, 24 (417): commentary on Luke 14.23 ('Compel them to come in . . . ').

[1] The *Circumcelliones* were farm workers, often vagabonds, who served as the Donatists' shock-troops.

Great Pontiff. In 380, Christianity was proclaimed as the state religion by Theodosius. Heretics were to be persecuted just as much as pagans: every pagan custom was prohibited in 392. This was a death blow for the old religion. Pagan festivals were no longer celebrated and the temples were demolished. Christians thought that they had a licence to perpetrate acts of violence against pagan people and places. By the beginning of the fourth century the reversal was complete; the pagans, once the persecutors, had become the persecuted, and vice versa. The power of the state, formerly at the service of paganism, was now at the service of Christianity. But the same mental processes were operating. How could it be otherwise? A separation between religion and the state was inconceivable. Religion was still the foundation and the cement of society. Only the religion had changed.

Persuasion or repression

Were Christians happy to accept the help of the authorities in the fight against paganism and heretical movements? It is certain that the majority were, and that in the end the emperors were only interpreting their wishes. But there had been some hesitation among certain bishops at the time of the condemnation of Priscillian. This Bishop of Avila, in Spain, had stirred up an excitable community, very austere and rather secretive, in the 380s. Two Spanish bishops accused him of Manichaeism before the ecclesiastical authorities, and then before the Emperor Maximus at Trier. Martin, Bishop of Tours, who happened to be at Trier, urged the prosecuting bishop to step down and the Emperor not to shed blood. 'It would be an unheard-of thing,' he said, 'and monstrous to have an ecclesiastical affair judged by a secular court.' Nevertheless the emperor condemned Priscillian to death along with several of his followers on the charge of immorality and practising magic (385). These were the first heretics to

die under the impact of state justice. Ambrose, Bishop of Milan, broke off relations with the bishops who had accused Priscillian, and cultured pagans were extremely indignant.

The situation could in fact be quite complex. Augustine, Bishop of Hippo, in an African church troubled by the Donastist schism, came to accept the collaboration of the imperial authorities in fighting against the dissidents, who often resorted to armed violence.

4. Society transformed by the gospel

Did the spirit of Christianity influence the institutions of the later empire? Without doubt the Christian calendar gave rhythms to social life from then on: since 325, Sundays, and the great Christian festivals, had been holidays. A Christian influence could be discerned in legislation which had to do with family matters. The law prohibited adultery with a slave. Obstacles were put in the way of divorce, no matter who was involved. No doubts were felt over slavery – the church herself had slaves – but it was forbidden to break up families of slaves, and they could be set free more easily, by a declaration read in church in the presence of a clergyman. A little more humanity was shown in the prisons; gaolers were not allowed to let the prisoners die of hunger, and they had to be able to see the light of the sun once a day. The clergy had the right to visit in the prisons.

Charitable institutions

Not being able to effect a major transformation in the way things were done, Christian concern showed itself in the creation of charitable institutions. In the very long term, it was through these that the structures would be transformed. Almsgiving, traditionally practised since the time of the Acts of the Apostles, flourished in the Christian empire. Basil, Bishop of Caesarea in Cappadocia, founded a truly Christian city which consisted of church, monastery, hospice and hospital. Travellers were welcomed there, and sick and poor people. The monks there were qualified people. In Alexandria, the bishop had an army of five hundred male nurses. The port of Ostia had a reception centre for pilgrims.

Limited Christianizing

However, the Christianizing of society was still limited. The newly baptized were not always anxious to change their ways. The law forbade infanticide, but not the exposure of children. The prohibition of gladiator fights remained more often than not a dead letter until the fourth century. Hesitations Christians felt over the army faded. The later empire became more and more of a totalitarian regime, a despotic police state. The application of justice frequently involved torture, though the bishops sometimes tried to oppose this kind of violence. The Emperor Theodosius, who had ordered the massacre of seven thousand people in Thessalonica, was required by Ambrose (in 390) to do penance before taking part in the eucharist again.

II · The Development of Worship and the Progress of Evangelization

1. The evolution of baptism and penance

(59)

Until the time of the peace of the church in 313, becoming a Christian meant running the risk of martyrdom. Then everything changed. In huge numbers, the inhabitants of the empire thought it would be to their advantage to become Christians, although they were not willing to accept the moral demands imposed by baptism. The rites of baptism and penance did not change, but the practice of them was much modified.

Baptism

(86)

Many were marked with the sign of the cross, received elementary instruction in the faith, tasted blessed salt, and then went no further. Their catechumenate stretched out indefinitely, and they postponed their baptism until extreme old age or death. In fact, since all sins were pardoned at baptism, and since penance could only be granted once in a lifetime, it was thought better to wait until bodily desires had spent themselves before making a definite commitment. Nor was the church particularly interested in this tentative group of catechumens, preferring to concentrate its attention on those who were asking for baptism at an early date.

The latter presented themselves as candidates at the beginning of Lent, which acted as a chronological framework for their preparation. The catechesis, backed by the bishop or his representative, progressively unfolded the content of the faith through a symbol of faith, or creed. For educational reasons – it was a matter of implementing this teaching, which also had to be lived out – the catechumens were asked to keep quiet about what they had learned, in front of the non-baptized. During meetings for worship, they were subjected to exorcisms, and had read to them in solemn fashion the Apostles' Creed, which they would have to recite on Holy Saturday. In some churches the Lord's Prayer was treated in the same way. The rite of Easter Eve stayed the same. The catechisms continued during the week following baptism. That is the reason why there was sometimes a distinction between baptismal catechisms before the baptism – which concentrated on the creed and moral

(59)

Different motives among baptismal candidates in the middle of the fourth century

Cyril (315–387), Bishop of Jerusalem, had an episcopacy troubled by the Arian crisis. He was exiled three times. His most famous work is the series of twenty-four catechetical lectures which he gave in the basilica of the Holy Sepulchre. The extract which follows is drawn from the catechesis welcoming those who were candidates for baptism at the beginning of Lent. Cyril is not deceived by the variety of motivations among the candidates.

We, the ministers of Christ, have admitted every one, and occupying, as it were, the place of doorkeepers, we left the door open: and possibly you entered with your soul bemired with sins and a will defiled. But you did enter, for you were allowed: your name was inscribed. Did you see the good behaviour of our congregation? Did you see the order and the discipline? Did you note the reading of the scriptures, the presence of the clergy, the course of our instruction? Lower your eyes in this place and be taught by what you see. Go out opportunely now and enter most opportunely tomorrow.

If you have a heart filled with avarice, come back in another dress. Take off the garment that you had and do not cover it with another. Put off debauchery and uncleanness and put on the shining garment of purity. As for me, this is the advice I give you before Jesus the bridegroom of your souls sees your fashions. You have time, for you have forty days for repentance; you have a full opportunity to put off, and to wash, and to put on and enter.

But if you persist in an evil purpose, the speaker is blameless, but you must not hope to receive grace: for the water will receive you but not the spirit. If anyone feels wounded, let him take the salve; if anyone has fallen, let him arise.

Possibly, too, you have come on another pretext. It is possible that a man is wishing to pay court to a woman and came on that account. The remark applies in like manner to women also in their turn. Perhaps a slave wishes to please his master, and a friend his friend.

I accept this bait for the hook and welcome you, though you came with an ill purpose, yet as one to be stayed by a good hope. Perhaps you did not know where you were coming or in what kind of net you were taken. You have come within the church's nets. Be taken alive, do not flee, for Jesus is angling for you, not in order to kill, but by killing to make alive; for you must die and rise again. For you have heard the apostle say, 'Dead indeed to sin but alive to righteousness.' Die to your sins, and live to righteousness; live from this very day.

Cyril of Jerusalem (313–387),
Catechetical Lectures, Prologue, 4,5.

conversion – and mystagogical catechisms after the baptism, focussed on the baptism itself and the eucharist.

In an age when the struggle against a hostile society had gone into its second phase, theology emphasized the efficacious value of the rite, signifying that God's gift came through grace. St Augustine, in the hope of encouraging the baptism of children, stressed original sin, which called for divine intervention even in the absence of all personal sin.

Penance

When their enthusiasm had worn off, Christians often lapsed into serious errors. But since penance could only be undertaken once in a lifetime, sinners put it off until the last possible moment, often until death was near.

Official or canonical penance was an exceptional practice, undertaken only by those who had committed a grave and scandalous offence which excluded them from the eucharist. These offences did not coincide exactly with what we call mortal sins. The majority of Christians therefore did not have occasion to make this solemn penance.

Anyone who had committed a grave sin confessed it, in principle in secret, to the bishop, who could also request sinners to come and do penance. This took place by stages in the framework of a liturgical assembly. As the sinners began their penance, the bishop laid his hands on their heads and clothed them in a hairshirt, a garment made of goat's hair. They then formed a special group (order) within the church and no longer took part in the offertory or in the communion. During Lent, the priests again laid their hands on the penitents. At the end of their time, which varied according to the gravity of the offence and could last for several years, the bishop absolved the penitents by a laying on of hands, generally on Maundy Thursday.

The conditions imposed on the penitent were very severe. He had to wear the garments of a pauper, go unwashed, fast, not eat meat, give alms. He was forbidden to engage in certain trades and had to abstain from sexual relations. Even after he had received forgiveness, the prohibitions on his trade and on sexual relations lasted until his death. Anyone who did not observe these restrictions was considered to be an apostate for whom there was no forgiveness, since penance could only be undertaken once. The only other thing he could hope for was to be given the last sacrament on his death bed.

The severity of this official penance came to rebound against itself. The catechumens postponed their baptism so that their sins might one day be pardoned without their having to suffer any particular hardships. As for sinners who were already baptized, they put off penance until the last possible moment because they were unwilling to commit themselves to abandoning their trades or their marital relationships. Besides, penance was refused to people who were still young. It became a pastoral measure for the old and the dying.

Because penance was a last-minute thing, sinners were invited to penitential acts during their daily life: mortification, prayer, giving alms, etc. They were also excluded from the eucharist. Those who had committed the most infamous sins were excommunicated by name, but many of them, having abstained for some time, communicated again without receiving absolution. Some of them even thought that taking communion washed away their sins. In the fifth century, the order of penitents was increasingly abandoned by sinners, who could not accept its severity. By contrast, the most exacting Christians submitted to official penance in a spirit of humility.

2. The splendour of worship

The eucharist displayed more and more pomp, through the richness of its buildings, the basilicas, its vestments and liturgical objects. Speeches, processions and sermons grew in number. In the West, the custom of a daily eucharist gradually evolved, while in the East customs varied.

The liturgical year

It seems that, from the end of the second century, the rejoicing of Easter was considered to extend into the fifty days that followed. But the festival of Pentecost as a celebration of the gift of the Spirit only dates from the end of the fourth century. Before long the two days before Easter were associated with it as a time of fasting and preparation, especially for the catechumens who were to be baptized on Easter Eve. Lent itself as we understand it, that is to say the forty days of preparation before Easter, came into being a little after the peace of the church. Then fasting, which had first of all been laid down just for the week before Easter, extended to the forty days, although this was calculated in various ways. The intention was to imitate the forty days during which Jesus fasted in the desert. Baptismal preparation continued to reinforce Lent.

Two festivals with fixed dates appeared during the fourth century. In the East, Epiphany on January 6 celebrated the appearance of God on earth: the birth of Jesus and his baptism. January 6 was the day of an Egyptian solar festival. In the West, round about the year 330, the birth of Jesus was celebated on December 25. This was the day of the pagan celebration of the victorious sun at the time when the days began to grow longer. At the end of the fourth century, the two festivals were celebrated in their two respective areas. In the West, Christmas was set aside for the celebration of the birth at Bethlehem and Epiphany for the other appearances of Jesus: the visit of the Magi, his baptism and the first miracle at Cana.

60 A pilgrimage to the Holy Land at the end of the fourth century

The identity of Egeria (or Etheria) is uncertain. In all probability she was a well-to-do Spanish lady (from Galicia) who lived at the end of the fourth century. She was perhaps a religious, or at least a virgin in the world, who undertook a pilgrimage to holy places and gave an account of her journey to her sisters. Her text gives us valuable information about the Christian Middle East at the end of antiquity and on the liturgy of Jerusalem. Moreover, Egeria shows us how credulity and piety give rise to the identification of geographical locations for and souvenirs of events in the Old and New Testament. Guides are always ready to satisfy the curiosity of pilgrims.

It was about four o'clock by the time we had come right down the Mount and reached the Bush. This, as I have already said, is the Burning Bush out of which the Lord spoke to Moses, and it is at the head of the valley with the church and all the cells. The Bush itself is in front of the church in a very pretty garden which has plenty of excellent water. Near by you are also shown the place where holy Moses was standing when God said to him, 'Undo the fastening of your shoes', and so on. Since it was already four in the afternoon by the time we got there, it was too late for us to be able to make the Offering, but we had a prayer in the church and also in the garden by the Bush, and as usual the appropriate passage was read from the book of Moses. Then, because it was late, we had our meal with the holy men in the garden near the Bush, and stayed there for the night . . . (4.7f.)

(From Mount Nebo) we saw the whole country of the Sodomites . . . We were also shown the place where Lot's wife had her memorial, as you read in the Bible. But what we saw, reverend ladies, was not the actual pillar, but only the place where it had once been.

The pillar itself, they say, has been submerged in the Dead Sea – at any rate we did not see it, and I cannot pretend we did. In fact it was the bishop there, the Bishop of Zoar, who told us that it was now a good many years since the pillar had been visible . . . (12.6f.).

Then I remembered that according to the Bible it was near Salim that holy John baptized at Aenon (John 3.23). So I asked if it was far away. 'There it is,' said the holy presbyter, 'two hundred yards away. If you like we can walk over there. It is from that spring that the village has this excellent supply of clean water you see.' Thanking him I asked him to take us, and we set off. He led us along a well-kept valley to a very neat apple-orchard, and there in the middle of it he showed us a good clean spring of water which flowed in a single stream. There was a kind of pool in front of the spring at which it appears holy John Baptist administered baptism (15.1f.).

Texts taken from *Egeria's Travels* ed. John Wilkinson, SPCK 1971.

The cult of martyrs and pilgrimages

The cult of martyrs enjoyed a luxuriant growth and sometimes borrowed from old pagan religiosity: for example, *refrigerium*, the custom of providing food on tombs. Huge basilicas were built on the mortal remains of the martyrs (such as St Peter at the Vatican). People had themselves buried in the vicinity. The taste for relics gave rise to more and more sensational discoveries: the cross of Christ, the remains of St Stephen, of the Apostles, and so on. It spread throughout the church. Interest grew to the same extent as interest in places connected with the Bible and the life of Christ. From this developed pilgrimages, the best known of which was that of Egeria to Jerusalem about 400. The credulity of the pilgrims facilitated the task of the guides, who 'discovered' an increasing number of souvenirs.

3. The progress of evangelization

Within the boundaries of the empire

Within the boundaries of the empire, the towns had become for the most part Christian. The time came when Christians who had forgotten the period when their ancestors were persecuted destroyed the last pagan temples (in Alexandria in 389 and in Carthage in 399). The bishops directed their efforts at evangelization towards the country areas which remained attached to the religion of the forces of nature. St Martin, Bishop of Tours from 370 to 397, is still the most famous of these missionaries to the countryside, although it is true to say that legend has magnified what he did. Certain stereotyped themes keep cropping up. The missionaries overturned statues of the gods, cut down the sacred groves, set fire to temples and sanctuaries and built churches and chapels on the ashes. Crowds of people underwent mass baptism. The old religion was able to hold its own and reappear in the guise of Christianity.

The evangelization of the countryside resulted in the creation of a large number of parishes, autonomous areas entrusted to priests who were sent out from the episcopal town. In many of the areas which were only slightly Christianized at the beginning of the fourth century, the episcopal sees grew in number during the century. In northern Italy they increased from five or six in 300 to about fifty in 400. In Gaul they were twenty-two in 314 and seventy in 400.

Beyond the empire

The Persian church, which was harshly persecuted in the middle of the fourth century, reorganized itself after the Council of Seleucia (Baghdad) in 410 and displayed a surge of missionary activity towards the East, the Persian Gulf and Central Asia. The Armenian church organized itself in the fourth century and Armenian became a civilized language in the fifth century with St Mesrop (441 onwards), who invented an alphabet. Christianity took hold in the Caucasian countries: St Nino, a slave girl snatched from the Romans, converted Georgia. Captives also evangelized Ethiopia and joined its church to that of Alexandria. Ulphilas (383 onwards) converted the Germans to Arian Christianity.

In the fifth century, most of the churches outside the empire did not accept the decisions of the Councils of Ephesus and Chalcedon (chapter 5, pp.96–99). They kept themselves apart from the churches within the empire, but this did not halt their missionary zeal.

Ravenna mosaic

III · The Beginnings of Monasticism

1. The origins of a life dedicated to the church

From the beginning, the choice of virginity and chastity for the sake of the kingdom was held in honour by Christian communities. This choice was based on the example and teaching of Jesus (Matt. 19.22,30) and of Paul (I Cor. 7). The company of widows in I Tim. 5; the four daughters of Philip, virgins who prophesied (Acts 21.8–9) – these were the first evidences of the dedicated life.

Throughout the second and third centuries there were more and more examples of men and

---

Monk comes from the Greek *monachos*, solitary; originally the **monastery** was the abode of a monk.

Hermit comes from *eremos*, desert, and denotes someone who lives in the desert away from human society.

Anchorite comes from *anachorein*, withdraw, take to the hills, and signifies someone who has left the world. The word is almost synonymous with hermit.

Cenobite comes from *koinos bios*, common life, and denotes someone who lives in an organized community.

Abba or **Apa** signifies father, abbot or superior.

Amma signifies mother, abbess, or superior.

Monasticism eventually came to denote the state of life of all those who had left the world to devote themselves fully to God. At that time monasticism took two main forms: solitary life (*anchoritism* or *eremetism*) and common life (*cenobitism*).

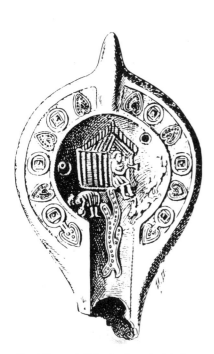

Dendrite monk, living in a tree, depicted on a Christian lamp from Carthage

St Alypius, a stylite, living on a column. Basilica of San Marco in Venice

women who chose the way of asceticism and chastity. To the Christian motivation – forsake all for the kingdom – could be added others. Distaste for the prevailing immorality led some to choose chastity; for women, virginity could be a way of freeing themselves from the social oppression of marriage – the beginning of emancipation.

Dedicated widows continued to live in their families and shared the life of all the faithful. They met together occasionally but did not wear any distinctive clothing. They were advised to practise poverty, and were expected to carry out works of mercy, to visit the poor and sick and meditate on the scriptures. From the third century there was a commitment, but it was made privately and was not necessarily binding.

Writings of the time set out a spirituality of virginity which was an extension of baptism. It was a restoration to the state before the Fall. The theme of marriage to Christ made its appearance. At the same time some deviations came to light. Some women were full of pride at their choice. Others lived together with men who had made the same choice, in a kind of mystical marriage. It is certain that in the end the exaltation turned to scorn of, even a prohibition of, marriage for Christians.

2. The first Eastern monks

With the peace of the church, the likelihood of martyrdom vanished. Becoming a Christian involved no risk, and many experienced a certain slackening off. Some, who wanted to live a more intense Christian life, less preoccupied with the affairs of the world, went off into the desert. This was the beginning of monasticism.

Antony (251–356), about whom we read in the romantic *Life* attributed to Athanasius, Bishop of Alexandria, is the father of the hermits and anchorites of the Egyptian deserts. Antony's example was followed by a great many Christians. St Augustine echoed it in his *Confessions*

61

(VIII, 6). In the upper valley of the Nile Pachomius (286–346) founded a communal monastic life for men (cenobitic), while his sister Mary set up the first community for women. This primitive monasticism spread rapidly in Egypt, Palestine, Syria and Mesopotamia. It did not have a very precise legal structure. A candidate placed himself under the direction of a spiritual master, a father or abbot, until he was able to stand on his own feet. The life of a hermit developed into an ascetic competition. Dendrites lived in trees; recluses huddled in hovels; stylites perched on the tops of pillars; Adamites threw off their clothes and left them behind. In short, this monasticism is evidence of a popular Christianity. It put the emphasis on a struggle against the demons which an animist mind saw everywhere, rather in the way that we see microbes today. Monasticism thought to lead humankind back to the state it was in before the Fall. That was why they tamed wild animals. Although they were contemplatives, the monks also showed hospitality. Their refusal to study often increased their obsessions and landed them in dubious ventures into dogma.

Basil, Bishop of Caesarea (330–379), reacted against monastic eccentricities. In his Rules, he required monks to live in communities; he encouraged them in intellectual work and in care for the poor. The first community in Jerusalem was the monk's ideal. His first duty was obedience to the abbot. The superior only interpreted and applied to everyday life the supreme rule of the gospel. Many Greek writers put forward a theology of the monastic life based on a Platonist anthropology that set little value on the body. The monastery became the ideal Christian society which would replace society here on earth.

3. Monastic life in the West

As had been the case in the past, many virgins and ascetics who had made a vow to God continued to live with their families. Travellers

Antony, father of the hermits

Going according to custom into the Lord's House, he communed with himself and reflected as he walked how the apostles left all and followed the saviour; and how they in the Acts sold their possessions and brought them and laid them at the apostles' feet for distribution to the needy, and what and how great a hope was laid up for them in heaven. Pondering on these things he entered the church, and it happened the gospel was being read, and he heard the Lord saying to the rich man, 'If you would be perfect, go and sell what you have and give to the poor; and come follow me and you shall have treasure in heaven.' Antony, as though God had put him in mind of the saints, and the passage had been read on his account, went out immediately from the church and gave the possessions of his forefathers to the villagers – they were three hundred acres, productive and very fair – that they should no longer be a clog upon himself and his sister. And all the rest that was moveable he sold, and having got together much money he gave it to the poor, reserving a little, however, for his sister's sake . . .

[Antony withdrew into increasingly rigorous solitude, where he proved victorious over the assaults of the devil.]

But the devil, who hates and envies what is good, could not endure to see such a resolution in a youth . . . First of all he tried to lead him away from the discipline, whispering to him the remembrance of his wealth, care for his sister, claims of kindred, love of money, the various pleasures of the table and the other relaxations of life, and at last the difficulty of virtue and the labour of it . . . The devil, unhappy soul, one night even took upon him the shape of a woman and imitated all her acts simply to beguile Antony. But he, his mind filled with Christ and the nobility inspired by him, and considering the spirituality of the soul, quenched the coal of the other's deceit . . . In the night the demons made such a din that the whole of that place seemed to be shaken by an earthquake, and the demons as if breaking the four walls of the dwelling seemed to enter through them, coming in the likeness of beasts and creeping things. And the place was on a sudden filled with the forms of lions, bears, leopards, bulls, serpents, asps, scorpions, and wolves, and each of them was moving according to its nature. The lion was roaring, wishing to attack, the bull seeming to toss with its horns, the serpent writhing but unable to approach and the wolf as it rushed on was restrained; altogether the noises of the apparitions, with their angry raging, were dreadful . . .

And so for nearly twenty years he continued training himself in solitude, never going forth, and seldom seen by any. After this, when many were eager and wishful to imitate his discipline, and his acquaintances came and began to cast down and wrench off the door by force, Antony, as from a shrine, came forth initiated in the mysteries and filled with the Spirit of God. Then for the first time he was seen outside the fort by those who came to see him. And they, when they saw him, wondered at the sight, for he had the same habit of body as before, and was neither fat, like a man without exercise, nor lean from fasting and striving with the demons, but he was just the same as they had known him before his withdrawal. And again his soul was free from blemish, for it was neither contracted as if by grief nor relaxed by pleasure, nor possessed by laughter or dejection, for he was not troubled when he beheld the crowd, nor overjoyed at being saluted by so many. But he was altogether even as being guided by reason, and abiding in a natural state. By him the Lord healed the bodily ailments of many present, and cleansed others from evil spirits. And he gave grace to Antony in speaking, so that he consoled many that were sorrowful and set those at variance at one, exhorting all to prefer the love of Christ before all that is in the world. And while he exhorted and advised them to remember the good things to come, and the loving-kindness of God towards us, who spared not his own Son but delivered him up for us all, he persuaded many to embrace the solitary life. And thus it happened in the end that cells arose even in the mountains, and the desert was colonized by monks, who came forth from their own people, and enrolled themselves for the citizenship in the heavens . . .

Antony was there daily a martyr to his conscience, and contending in the conflicts of faith. And his discipline was much severer, for he was ever fasting, and he had a garment of hair on the inside, while the outside was skin, which he kept until his end. And he neither bathed his body with water to free himself from filth nor did he ever wash his feet, nor even endure so much as to put them into water, unless compelled by necessity. Nor did any one even see him unclothed, nor his body naked at all, except after his death, when he was buried.

Life of Antony,
attributed to Athanasius, 2, 5, 9, 14, 47.

coming from the East, Athanasius and Jerome, for example, spread propaganda for the monastic life. The great number of virgins, the possibilities for abuse and backsliding, the example of the East and the general tendency to develop institutions all helped towards an organization of the religious life. Several communities existed in Rome around 350, founded by women of high birth. A liturgy for the dedication of virgins, or the ceremony of taking the veil, was established, drawing its inspiration from the symbolism of marriage. Ambrose suggested the virgin Mary as a model for virgins.

Jerome (347–419), who had been a monk in the East, spoke up for the monastic life among women of the Roman aristocracy. Gravely and passionately, he defended the superiority of the virgin state over marriage against those who opposed him. When he returned to Palestine with his friend Paula he founded communities of women in Bethlehem, arranged according to their social status, and a community of men amongst whom he lived. What monasticism most owes to Jerome is a taste for the culture of the Bible. The monk made an intellectual effort to understand the scriptures, which then became

 62

The addressees and aims of the Rule of St Benedict

Prologue

Son, listen to the precepts of your master; take them to your heart willingly. If you follow the advice of a tender father and travel the hard road of obedience, you will return to God, from whom by disobedience you have gone astray.

I will address my discourse to all of you who will renounce your own will, enter the lists under the banner of obedience, and fight under the lead of your lawful sovereign, Christ the Lord . . .

I am to erect a school for beginners in the service of the Lord: which I hope to establish on laws not too difficult or grievous. But if, for reasonable cause, the retrenchment of vice or preservation of charity, I require some things which may seem too austere, you are not thereupon to be frightened from the ways of salvation. Those ways are

always strait and narrow at the beginning. But as we advance in the practices of religion and in faith, the heart insensibly opens and enlarges through the wonderful sweetness of his love, and we run in the way of God's commandments. If then we keep close to our school and the doctrine we learn in it, and persevere in the monastery till death, we shall here share by patience in the passion of Christ and hereafter deserve to be united with him in his kingdom. Amen.

Conclusion

I have written this Rule with the object of showing that monks who keep it have at least something of virtuous character and must have begun to live a truly good life. But men aspire to the perfect life; and for them there are the teachings of the holy fathers, which will lead those who follow them to true perfection.

What page – even sentence – of the inspired Old and New Testaments is there that is not an excellent rule of life? What book of the holy Catholic fathers is there that does not point out the nearest way to come to our Creator? The Conferences of the fathers, their Institutes[1] and their Lives; the Rule of our father, St Basil – there are instruments to help the monk who follows them, to lead a good life; to us, idle and neglectful sinners, they are a reproach and a shame.

Whoever you are, who desire to advance apace to the heavenly country, practise first, through Christ's help, this little Rule for beginners. And in the end, under God's protection, you will climb those greater heights of knowledge and virtue to which the holy fathers beckon you.

Rule of St Benedict.

[1] Works of Cassian

his spiritual food. Jerome is the prototype of that kind of monk who devoted himself to Christian culture and culture generally, after classical civilization had collapsed under the onslaught of the barbarians.

Augustine (354–430), who, after his conversion, chose to live as a monk, wanted his clergy to adopt the hallmarks of the monastic life. This is the beginning of a new tendency, the assimilation of the priest to the monk. Priests were chosen for preference from among the monks, and they were required to adopt certain aspects of the monastic life, such as celibacy. *The Rule of St Augustine*, which he added to a letter written in 211, sketched out general observations and advice on the religious life.

John Cassian (360–435) came from Roumania, and after visiting monasteries in the East founded two in Marseilles, St Victor for men and St Saviour for women. His writings, *The Monastic Institutions* and the *Conferences*, formed a bridge between the monks of the East and those of the West. For him discretion became the prime monastic virtue. The islands of Lerins were also a thriving focus of the monastic life.

The Rule of St Benedict

While the Irishmen Patrick, Columba and Columbanus were setting up a monastic life which associated them with the anarchy of the first Eastern monks (fifth to seventh centuries), the Rule of St Benedict (about 480 to about 547) was to be the inspiration of all the monasteries of the West right up until the twelfth century. The Rule inherited all the earlier monastic tradition which it commended warmly. It insisted on stability: the monk had to promise to live in his monastery. The abbot was the lynch-pin of cenobitism, having the dual role of spiritual master and head of the community. He was elected for life by the monks, who owed him absolute obedience. This obedience allowed them to ascend the ladder of

---

The abbot in the Rule of St Benedict

It is well-known that there are four sorts of monks. The first is of cenobites, who dwell in convents under the direction of a rule and an abbot . . . (ch. 1).

An abbot qualified to govern a monastery ought always to remember the name he bears, and to maintain by his good life the title of superior; for he is esteemed to supply the place of Christ in the monastery, being called by his name; according to the apostle: 'You have received the spirit of the adoption of sons, whereby we cry Abba, Father' . . .

When anyone takes upon him the office of abbot, he is to instruct his disciples in two ways. That is: he is to lay before them what is good and holy, more by example than by words; to teach the law of the Lord by word of mouth to such as are of a quicker comprehension, and by example to those of harder hearts and meaner capacities. He ought to create by his conduct an aversion from the thing which he condemns in his discourse; then he will not prove a castaway while he preaches to others . . . (ch. 2).

Whenever any matter of moment is to be debated in the monastery, the abbot is to assemble the whole community, and to lay open the business before them; and after having heard their opinions, and maturely debated with himself, he may resolve on what he judges most profitable. We have for this reason ordained that the whole community shall be assembled because God often reveals what is best to the young (ch. 3).

The first degree of humility is a prompt and ready obedience. This is fitting for those who love Christ above all else. By reason of the holy duty they have undertaken, or for fear of hell, or for eternal glory, they make no more delay to comply, the very instant anything is appointed them, than if God himself had given the command (ch. 5).

Rule of Benedict.

humility, which was the bedrock of spiritual progress. Stability, obedience and humility made for an inner ascetism. Benedict introduced monasticism to a moderate country and rejected the excesses of the East. The monks led a life dedicated to poverty, but its austerities were tempered when it came to sleep, clothing, food and prayer. The day was divided between the *opus Dei*, work of God (prayer and worship), reading and meditating on the scriptures, and manual work and rest. Study of the scriptures was the starting point for intellectual work.

The beam of light shed by the Benedictine Rule penetrated a long way, because it provided a definite enough basis for monastic life, while remaining flexible. The Benedictine monasteries contributed to the birth of Europe, after the empire ebbed away in the West (see chapter 7).

For further reading

D. J. Chitty, *The Desert a City: An Introduction to the History of Egyptian and Palestinian Monasticism under the Christian Empire*, Blackwell 1966

S. L. Greenslade, *Schism in the Early Church*, SCM Press 1953

S. L. Greenslade, *Shepherding the Flock*, SCM Press 1967

Alastair Kee, *Constantine versus Christ*, SCM Press 1982

T. F. Lindsay, *St Benedict*, Burns and Oates 1949

Christ monogram on a sarcophagus, Lateran

5
The Formation of the Creed

Fourth and Fifth Centuries
The First Ecumenical Councils in the Church's Life

The first Christians did not put forward a philosophy or a theology right away. They bore witness to Jesus, who had spoken to them about the one God of scripture as his Father. Jesus was dead, but 'God has made this Jesus, whom you crucified, Lord and Christ' (Acts 2.24,36). 'Lord' is the title given to God in scripture. And so God gave his own name to his Son Jesus (Phil. 2.6–11). That is to say that Jesus, the Christ, is close to God. Before becoming man he was already with God, like Wisdom in Proverbs 8. He took part in creation (Col. 1.15f.). In the beginning of the Gospel of John, Jesus is the Word of God made flesh, this Word by whom the world was made. Word is *logos* in Greek, *verbum* in Latin. The term *logos* is biblical, often indicating the word of God in the Old Testament. But the Greek philosophers also spoke of *logos* as

thought, or divine will, so there was a meeting point there.

We find the first confessions of faith in the New Testament, the outline of a creed. The liturgies of baptism and the eucharist included a profession of faith. Christians affirmed their faith by means of phrases from the scriptures. But they also had to make this faith comprehensible to the world in which they lived, and it was necessary for them to explain things that, in the first instance, appeared incompatible. How could God be unique and at the same time Father and Son? How could a man who was born, lived and died, be God, let alone a God who was by definition beyond all change? Christian theology came into being as an answer to these questions. But thought went off in different directions, and one day different positions had to be reconciled.

This was the work of the councils, which brought together the bishops who were the leaders of the church.

Every Sunday in our churches we proclaim our faith by means of the Nicene Creed. This text did not evolve through the peaceful exchange of ideas, but often through violent arguments which went beyond questions of dogma. Conflicts between people, cultures, regions; exiles; bloody skirmishes and interventions by the army and the police are the background to the formation of our creed.

I · How can Jesus Christ and the Holy Spirit be God?

1. The beginning of the Arian crisis

From the second century, Christian thought was propelled in various directions as it tried to safeguard both biblical monotheism and the baptismal profession of a trinitarian faith. Some thought that God was at the same time both Father and Son, and that one could say that the Father had suffered as well as the Son. Others insisted on making a distinction between the Father and his Son, between the Father and his Word (Logos). The Son was God but not in the same way as the Father; the Son (the Logos) was subordinate to the Father. Jesus could have been

---

Confrontation of Doctrines

Arius	Alexander
The Word did not coexist with the Father from all eternity.	The Word has coexisted with the Father from the beginning.
The Word was created from nothing.	The Word was not created, but is the one who created all things.
The Word is not Son by nature and is not strictly of the Father.	The Word is Son, not by adoption but by nature.
The nature of the Son does not proceed from that of the Father.	The Word has a nature equal to that of the Father.
The Word began to exist by an act of the Father's will.	The Word exists by the communication of the essence of the Father.
The Word is by nature subject to change, physical and moral.	The Word, who by his nature is divine, is subject to neither change nor suffering.

a man made divine through adoption by the Father. Certain scriptural references could be interpreted as having this meaning (John 14.28). Writers used Greek and Latin words in different ways, giving rise to some confusion.

Before the peace of the church the disagreements were fairly localized, but after 313 they spread rapidly throughout the whole of the empire. So a crisis which arose within the church in Alexandria soon stirred up the whole church in the East. Arius, a strict and highly respected priest from a parish in Alexandria, wanted, like many others before him, to safeguard the position of a unique God, a being who alone had no beginning. If this God was Father, it was because at a certain moment he begat a Son. So the Son had a beginning. He was not of exactly the same nature as the Father, and was subordinate to him. Arius used Prov. 8.22 and John 14.28 to support his affirmations. Finally, Jesus saved

64

humanity by urging people to follow his own example in order one day to be glorified with him.

Alexander, Bishop of Alexandria, did not accept this theology. The Son, the Word (Logos) of God, had existed from all eternity as the equal of the Father. If the Word were not fully God, man could not be fully divine, because it would not have been God who became incarnate in a man. So man could not be saved. When meeting and discussion had no effect, Arius and a dozen of his followers were excommunicated (318). Of course, Arius did not accept this condemnation: he went the rounds of his followers, of whom there were a large number in the East, where many considered his view to be the tradition. Trouble flared up in Alexandria. Theological insults were hurled in the theatres and in the market places. Arius composed works, and songs too, to defend his ideas.

65

65

The Thalia (Banquet) of Arius

This work, in which Arius presents his teaching, is only known from quotations by his opponents. It has not only a prose text but also passages in verse which the supporters of Arius learned by heart. Perhaps these poems should not be confused with the songs which Arius is also said to have composed.

God was not always Father. There was a time when he was not yet Father; then he became Father. The Son was not always: for all things were made from the non-existent, and all existing creatures and works were made; so also the Word of God himself was made from the non-existent, and there was when he did not exist, and he was not before he was

made, but he also had a beginning of creation. For God was alone, the word and wisdom did not yet exist . . .

By nature the Word is, like all of us, subject to change, but free in himself; he remains good as far as he wills. If he wills, he can change like us since he is by nature subject to change . . .

The Word is not truly God. But if he is called God, nevertheless he is not truly; but by participation of grace . . . Just as all things are by nature alien to God and different from him, so too the Word is absolutely alien to the essence and property of the Father; he is of the order of works and creatures: he is one of them . . .

The essences of the Father, Son and Holy Spirit are divided by nature, estranged, disjunct and without exchanges between them: thus they are totally dissimilar in essence and glory . . .

Constantine's point of view on quarrels over dogma

Having first lived in the West, Constantine, victor over Licinius in 324, installed himself at Nicomedia, the capital of the East. There he learned of a theological quarrel which arose at Alexandria and set all the East in a ferment. Anxious to maintain order, he sought to appease the two adversaries who seemed to him to be quarrelling over words. The failure of his attempt led him to summon the Council of Nicaea.

Victor Constantine, Maximus Augustus, to Alexander and Arius: I understand that the origin of the present controversy is this. When you, Alexander, demanded of the presbyters what opinion they severally maintained respecting a certain passage in the divine Law (Prov. 8.22), or rather, I should say, that you asked them something connected with an unprofitable question, then you, Arius, inconsiderately insisted on what ought never to have been conceived at all, or if conceived, should have been buried in professed silence. Hence it was that a dissension arose between you, fellowship was withdrawn, and the holy people, rent into diverse parties, no longer preserved the unity of the one body. Now therefore you must both show an equal degree of forbearance, and receive the advice which your fellow-servant righteously ignores. What then is this advice? It was wrong in the first instance to propose such questions as these, or to reply to them when propounded. For those points of discussion which are enjoined by the authority of no law, but rather suggested by the contentious spirit which is fostered by misused leisure, even though they may be intended merely as an intellectual exercise, ought certainly to be confined to the region of our own thoughts, and not hastily produced in the popular assemblies, nor unadvisedly entrusted to the general ear. For how very few are there able either accurately to comprehend, or adequately to explain subjects so sublime and abstruse in their nature?

The cause of your difference has not been any of the leading doctrines or precepts of the divine law, nor has any new heresy respecting the worship of God arisen among you. You are in truth of one and the same judgment: you may therefore well join in communion and fellowship. For as long as you continue to contend about these small and very insignificant questions, it is not fitting that so large a portion of God's people should be under the direction of your judgment, since you are thus divided between yourselves . . .

You know that philosophers, though they all adhere to one system, are yet frequently at issue on certain points, and differ, perhaps, in their degree of knowledge; yet they are recalled to harmony of sentiment by the uniting power of their common doctrines. If this be true, is it not far more reasonable that you, who are the ministers of the Supreme God, should be of one mind respecting the profession of the same religion . . . The dignity of your synod may be preserved, and the communion of your whole body maintained unbroken, however wide a difference may exist among you as to unimportant matters . . . as far then as regards the divine providence, let there be one faith, and one understanding among you, one united judgment in reference to God . . . And now let the preciousness of common affection, let faith in the truth, let the honour due to God and to the observance of his law continue immovably among you . . .

Eusebius, *Life of Constantine,*
II, 69–71.

The sole master of the empire since his victory over Licinius, Constantine wanted to see peace restored in the East. It was only a matter of disagreeing over words, he said. Everyone should make an effort to be reconciled. As the disturbances went on, he decided to call the bishops together for a great council.

The Council of Nicaea. Sixteenth-century Bulgarian fresco

2. The Council of Nicaea (325)

Several local councils had been held during the preceding centuries. In calling all the bishops together at Nicaea in Bithynia, a little way south of the Bosphorus, Constantine created a new institution in the church, the ecumenical (world-wide) council. It is reckoned to be the first of its kind and Vatican II the twenty-first. The Council of Nicaea brought together about 300 bishops, of whom we still have the names of 220. These were mostly bishops from the East, with a Greek cultural background; they were the nearest, and most worked up over dogmatic quarrels. From the West we know only of Caecilian of Carthage, from Calabria, and two priests representing Sylvester, the Bishop of Rome (one called Nicasius, Bishop of Dia in Gaul, and Hosius, Bishop of Cordoba, who acted as ecclesiastical adviser to Constantine). The assembly made a great impression. Never before had so many of the church's dignitaries come together at the same time. The bishops still bore traces of the recent persecution. High and mighty bishops rubbed shoulders with lowly ones, and all of them marvelled at the welcome given them by the emperor, the gilt furnishings of the palace and the uniforms of the soldiers who paid them honour. Could the kingdom of God be more splendid?

The First Ecumenical Council, Nicaea, 325

In effect, the most distinguished of God's ministers from all the churches which abounded in Europe, Libya and Asia were here assembled. And a single house of prayer, as though divinely enlarged, sufficed to contain at once Syrians and Cilicians, Phoenicians and Arabians, delegates from Palestine, and others from Egypt; Thebans and Libyans, with those who came from the region of Mesopotomia. A Persian bishop too was present at this conference, nor was even a Scythian found wanting to the number. Pontus, Galatia and Pamphylia, Cappadocia, Asia and Phrygia, furnished their most distinguished prelates, while those who dwelt in the remotest districts of Thrace and Macedonia, of Achaea and Epirus, were notwithstanding in attendance. Even from Spain itself one whose fame was widely spread (Hosius) took his seat as an individual in the great assembly. The prelate of the imperial city (Rome)

was prevented from attending by extreme old age, but he was represented by the presbyters of his church . . .

The bishops entered the great hall of the palace and sat down according to their rank on the seats that had been prepared for them . . . And now, all rising at the signal which indicated the emperor's entrance, at last he himself proceeded through the midst of the assembly, like some heavenly messenger of God, clothed in raiment which glittered as it were with rays of light, reflecting the glowing radiance of a purple robe, and adorned with the brilliant splendour of gold and precious stones . . .

(Towards the end of the Council) the emperor completed the twentieth year of his reign. On this occasion public festivals were celebrated by the people of the provinces generally, but the emperor himself invited and feasted with those ministers of God whom he had recon-

ciled. Not one of the bishops was wanting at the imperial banquet, the circumstances of which were splendid beyond description. Detachments of the bodyguard and other troops surrounded the entrance to the palace with drawn swords, and through the midst of these the men of God proceeded without fear into the innermost of the imperial apartments, in which some were the emperor's own companions at table, while others reclined on couches arranged on either side. One might have thought that a picture of Christ's kingdom was thus shadowed forth, and a dream rather than reality. After the celebration of this brilliant festival the emperor courteously received all his guests, and generously added to the favours he had already bestowed by personally presenting gifts to each individual according to his rank.

Eusebius, *Life of Constantine,*
III, 7, 10, 15, 16.

91

Most of the bishops confirmed the condemnation of Arius. As they had to make a positive statement of doctrine, Eusebius of Caesarea put forward the creed of his church. The Council accepted it, but at the request of Constantine, on the advice of Hosius, the bishops added the adjective *homoousios* in speaking of the Son of God; that is to say that the Son is of the same *ousia*, the same substance, as the Father, or consubstantial with him. This term affirms the absolute equality between the Father and the Son. Since it was the emperor who proposed the amendment, all the bishops ratified it with the exception of two who were sent into exile with Arius.

The Council also afforded the opportunity to sort out certain points of church discipline. It was decided that the date of Easter would be that

---

The Nicene Creed

We believe in One God, the Father, Almighty, Maker of all things visible and invisible;

And in one Lord Jesus Christ, the Son of God, begotten of the Father, Only-begotten, that is, from the substance of the Father; God from God, Light from Light, Very God from Very God, begotten not made, Consubstantial with the Father, by Whom all things were made, both things in heaven and things in earth; Who for us men and for our salvation came down and was incarnate, was made man, suffered, and rose again the third day, ascended into heaven, and is coming to judge living and dead.

And in the Holy Spirit.

And those who say 'There was when he was not' and 'Before his generation he was not', and 'He came to be from nothing', or those who pretend that the Son of God is 'Of other hypostasis or substance', or 'created' or 'alterable' or 'mutable', the Catholic and Apostolic Church anathematizes.

Stephenson, *A New Eusebius*, 366.

Bishop Paphnutius and the married life of the clergy, at the Council of Nicaea

Socrates (380–440), a lawyer at Constantinople, takes over from Eusebius of Caesarea by relating the religious events between 305 and 439. As he reproduces his sources literally, he is an inestimable source of information.

Paphnutius then was bishop of one of the cities in Upper Thebes: he was a man so favoured divinely that extraordinary miracles were done by him. In the time of the persecution he had been deprived of one of his eyes. The emperor honoured this man exceedingly, and often sent for him to the palace, and kissed the place where the eye had been torn out . . .

It seemed fit to the bishops to introduce a new law into the church, that those who were in holy orders, I speak of bishops, presbyters and deacons, should have no conjugal intercourse with the wives whom they had married when they were still laymen. Now when discussion on this matter was impending, Paphnutius having arisen in the midst of the assembly of bishops, earnestly entreated them not to impose so heavy a yoke on the ministers of religion: asserting that 'marriage itself is honourable, and the bed undefiled'; urging before God that they ought not to injure the church by too stringent restrictions. 'For all men,' he said, 'cannot bear the practice of rigid continence; neither perhaps would the chastity of the wife of each be preserved'; and he termed the intercourse of a man with his lawful wife chastity.

It would be sufficient, he thought, that such as had previously entered on their sacred calling should abjure matrimony, according to the ancient tradition of the church: but that none should be separated from her to whom, while yet unordained, he had been united. And these sentiments he expressed, though himself without experience of marriage and, to speak plainly, without ever having known a woman: for from a boy he had been brought up in a monastery, and was specially renowned above all men for his chastity.

The whole assembly of the clergy assented to the reasoning of Paphnutius; wherefore they silenced all further debate on this point, leaving it to the discretion of those who were married.

Socrates, *Ecclesiastical History*, I,11.

adopted by Rome and Alexandria. A certain number of rules were laid down about the episcopate, to which we shall return a little later on. Some restrictions were imposed on clergy living with their wives. According to the historian Socrates (beginning of the fifth century), the bishops wanted to force married clergy to give up marital relations, a rule which seems to have been adopted in Spain. Bishop Paphnutius, though himself celibate, opposed this demand, and the Council allowed freedom in this respect to bishops, priests and deacons. Several decisions were made in sorting out the consequences of the persecutions, such as the reconciliation of heretics, the forms of liturgical penance, and so on.

3. A troubled half-century

The agreement reached at Nicaea was soon in jeopardy. Many rejected the term *homoousios* because it was not to be found in scripture. Others remembered that the word had been used by heretics who made little distinction between the Father and the Son. Very soon, the majority of those in the East had rejected the formula of Nicaea, with the exception of Athanasius, who had been Bishop of Alexandria since 328. The Latin West on the whole remained loyal to Nicaea.

The Emperor Constantine, who had wholeheartedly lent his support to the Nicene Creed, was anxious to keep on friendly terms with the East and so changed his mind. Outbreaks of violence and the settling of accounts soon followed. Athanasius, who did not want to reinstate Arius, was deposed by the Council of Tyre in 335 and sent into exile in Trier on the German border. He was to experience exile on four further occasions for his loyalty to Nicaea.

During the reign of Constantine's son, the disagreements intensified. The Council of Sardica (Sofia) in 342–3 saw a clash between the bishops of the West and those of the East, who parted company angrily. Constantius, who had been sole emperor since 351, came down completely in favour of Arianism. This time it was the Latin bishops who were sent into exile in the East: Liberius, Bishop of Rome, Hilary of Poitiers, Hosius of Cordoba. Councils produced decrees in increasing numbers which satisfied no one. In 359 the emperor succeeded in imposing a rather vague formula, 'The Son is like (*homoios*) the Father.' 'The whole earth groaned,' said St Jerome, 'surprised to find itself Arian.'

These arguments even sowed division within the local churches. There were up to five communities in Antioch, each with its own bishop; in this way all the theological nuances were represented. The divisions in the Roman church made matters difficult when a successor had to be chosen to Bishop Liberius (366). Two candidates put themselves up. Damasus won, but at the cost of fighting in which thirty-seven people were killed.

4. The Council of Constantinople (381) and the resolution of the crisis

Through the troubles, theological thinking made some progress. The vocabulary became clearer. A distinction came to be made between *ousia* (substance) and *hypostasis* (person), which allowed the recognition of the equality of the Father and the Son in one substance and their distinction in two persons.

Basil, Bishop of Caesarea (370–379), achieved some union primarily through theological thinking. A fresh question arose: Is the Holy Spirit God? The Arians said no, and this earned them the title *pneumatomachoi* (those who fight against the Spirit). In his *Treatise on the Holy Spirit*, Basil demonstrated that the Spirit, too, is of the same substance as the Father. His friend Gregory of Nazianzus wrote along the same lines. Moreover, Basil approached the other Eastern bishops and asked Athanasius to establish a bond with the West. In a letter to the bishops of

The Council of Constantinople (381)

(70) The Spirit is God

What titles which belong to God are not applied to the Spirit? . . . They who say and teach these things, and moreover call him another Paraclete in the sense of another God (John 14.16), who know that blasphemy against him along cannot be forgiven (Matt. 12.31), and who branded with such fearful infamy Ananias and Sapphira for having lied to the Holy Spirit, what do you think of these men? Do they proclaim the Spirit of God or something else? Now really you must be extraordinarily dull and far from the Spirit if you have any doubt about this and need someone to teach you.

Gregory of Nazianzus,
Fifth Theological Oration, 29, 30.

(71) Theology in the streets

Every part of the city is filled with such talk: the alleys, the crossroads, the squares, the avenues. It comes from those who sell clothes, money changers, grocers. If you ask a money changer what the exchange rate is, he will reply with a dissertation on the begotten and the unbegotten. If you enquire about the quality and the price of bread, the baker will reply: 'The Father is greatest and the Son is subject to him.' When you ask at the baths whether the water is ready, the manager will declare that the Son came forth from nothing. I do not know what name to give to this evil, whether frenzy or madness . . .

Gregory of Nyssa,
On the Divinity of the Son and the Holy Spirit, V.

(72) Squabbling among bishops

Gregory of Nazianzus, Bishop of Constantinople, tried in vain to unite bishops on disputed questions.

The bishops chattered like a flock of magpies. It was a childish hubbub, the noise of a workshop starting up, a dust storm, a real hurricane . . . The discussion was chaotic; like wasps, they went straight for the face, all at the same time. Venerable greybeards, far from restraining the young, fell into line with them.

Gregory of Nazianzus,
Poem on his Life, 168off.

(71) Gaul and Italy Basil described the distress felt by the East. However, Damasus, Bishop of Rome, made little effort at reconciliation.

The death of the Arian Emperor Valentius in battle against the Goths during the catastrophe at Andrinopolis (378) seemed like a divine judgment. The two emperors, Gratian in the West and Theodosius in the East, decided to put an end to the theological quarrels which were even causing brawling in the street.

Peace returns

In 380, Theodosius made Christianity the state religion, appointed Gregory of Nazianzus Bishop of Constantinople and convened a council in his capital (381). This was just an Eastern council, and only four of its canons have been preserved: the faith professed at Nicaea had to be preserved and the various heresies which had recently appeared had to be rejected. So the council reaffirmed the Nicene Creed, to which it added a statement about the Holy Spirit. 'We believe in the Holy Spirit, the Lord and Life-giver, who proceeds from the Father, who with the Father and Son is worshipped and glorified.' And so the creed which we recite every Sunday was drawn up. In the eighth century the Latin bishops added the famous *filioque* (who proceeds from the Father *and the Son*); this was one of the causes of the break in the eleventh century between the Latin and the Greek churches.

(72) The council was also the setting for a personal quarrel. The election of Gregory of Nazianzus to the see of Constantinople was contested, because previously he had only been bishop of a medium sized village. Disheartened by the fuss,

94

Gregory withdrew to his own estates – a retired official was chosen to replace him.

In the West, the council called by the Emperor Gratian in the same year at Aquileia (on the Adriatic, near Trieste) only brought together a few bishops from northern Italy and Gaul. The Arian bishops were dismissed and the Emperor was called upon to see that the sentence was carried out. Gradually Arianism disappeared from the empire, but it remained among the Germanic barbarians evangelized by Ulphilas, who had been consecrated bishop by one of the Arian leaders, Eusebius of Nicomedia.

II · How are God and Man united in Jesus Christ?

1. The beginning of the christological controversy

The thinking and the talking never stopped. Once the equality of Father, Son and Holy Spirit was agreed on, people wondered how to explain the union between the divinity of the Word and the humanity of Jesus. The Word of God is eternal, but Jesus was born, suffered and died. Could it be said that God was born, that he knew hunger, that he suffered and died? If one were to make too much of a distinction between God and man in Jesus, how could one speak of the incarnation, of this flesh assumed by the Word?

Apollinarius, Bishop of Laodicea in Syria (310–390) and a great friend of Athanasius, thought that he had found the answer. Jesus, like all men according to the anthropology of the time, was thought to consist of flesh, that is to say, of a living body, and spirit (soul). But in Jesus the place of the spirit was taken by the Word. So Jesus was incapable of sin because he did not have a human soul which was capable of sin and error. Some people very soon gained the impression that Apollinarius was endangering the doctrine of redemption because 'only that which has been assumed by Christ can be saved in man'. If Christ did not have a human soul, man's will cannot be saved. Apollinarius was condemned on several occasions.

Unity and distinction

Two theological tendencies or trends now made themselves felt. In Alexandria, the emphasis was on the unity of Christ, starting from the Logos (Word). Christ was the Word (God) who appeared in the flesh. That was the condition for the divinization of man. In Antioch the emphasis was put on the two aspects of Christ's being. The starting point was the two natures and the goal was their unity. There was a concern to maintain the complete humanity of Christ. Here again, the vocabulary was not very clear. The word *physis* (nature) was used in two different senses; for some people there was only one nature in Jesus, for others two.

These differing points of view were soon to turn into a sharp confrontation between two rival bishops, Cyril of Alexandria and Nestorius of Constantinople. Round about 428, Nestorius, who originally came from Antioch, attacked the popular piety which called on Mary as *theotokos*, i.e. Mother of God. As far as Nestorius was concerned, this term was not in scripture, and Mary could only be the mother of the man Jesus. In opposition to him, Cyril set out to defend the

unity of Christ and the common faith of Christians. He argued for one single nature in Christ. Cyril joined forces with Celestinus, Bishop of Rome, who condemned Nestorius (430). Cyril then requested that Nestorius should sign a statement affirming that, in Jesus, the Word and the man were united in one single nature. Nestorius appealed to his friends in Antioch, John and Theodoret, and accused Cyril of Apollinarianism. In the face of such an uproar, the Emperor Theodosius II called a council at

Seventh-century Virgin and child. Subbiaco

Ephesus in November 430, requesting that all the provinces be represented. Celestinus, Bishop of Rome, was invited, as was Augustine of Hippo, but Augustine died on 30 August of the same year.

2. The Council of Ephesus (431)

The historians of the time have described the stormy progress of this Council. Cyril had come to Ephesus with the firm intention of eliminating his rival of Constantinople. It was dangerous to oppose the Bishop of Alexandria, who did not

---

The Council of Ephesus according to a historian of the time

Not long afterwards a mandate from the emperor directed the bishops in all places to assemble at Ephesus. Immediately after the festival of Easter, therefore, Nestorius, escorted by a great crowd of his adherents, went to Ephesus, and found many of the bishops already there. Cyril, Bishop of Alexandria, was delayed, and did not arrive till near Pentecost. Five days after Pentecost, Juvenal, Bishop of Jerusalem, arrived. While John of Antioch was still absent, those who were now congregated started to consider the question; and Cyril of Alexandria began a sharp skirmish of words, aimed at terrifying Nestorius, for he had a strong dislike of him. When many had declared that Christ was God, Nestorius said: 'I cannot term him God who was two or three months old. I am therefore clear of your blood, and shall in future come no more among you.' Having uttered these words, he left the assembly, and afterwards held meetings with the other bishops who entertained sentiments similar to his own. Accordingly those present were divided into two factions.

That section which supported Cyril, having constituted themselves a council, summoned Nestorius: but he refused to meet them, and put them off until the arrival of John of Antioch.

The partisans of Cyril therefore proceeded to the examination of the public discourses of Nestorius which he had preached on the subject in dispute; and after deciding from a repeated perusal of them that they contained distinct blasphemy against the Son of God, they deposed him. This being done, the partisans of Nestorius constituted themselves another council apart, and in it deposed Cyril himself, and together with him Memnon, Bishop of Ephesus. Not long after these events, John Bishop of Antioch made his appearance. Being informed of what had taken place, he pronounced unqualified censure on Cyril as the author of all this confusion, in having so precipitately proceeded to the deposition of Nestorius. Thereupon Cyril combined with Juvenal to revenge themselves on John, and they deposed him also.

When affairs reached this confused condition, Nestorius saw that the contention which had been raised was thus tending to the destruction of communion. So in bitter regret he called Mary Theotokos, and cried out: 'Let Mary be called Theotokos, if you will, and let all disputing cease.' But although he made this recantation, no notice was taken of it; for his deposition was not revoked, and he was banished to the Oasis, where he still remains . . .

John, having returned to his bishopric and convened several bishops, deposed Cyril, who had also returned to his see: but soon afterwards, having set aside their enmity and accepting each other as friends, they mutually reinstated each other in their episcopal chairs. But after the deposition of Nestorius there was great agitation among the churches of Constantinople. For the people were divided on account of what we have already called his unfortunate utterances; and the clergy unanimously anathematized him.

Socrates, *Church History*, VII, 34.

The Theotokos. Cave church in Cappadocia

care what methods he used when his episcopal see and doctrine were at stake. Cyril had brought with him about fifty Egyptian bishops who were loyal to him, along with numerous gifts. Cyril is a saint, but it cannot be said that all his actions were saintly!

Despite the number of absentees on the opening date, and despite protests from the imperial officers and about sixty bishops, Cyril opened the Council on 22 June 431. Nestorius was deposed as a new Judas, a heretic, and so on, by two hundred bishops. The crowd went wild with joy, and accompanied the bishops back to their lodgings with a torchlight procession. For these honest folk, Christ had overcome heresy. Although it had not been explicitly in question, the *theotokos* had triumphed.

A number of Nestorius' followers arrived soon afterwards, as did some bishops who were very put out by Cyril's behaviour and condemned him and his friends. It is hardly possible to make out which among the bishops was not condemned. The emperor's representative tried to make everyone happy by deposing both Nestorius and Cyril. The latter succeeded in escaping and returned in triumph to Alexandria. Nestorius spent the rest of his life in exile.

The dogma of Ephesus?

The dogmatic content of the Council appears to have been thin, since the only official document is the condemnation of Nestorius. In fact, the Council of Ephesus reinforced the authority of Nicaea and the emphasis on the unity of Christ. The term *theotokos* was no longer to be in dispute. Moreover in 433, John of Antioch, one of Cyril's opponents, proposed a formula of union and reconciliation: 'Union of two natures had been achieved . . . and because of this union we confess that the holy virgin is *theotokos*, because the Word of God had been made flesh and been made man.' Cyril accepted this enthusiastically, and Sixtus, Bishop of Rome, congratulated the two men on their harmony when he approved the statement.

3. Further controversies leading up to the Council of Chalcedon (451)

The union of 433 left the extremists of both parties unsatisfied. Many of the protagonists had disappeared from the scene when the quarrel sprang up again between Theodoret, Bishop of Cyrus in Syria, who continued to defend the two natures of Christ without being able to give a satisfactory explanation of the 'union without confusion', and Eutyches, an old monk from Constantinople, who claimed that in Christ the divine nature absorbed the human nature. For Eutyches, the body of Christ was not made of the same substance as ours. The monk was condemned and excommunicated during a synod convoked by Flavian, Bishop of Constantinople. Eutyches appealed to Leo, Bishop of Rome, and Dioscorus, Bishop of Alexandria.

The Robber Synod of Ephesus

Theodosius II, who was a friend of Eutyches, convened a council to which he invited virtually only supporters of Eutyches and the Bishop of Rome. Leo had entrusted to the delegates who were to represent him an account of the incarnation, the *Tome*, addressed to Flavian. Leo's position was clear: Christ had a real body, of that same nature as that of his mother. The two

74

97

natures were safeguarded; they were united in one person. In Latin the distinction between nature and person had long been clarified, but this was not the case in Greek (*physis* and *hypostasis*).

The Council which met at Ephesus in 449 comprised mainly supporters of Eutyches, among whom was Dioscorus of Alexandria, who had brought with him a crowd of unruly monks. The representatives of the Bishop of Rome – who did not know Greek – could not make themselves heard. During the course of a stormy session, Flavian was deposed, along with all those who spoke in terms of two natures. Flavian, who had been wounded in the brawl, in which police had intervened, died soon afterwards. Theodoret

appealed to Rome, where Leo expressed great indignation at the 'Robber Synod of Ephesus'.

The Council of Chalcedon

A new emperor, Marcian, went in for a change of religious policy. He requested Leo to come and preside at a council. Leo was unable to make the journey, because the Huns had invaded the West. The Bishop of Rome sent a legate and the Council met in 451 at Chalcedon, facing Constantinople on the other shore of the Bosphorus. It was the first time that an ecumenical council had been presided over by the Bishop of Rome. We shall examine later the conditions necessary for a council to be considered ecumenical. The two old-established camps met again in the

Dogmatic definition of the Council of Chalcedon (451)

The wise and salutary Creed of Nicaea and Constantinople, therefore, derived from divine grace, suffices for the perfect acknowledgment and confirmation of godliness . . . But since those who, taking in hand to set aside the preaching of the truth by heresies of their own, have uttered vain babblings, some daring to pervert the mystery of the dispensation, which for our sakes the Lord undertook, and denying the propriety of the name Theotokos, *as applied to the Virgin, and others bringing in a confusion and mixing of natures, and fondly feigning that there is but one nature of the flesh and Godhead, and by this confusion absurdly maintaining that the divine nature of the only-begotten is passable – for this reason, the holy, great, ecumenical council now in session, being desirous of precluding every device of theirs against the truth, teaching in its fullness the doctrine*

which from the beginning has remained unshaken, has decreed, in the first place that the Creed of the 318 fathers (Nicaea) remain inviolate; and on account of those who impugn the Holy Spirit, it ratifies and confirms the doctrine delivered subsequently, concerning the essence of the Spirit, by the 150 holy Fathers (Constantinople 381), who were assembled in the imperial city, which they made known to all, not as though they were supplying some omission of their predecessors, but distinctly declaring by written testimony their own understanding concerning the Holy Spirit, against those who were endeavouring to set aside his sovereignty . . .

Wherefore following the holy Fathers, we all with one voice confess our Lord Jesus Christ one and the same Son, the same perfect in Godhead, the same perfect in manhood, truly God and

truly man, the same consisting of a reasonable soul and a body, of one substance with the Father as touching the manhood, like us in all things apart from sin; begotten of the Father before the ages as touching the Godhead, the same in the last days, for us and for our salvation, born from the Virgin Mary, the Theotokos, as touching the manhood, one and the same Christ, Son, Lord, Only-begotten, to be acknowledged in two natures, without confusion, without change, without division, without separation; the distinction of natures being in no way abolished because of the union, but rather the characteristic property of each nature being preserved, and concurring into one person and one subsistence . . .

T. H. Bindley,
Oecumenical Documents of the Faith, Methuen 1906, pp. 191–3.

assembly, separated by a copy of the Gospels. Flavian was rehabilitated. The Niceno-Constantinopolitan creed was read aloud (from then on it was to serve as a point of reference) together with letters of Cyril and the *Tome* of Leo. This last text aroused great enthusiasm. 'This is the faith of the Fathers, the faith of the Apostles! This is what we all believe! Anathema on those who do not believe! Peter has spoken through Leo . . . ! This is what Cyril taught! Leo and Cyril taught the same thing!'

Dioscorus was deposed and exiled. Accounts were settled with those who had taken part in the Robber Synod of Ephesus, and a statement of faith was formulated which drew its inspiration from the *Tome* and developed the Niceno-Constantinopolitan creed: Christ is one person in two natures. This was the basis of christology from then on. It does not prevent us looking for new and complementary formulas when cultures change.

Some disciplinary measures were also taken. Later on we shall return to canon 28. The emperor, the 'new Constantine', approved the council's decisions, but the pope only recognized those which concerned dogma.

4. The first separated churches and the consequences of the christological controversies

In spite of its balanced formulation, the Council of Chalcedon did not bring peace. A council has never been able to solve problems completely – we see that clearly in our own day. The christological controversies went on. Those who opposed the Chalcedonian Definition parted company with the official church. The Monophysite churches thought they were remaining faithful to Cyril in speaking of a single nature in Christ; the Nestorian churches wanted to safeguard the duality of man and God in Christ. However, in the majority of cases, particularly where present-day communities are concerned, it is important to beware of speaking of heresy in the stronger sense of the word. Choices have always been as much political as dogmatic.

Within the frontiers of the empire

The imperial government of Constantinople took it upon itself to impose the orthodox doctrine (the 'right doctrine') of Chalcedon upon its territories. Many of the provinces or regions rejected it in order to show their cultural and religious independence from the Greek imperialism of Constantinople. In Egypt, through loyalty to Dioscorus and Cyril, Christians chose Monophysitism as the national religion of a church whose language was Coptic, while the few Chalcedonians found recruits from among the Hellenistic minorities close to the seat of power. It was the same in Syria, where Monophysitism became the religion of those Christians who spoke Syriac. The Chalcedonians were given the name 'Imperials' (*melkites* in Syriac). The Monophysites introduced the Niceno–Constantinopolitan creed into their liturgy to show their loyalty to a tradition older than the innovations of Chalcedon.

Beyond the empire

Beyond the eastern frontiers of the empire it was equally either political circumstances or chance which made the churches of these regions choose Monophysitism or Nestorianism. At the end of the fifth century, the emperor closed the school of theology at Edessa (Urfa, between the Euphrates and the Tigris), which he deemed to be Nestorian. It was re-established in Persian territory at Nisibis. At the Synod of Ctesiphon in 486, Nestorianism became the official religion of Christians in the Persian empire. At the same time, Persian Christians hoped to escape the accusation of being spies in the service of the Emperor of Constantinople. Cut off from the West, Persian Nestorians made great missionary forays as far as Central Asia and China. The stele of Si-Ngan-fou, a Syriac-Chinese inscription engraved on stone, erected in 781 in the town of that name, the then capital of China, bears witness to this missionary zeal. As for the Armenians, they adopted Monophysitism in opposition to the Nestorian Persians and the Greeks of Constantinople. The Ethiopians who were dependent on Alexandria also opted for Monophysitism.

The emperors always cherished hopes of achieving dogmatic and political unity through compromise formulas. To no avail. They resulted in more arguments and more violence. Two ecumenical Councils (Constantinople II, 553, and Constantinople III, 681) again dealt with christological dogmas. Constantinople III condemned new forms of Monophysitism: Monothelitism (one will in Christ) and Monergism (one operation or energy).

III · The Organization of the Church and Church Unity

The ecumenical councils did not just promulgate definitions of dogma. They were the occasions for all the bishops of the empire to meet together. Each local church already had its own traditions. The councils of the fourth and fifth centuries tried, without always succeeding, to standardize the rules by which the communities were organized, in particular those relating to the appointment of bishops and the defining of relationships between the churches.

1. Bishops and metropolitans

Naturally enough, church organization was modelled on political, administrative and economic organization. The bishop was the head of the Christian community in a city. Each city was part of a province. The bishop of the capital of a province, the metropolis, played a particularly important role. He could call a provincial council. He confirmed and installed bishops in the province. That is recalled by canon 4 of Nicaea. This canon points to a collegial method for the election of bishops.

In the episcopate, as elsewhere, some places were better than others. It was therefore tempting to try to change one's episcopal see. However, canon 15 of the Council of Nicaea opposed this practice. The bishop, made in the image of Christ, was thought of as the husband of his church. He could not leave her for another one. It was because of this rule that Gregory of Nazianzus gave up the see of Constantinople, because he had formerly been bishop of a medium-sized town. The rule was abandoned later on.

2. The origin of the five patriarchates

Since the earliest times of the church, it was the episcopal sees which had a special role to play, although they were under the metropolitans. The sees of the principal towns of the empire had also been the bases for evangelization: Rome, Alexandria, Antioch and also Carthage. The bishops of these towns played a part in the affairs of an area which was much bigger than the single province where they were situated, calling councils, appointing bishops etc.

From the time of Diocletian, the provinces were grouped in larger areas called dioceses (there were fifteen of them at the end of the fourth century). In the eastern part of the empire, the bishops of the capitals of the dioceses, sometimes called exarchs, had a privileged role:

Church organization and links between churches

75) The canons of the Council of Nicaea (325)

4. The bishop should be appointed by all the bishops in the province: but should this be difficult, either on account of urgent necessity or because of distance, three at least should meet together, and the suffrages of the absent also being given and communicated in writing, then the ordination should take place. But in every province the ratification of what is done should be left to the metropolitan.

6. Let the ancient customs in Egypt, Libya and the Pentapolis prevail, that the Bishop of Alexandria have jurisdiction in all these, since the like is customary for the Bishop of Rome also. Likewise in Antioch and the other provinces, let the churches retain their privileges.

15. On account of the great disturbance and discords that occur, it is decreed that the custom prevailing in certain places, contrary to the canon, must wholly be done away; so that neither bishop, presbyter, nor deacon shall pass from city to city. And if any one, after this decree of the holy and great synod, shall attempt any such thing, or continue in any such course, his proceedings shall be utterly void, and he shall be restored to the church for which he was ordained bishop or presbyter.

76) The canons of the Council of Constantinople (381)

2. The bishops are not to go beyond their dioceses to churches lying outside their bounds, nor bring confusion into the churches; but let the Bishop of Alexandria, according to the canons, alone administer the affairs of Egypt: and let the bishops of the East manage the East alone, the privileges of the church in Antioch, which are mentioned in the canons of Nicaea, being preserved; and let the bishops of the Asian diocese administer the Asian affairs only; and the Pontic bishops only Pontic matters; and the Thracian bishops only Thracian affairs . . .

The Bishop of Constantinople, however, shall have the prerogative of honour after the Bishop of Rome; because Constantinople is New Rome.

77) Canon 28 of the Council of Chalcedon (451)

Following in all things the decisions of the holy Fathers, and acknowledging the canon, which has been just read, of the 150 bishops beloved of God who assembled in the imperial city of Constantinople (Constantinople 2, see below), which is New Rome, in the time of the Emperor Theodosius of happy memory, we also do enact and decree the same things concerning the privileges of the most holy church of Constantinople, which is New Rome. For the Fathers rightly granted privileges to the throne of old Rome, because it was the royal city. And the 150 most religious bishops, actuated by the same consideration, gave equal privileges to the most holy throne of New Rome, justly judging that the city which is honoured with the sovereignty and the senate, and enjoys equal privilege with the old imperial Rome, should in ecclesiastical matters also be magnified as she is, and rank next after her; so that, in the Pontic, the Asian and the Thracian dioceses, the metropolitans only and such bishops also of the dioceses aforesaid as are among the barbarians, should be ordained by the aforesaid most holy throne of the most holy church of Constantinople . . .

Church organization and links between churches

78. The Bishop of Rome has inherited the promises made to Peter

From all the world, Peter alone was chosen to be overseer at the call of all the peoples; he alone was put at the head of all the apostles and all the fathers of the church. So although in the people of God there might be numerous priests and numerous pastors, Peter would govern in his personal capacity all those who are also governed by Christ as head. In his goodwill, beloved, God accorded this man a great and wonderful part in the exercising of his power.

St Peter was told, 'I will give you the keys of the kingdom of heaven . . .' Indeed the right of exercising this power also passed to other apostles, and the institution which was born of this deci-sion has extended to all the principali-ties of the empire. However, there was a reason why one individual was entrusted with what must be signified to all. If, in fact, this power was given to Peter in a personal way, it is that the rule of Peter is set before all the leaders of the church. The privilege of Peter always remains where a judgment is given by virtue of his equity . . . To Peter, this good shepherd, we offer this anniversary of our entry into office; to him we offer this festival, since it is by his protection that we have been worthy to be associated with his see . . .

Leo the Great, *Sermon IV* (95).

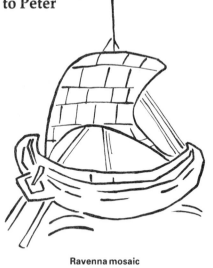

Ravenna mosaic

this was the position of Alexandria and Antioch. Some of them had the right to consecrate metro-politan bishops. That is the significance of canon 6 of Nicaea and canon 2 of Constantinople.

Because of the political importance of his position, the Bishop of Constantinople came to hold the place of honour after the Bishop of Rome (canon 3 of Constantinople). This decision was not directed against Rome but against Alex-andria, which for a long time had been the second most important city in the empire and in the church. The councils mentioned earlier have shown us the hostility of the Bishops of Alexan-dria towards those of Constantinople. In a simi-lar way, the see of Jerusalem thought that it ought to be accorded particular honour because of its religious role. Canon 28 of Chalcedon determined the position of Constantinople by giving it jurisdiction over a vast area: the three dioceses of Pontus, Asia and Thrace, and the newly evangelized territories. Thus the four eastern districts of Constantinople, Antioch, Jerusalem and Alexandria were set up, to which that of Rome was added in the West. These were the five patriarchates which were given legal sanction under Justinian. People sometimes des-cribed this as the 'pentarchy', government of five.

3. Assertion of the primacy of Rome

We cannot speak of the papacy or of the pope in the present-day sense until the sixth century. The word 'pope' was commonly used for any bishop whatsoever, denoting his role as father.

Without going into detail, we might say that the Bishop of Rome occupied a position in the Latin West comparable to that which the Bishop of Alexandria, for example, could occupy in Egypt and in Libya. However, from the beginning, the church of Rome held a particularly important place in the universal church. She owed this to the presence of the two apostles Peter and Paul and her situation in the capital of the empire. On the one hand, the Bishops of Rome intervened in the life of the other churches. We might recall how Clement of Rome called the church of Corinth to order in 96, how around 190 Victor excommunicated the bishops who did not celebrate the festival of Easter on the same day as Rome; and how Stephen of Rome criticized Cyprian for baptizing heretics, etc. It must be understood that these interventions did not always go down very well (see p.65). Irenaeus had nothing good to say about Victor's actions. On the other hand, all the Eastern churches had always accorded the place of honour to the church of Rome. They appealed to Rome in difficult cases, for example at the time of the Arian crisis, or in the christological disputes (the appeal to Leo).

The Bishops of Rome took a dim view of the rise of Constantinople. They feared that the political decline of Rome would bring with it the decline of the church. Moreover, from the middle of the fourth century they recalled that their primacy derived from their succession from Peter, and they gave the see the title the 'apostolic see'. Leo the Great rejected canon 28 of Chalcedon, because it seemed to him that the jurisdiction of Constantinople was being extended disproportionately.

The Council of Chalcedon made much of the doctrinal role of the Bishop of Rome. 'Peter has spoken through Leo.' Precisely as a Roman council had done already in 382, Leo used Matt. 16.18–19 as a basis from which to develop a theology of primacy. He recognized his right and his duty to control the whole church as Peter's successor. The other bishops were only called on to 'share in his pastoral concern, but not in the fullness of his power'. For Leo, the Bishop of Rome emerged as a universal bishop, a bishop of bishops, the source of episcopal authority. Much later, Gregory the Great considered the pope to be more like a bishop amongst other bishops, of whom he was just the chief. Today we speak of collegiality, a theology nearer to that of the East and therefore more ecumenical.

For further reading

A. Grillmeier, *Christ in Christian Tradition*, Mowbray, second edition 1975

J. N. D. Kelly, *Early Christian Doctrines*, A. & C. Black, third edition 1977

J. N. D. Kelly, *Early Christian Creeds*, Longman, third edition 1972

G. L. Prestige, *God in Patristic Thought*, SPCK 1936

Alan Richardson, *Creeds in the Making*, SCM Press 1935

Frances Young, *From Nicaea to Chalcedon*, SCM Press and Fortress Press 1983

6

The Church Fathers

The Christian Writers of the First Centuries

Bread and fish. Fifth-century Palestinian mosaic

Throughout the preceding chapters, we have been made aware of events, doctrines or liturgical prayers by means of the writings of Christians such as Eusebius, Tertullian, Origen, Irenaeus, Augustine, Athanasius – to name only a few. These authors are often called 'Church Fathers'. They are interesting not only because they can give us historical information, but also because even today they play a decisive role in our faith and in our Christian life. In fact, as we saw in the Introduction, the transmission of the gospel is not just the transmission of a text, but the absorption of a message by people of different mentalities and cultures, living in communities each of which was unique.

In this chapter, we shall try to find out more about what we owe to these first Christian writers. The subject is a huge one. Study of the Fathers, called 'patristics', is a special discipline which has given rise to thousands of books. A dozen pages or so on the subject can only afford a tiny glimpse which might encourage you to find out more by consulting other works; there are many very accessible ones.

I · Who were the Church Fathers?

1. Fathers

The word 'father' points us towards the start, towards what stands at the beginning of something. The term is often synonymous with ancestor. We speak of our 'fathers in the faith'. Sometimes we might have occasion to speak of 'Pilgrim Fathers' or 'founding fathers'. But a father is also someone who has children, who brings them up and guides them towards maturity. And so, in ancient times, a master was called a father, someone who passed on a wisdom which was at the same time knowledge and a way of life. And in spite of Jesus' hesitations (Matt. 23.8–11), the word father was to undergo a considerable revival in the church. In I Cor. 4.15 Paul exclaims: 'For though you have countless teachers in Christ, you do not have many fathers. For I became your father in Christ Jesus through the gospel.' Irenaeus said, 'When someone has received his teaching from the lips of another, he is called the son of the one who taught him, and the latter is called his father.' We have seen the importance of the father (abbot) in the beginnings of the monastic life (see p.85). In the first centuries of the church, the duty to instruct was laid on the bishop, who was quickly given the title of father, sometimes in the form of 'pope'. By analogy, many others, teachers and those who preached the gospel, were called fathers even without being bishops. There is a feeling of security and trust in the word. A father is the upholder of a tradition. All these connotations of the word 'father' help us to understand the place of the Church Fathers.

2. Close to the source

The writings of the Fathers take us back to the sources of our faith in Jesus, as they are nearer to them in time than we are. This return to the sources, of which we are very aware today, is not a step backwards. But we like to find Christian life and thought when they first spring up, when they have not yet been subjected to the test of time. In particular, the Fathers were the first readers of the New Testament, which they offered as food to Christians in a language which was not yet systematized. At the same time, they suggested a reading of the Old Testament in the light of Christ. They encouraged Christians to read scripture in a thoroughly christological way, under the guidance of the Holy Spirit. That is why, without wanting to gloss over fifteen or twenty centuries of church life, by going back to the writings of the Fathers we are better able to grasp the Christian message unencumbered by the deposits and the encrustations which can conceal it from us.

It is rather an arbitrary judgment, but tradition has it that the patristic age begins with the writings which came after the New Testament and ends in the eighth century. This finishing date corresponds to a certain drying up of Christian literature, particularly in the West (see chapter 7). At the same time this literature gradually developed: the tendency was for it to become specialized and break away from being a plain commentary on scripture. But the break was not a clean one; some people have said that Bernard of Clairvaux, who lived in the twelfth century, was the 'last of the Fathers' (see chapter 8).

3. Witnesses to the meeting of gospel and culture

The Fathers did not confine themselves to a plain meditation on scripture, or to a moral exhortation for the internal use of their communities. Circumstances obliged them to defend Christianity when it was attacked in the name of reason. When preaching the gospel they made use of Greek and Latin culture in order to be understood by those whom they were addressing. They looked for the meeting point between Greek learning and the Christian message. The austere morality of the Stoics and their submission to the order of things came face to face with the Creator God and providence of the Christians. In common with the Platonists, Christians thought that in leaving the visible world behind it was possible to ascend to God, its invisible author. Gradually the Fathers took over and Christianized the whole of ancient culture, but this was not always accomplished without difficulty. In the second and third centuries the Fathers had to busy themselves in countering the threats posed to the gospel message by strange doctrines. The arguments over the Trinity and the person of Christ arose because of the difficulty of evolving a language that was capable of explaining Christian dogmas (see chapters 3 and 5). So the circumstances gave rise to a theology, or rather several theologies.

Diversity in language and culture

It was not a matter of a monolithic system. The Fathers expressed themselves in the two main languages of the time, Greek and Latin, but in the East some of them used Syriac, Coptic, Armenian and so on. Each language had its own particular culture which left its stamp on Christianity in the various regions.

It does not do to idealize the past: we have seen that the confrontations between theologies were sometimes violent. However, the example of the Fathers encourages us to look for a language in which to preach the gospel which can be understood by our contemporaries. Moreover, present-day ecumenism finds in the writings of the Fathers a kind of common root of theology before the main divisions, and a diversity of expression which is compatible with the unity of the church.

4. Guarantors of the faith and sanctity of the church

The Fathers were the privileged witnesses of church tradition, that is to say, of how the gospel was lived out in the early centuries. That is why, if Christian tradition demanded orthodoxy, i.e. right thinking, of a Father, then it also required sanctity. A Father was someone who lived his life according to the teaching he was giving.

Sanctity and orthodoxy

However, we must understand this sanctity and orthodoxy in the right way. It was a question of communal sanctity, which was enough to obtain a kind of popular canonization. That should not stop us from realizing that St Jerome was not a very pleasant character, that he was unfair to his opponents and atrociously unfair to John Chrysostom. Orthodoxy signified that there was an agreement amongst the Fathers, a consensus of opinion on essential points of doctrine at a given moment. Certain statements of the second and third centuries appeared ambiguous two centuries later. Despite some assessments, it is not fair to judge these statements according to later criteria. An explanation and development of the dogmas occurred during the course of the centuries.

St Vincent of Lérins, in about 434, gives a good summary of how the church understood the role of tradition, and within it that of the Fathers, by reference to the scriptures and to statements of faith.

A few Christian writers, such as Tertullian, broke away from the main body of the church, becoming schismatics or heretics according to the criteria of the times. They are not thought of as being 'Fathers of the Church' in the strict sense, but they are no less valuable witnesses to Christian life and doctrine. That is why they appear here with the others.

II · The Golden Age of the Church Fathers

We have encountered some of the Church Fathers earlier on as exponents of the first theologies: Irenaeus, Origen, Tertullian, and so on. In the history of patristics, the Council of Nicaea (325) was the beginning of a new period. In fact the peace of the church and the meeting of the great Councils enabled Christian literature to blossom. The period between Nicaea (325) and Chalcedon (451) is spoken of as a golden age. Only some names can be mentioned here.

1. New arrivals

In addition to the Greek and Latin Fathers of the preceding period, there were new arrivals, those who wrote in Eastern languages. Among them,

the most important was Ephraem of Nisibis or Edessa (306–373), who was a deacon and a poet.

Ephraem lived in those areas of Mesopotamia which were the subject of dispute between the Roman empire and the Persian empire. When the town of Nisibis, where he was born, fell into the hands of the Persians, he took refuge at Edessa, the centre of a very old Syriac-speaking church. There it was he died, during a plague epidemic, a victim of his own self-sacrifice. In his role as deacon he preached, expounded the scriptures and led prayer. His work consists of sermons, exegetical treatises, and above all some 450 hymns, some of which have been translated into several languages. Ephraem's theology, like that of several other Syriac writers, was close to

---

Ephraem of Nisibis (306–373)

The hymns of Ephraem, written in Syriac, are rhythmic texts interspersed with refrains which the faithful learned by heart. In *Hymns on Paradise* Ephraem constantly draws parallels between Adam, the figures of the Old Testament, and Christ.

Refrain

Make me worthy in thy goodness
That we may enter thy paradise

Naked, Adam was handsome:
  His diligent wife
toiled to make him
  a garment of filth.
The garden saw it and,
  finding it hideous, cast him out.
But a new tunic
  was made for him by Mary.
Clothed in this finery and
  according to the promise,
  the villain looked splendid.
The garden, seeing Adam again
  in his image, welcomed him.

Moses doubted, yet lived,
  but he never entered
the promised land
  bounded by the Jordan.
After his sin, Adam
  left the Garden of Life,
guarded by the cherubim,
  but through our Lord,
both of them, having been buried,
  were able to enter by the resurrection:
Moses, the Promised Land;
  Adam, Paradise.

Athanasius (295–373)

God became man that we might become God

The Word of God, incorporeal and incorruptible, came among us, though he had never been far off. For he left no part of the creation void of his presence, but filled all things, living as he does with the Father. But he came among us to help us by showing us his love. . .

Filled with compassion for our race, taking pity on our weakness, condescending to our corruption, refusing to allow death to have dominion over us, in order that what had begun should not perish and that the work of his Father should not be useless, he took a body, a body no different from ours . . .

Those who talk of the human aspects of the Word also know what appertains to his divinity . . . When they speak of his tears they know that the Lord shows his humanity by his tears and his divinity by raising Lazarus; they know that the Lord experienced hunger and thirst, while feeding in a divine manner five thousand people with five loaves;

they know that his human body lay in the tomb and was raised as the body of God . . .

The Word was made man that we might be made God: he was made visible by his body that we might have an idea of the invisible Father; he endured the outrages inflicted on him by men that we might share in his immortality. He did not undergo any harm, since as Word of God he was impassable and incorruptible. But in this way he saved from danger the suffering humanity for which he endured all this.

Extracts quoted in Quasten, *Patrology*, III, 113f.

79

its biblical origins, and very little influenced by Greek culture.

St Athanasius. Palermo mosaic

80

61

2. The main Greek writers

The main Christian writers of the fourth century came from a Greek cultural background, because the dogmatic conflicts which arose in the East stimulated theological thought.

Athanasius grew up at the time of the Arian controversy in a divided Egyptian church. As a deacon he accompanied the Bishop of Alexandria to the Council of Nicaea (325). In 328, he himself became Bishop of Alexandria. During an eventful episcopate, he defended the faith of Nicaea against the Arians and those who were presumed to be Arians. Five times he was hounded from Alexandria. One of his periods of exile brought him to the West, as far as Trier. His work was mainly devoted to the defence and presentation of the theology of the Word Incarnate, the equal of the Father, e.g. his *On the Incarnation*. The *Life of St Antony*, which is attributed to him, enjoyed a huge success. He

inspired many monastic vocations, such as that of St Augustine.

Cappadocia, in the heart of Asia Minor, was the homeland of three important Fathers. Baptized as an adult after a thorough literary education, Basil (330–379) several times opted for the monastic life before becoming Bishop of his home town, Caesarea, in 370. His episcopate was marked by a threefold concern: the organization of charity during a period of frequent famine (he set up a relief city); the organization of a community living the monastic life (he composed Major and Minor Rules); and a concern for orthodoxy and unity in a period troubled by the Arian disputes. He pointed out how young Christians could make good use of pagan authors. He wrote commentaries on the scriptures and defined the role of the Spirit in his *Treatise on the Holy Spirit*. A moderate man concerned for dialogue, Basil, who was surnamed the Great, did not live long enough to see his efforts towards peace in the church bear fruit.

Gregory of Nazianzus (330–390) was a compatriot and friend of Basil. We have already seen his

8

short passage about the episcopal see of Constantinople. An indecisive man, he was not cut out to be a governor. He was better at writing, and has left some *Theological Discourses*, some panegyrics, some poems, and a vast correspondence.

Gregory of Nyssa (335–394), brother of Basil, married and then entered a monastery, before becoming Bishop of Nyssa. A good theologian, he played an important part in the Council of Constantinople. The most original aspect of his thought concerns mystical theology and contemplation. This is the subject of many of his works: the *Creation of Man*, the *Treatise on Virginity*. Man, made in the image of God, is capable of knowing God and returning to him after a long purification. Gregory declaimed many funeral orations.

John Chrysostom (345–407) was the most prolific of the Greek Fathers. Born in Antioch, John led a monastic life in the desert before becoming deacon and then priest in Antioch. He was an enormous success as a preacher, which led to his being made Bishop of Constantinople in 397, against his will. This was a bad move. Neither a man of the world nor a political animal, he could not adapt himself to the atmosphere of the imperial court. He was inflexible in his wish to reform the morals of the clergy and the courtiers. He attracted the animosity of the empress, and the dubious Bishop of Alexandria, Theophilus, plotted against him. Deposed and exiled for the first time in 403, thanks to public pressure he was able to remain in Constantinople. A second exile in 404 took him far from

Basil of Caesarea

Basil of Caesarea (330–379)

Homily for a time of famine and drought

The torments of the famished, the pangs of hunger, are indeed an evil to be pitied. Of human ills hunger is the chief, and of deaths it is the most painful . . . Hunger is slow torture, prolonged pain, an evil hovering and ever-present, a death which is always there and yet always delayed . . . The body becomes livid as a result of the pallor and blackness which accompany this affliction . . . The eyes become withdrawn into the head, loose in their sockets like dried nuts in their shells. The belly is empty, contracted, formless, without substance; the intestines no longer have their normal tension, and the bones are stuck to the back.

What punishment is too much for anyone who passes by such a body with indifference? Can he rise to any greater cruelty? Is he not worthy to be counted among the most inhuman of beasts, of being regarded as a criminal and a homicide? Yes, anyone who has the power to succour this evil and deliberately, through avarice, postpones doing so, is fully worthy of being condemned as a murderer.

Are you poor? There are others poorer than you are. Have you two days' provisions? They have only one. Be good and gracious, and share what you have with the needy. Do not hesitate to give away the little that you have; do not put your personal interest above the common danger. Even if your food is reduced to one loaf, if there is a beggar at the door, take this loaf out of your larder, hold it up to heaven in your hands and say these sad but generous words. 'Lord, the loaf which you see is my last and danger is imminent; but I am remembering your command and am giving of the little that I have to my brother who is hungry. Do you give also to your servant who is in peril. I know your goodness, and I trust in your power. Do not delay your goodness for long, but if it seems good to you, bestow on us your gifts.'

If you speak and act like this, this bread which you have given in your need will be the seed of a harvest: it will produce abundant fruit and will be the pledge of your food, having been the ambassador of mercy.

Basil of Caesarea,
Homily for a Time of Famine.

Gregory of Nyssa (335–394)

The image and similitude of God in man

It is true, indeed, that the divine beauty is not adorned with any shape or endowment of form, with any beauty of colour, but is given the form of excellence in unspeakable bliss. As painters transfer human forms to their pictures by means of certain colours, laying on their copy the proper and corresponding tints, so that the beauty of the original may be accurately transferred to the likeness, so I would have you understand that our Maker also, painting the portrait to resemble his own beauty, by the addition of virtues, as it were with colours, shows in us his own sovereignty; and manifold and varied are the tints, so to say, by which his true form is portrayed; not red, or white, or the blending of these, whatever it may be called, nor a touch of black that paints the eyebrow and the eye, and shades, by some combination, the depressions in the figure, and all such arts which the hands of painters contrive, but instead of these, purity, freedom from passion, blessedness, alienation from all evil, and all those attributes of the like kind which help to form in man the likeness of God: with such hues as these did the maker of his own image mark our nature.

And if you were to examine the other points also by which the divine beauty is expressed, you will find that to them too the likeness in the image which we present is perfectly preserved. The Godhead is in minds and word: for 'in the beginning was the Word', and the followers of Paul 'have the mind of Christ' which 'speaks' in them: humanity too is not far removed from these: you see in yourself word and understanding, an imitation of the very mind and word. Again, God is love, and the fount of love: for this the great John declares, that 'love is of God', and 'God is love': the fashioner of our nature has made this to be our feature too: for hereby, he says, 'shall all men know that you are my disciples, if you love one another': thus, if this be absent, the whole stamp of the likeness is transformed.

Gregory of Nyssa,
On the Making of Man, V.

John Chrysostom (354–407)

Every Christian must be concerned for the salvation of his brothers

Many things Christ leaves to be done by ordinary human wisdom that we may learn that his disciples were human, that it was not all everywhere to be done by grace: for otherwise they would have been mere motionless logs: but in many things they managed matters themselves. This is not less than martyrdom – to shrink from no suffering for the sake of the salvation of the many.

Nothing is more frigid than a Christian who does not care for the salvation of others. You cannot plead poverty, for she who cast down the two mites will be your accuser. And Peter said, 'Silver and gold have I none.' And Paul was so poor that he was often hungry and lacked necessary food. You cannot plead lowness of birth; for they too were ignoble men and of ignoble parents. You cannot allege lack of education, for they too were unlearned men. So even if you are a slave, indeed a runaway slave, you can play your part, for such was Onesimus: yet see to what Paul calls him, and to what great honour he advances him: 'that he may communicate with me,' he says, 'in my bonds'. You cannot plead infirmity, for such was Timothy, having often infirmities: 'For,' says the apostle, 'use a little wine for your stomach's sake and your frequent infirmities.'

Everyone can profit his nature if he will fulfil his part . . . Those who are solely concerned with their own interests are useless . . . Such too were those virgins, chaste indeed, and decent, and modest, but profitable to none. That is why they are burned. Such are those who are not nourished by Christ. For observe that none of those are charged with particular sins of their own, with fornication, for instance, or with perjury; in short with no sin but having been of no use to another. Such was he who buried his talent, showing indeed a blameless life, but not being useful to another.

John Chrysostom,
Twentieth Homily on Acts.

Constantinople into Asia, where he died in 407. John, whose fame as an orator earned him the name 'Golden Mouth', was first and foremost a pastor who expounded the scriptures in his sermons, prepared candidates for baptism (*Baptismal Homilies*) and encouraged Christians in their different stations of life, with treatises on *Priesthood, Marriage, Virginity* and so on.

In the preceding chapters we have also made the acquaintance of Cyril of Jerusalem (313–387) and Cyril of Alexandria (died 444).

3. The main Latin writers

With the exception of Augustine, the thinking of the Latin Fathers was less original than that of the Greek Fathers, from whom they borrowed a great deal.

Ambrose (340–397), Governor of Milan and still a catechumen, was keeping a careful eye on the difficult election of a new bishop, when a child's voice shouted out, 'Ambrose for bishop!' Within a few days, the catechumen had been

St Ambrose. Masolino (fifteenth century)

84

Ambrose of Milan (333–397)

Advice on prayer

Now hear how we should pray . . . The apostle says: 'I would that men should pray in every place, raising up pure hands, without wrath and without disputes.' And the Lord says in the gospel: 'When you pray, enter your room, close the door and pray to your Father.' Does there not seem to you to be a contradiction here? The apostle says, 'Pray in every place,' whereas the Lord says, 'Pray in your room.' But there is no contradiction. You can pray in your room everywhere and always. You have a room everywhere. Even if you are among the pagans, among the Jews, you always have a secret room. Your room is your spirit. Even if you are in the midst of a crowd, you have within you your closed and secret room.

When you pray, enter your room. He is right to say, 'Enter', lest you pray like the Jews who were told: 'This people honours me with their lips but their heart is far from me.' Let your prayer then rise not just from your lips. Devote all your attention to it, enter the depths of your heart, go right into it . . .

What is this closed door? Learn that you have a door to close when you pray. It has pleased God that women understand this . . . When you pray, do not raise your voice in a cry, do not keep on in your prayers and do not strike attitudes in the crowd. Pray secretly in yourself, certain that he who sees and hears everything can hear you in secret. And pray to your Father secretly. For he who sees what is hidden knows your prayer . . .

Why should we pray in secret rather than raising our voices? Look around. If you want something from someone who has good hearing, you do not think it necessary to shout: you simply ask in a quiet tone of voice. It is when you are trying to attract the attention of a deaf person that you begin to raise your voice so that he can hear you. So those who shout think that God can only hear them if they shout, and in calling on him, they reduce his power. By contrast, those who pray in silence prove their faith and recognize that God examines the reins and hearts, and that he hears your prayer before it leaves your mouth.

Ambrose, *De sacramentis*, 6, 11–16.

Jerome (347–420)

Advice on the education of a granddaughter (about 400)

Jerome gives Laeta advice on educating her daughter of Paula, the granddaughter of Paula, Jerome's friend, who lived with him in Bethlehem. The Bible has pride of place in this education.

The very words which she tries bit by bit to put together and to pronounce ought not to be chance ones, but names specially fixed upon and heaped together for the purpose, those for example of the prophets or the apostles or the list of patriarchs from Adam downwards as it is given by Matthew and Luke. In this way, while her tongue will be well trained, her memory will be likewise developed.

Let her take as a model some aged virgin of approved faith, character and chastity, apt to instruct her by word and by example. She ought to rise at night to recite prayers and psalms; to sing hymns in the morning; at the third, sixth and ninth hours to take her place in the line to do battle for Christ; and lastly, to kindle her lamp and to offer her evening sacrifice.

Let her treasures be not silks or gems but manuscripts of the holy scriptures; and in these let her think less of gilding, and Babylonian parchment, and arabesque patterns, than of correctness and accurate punctuation. Let her begin by learning the psalter, and then let her gather rules of life out of the proverbs of Solomon. From the Preacher let her gain the habit of despising the world and its vanities. Let her follow the example set in Job of virtue and of patience. Then let her pass on to the Gospels, never to be laid aside when once they have been taken in hand. Let her also drink in with a willing heart the Acts of the Apostles and the Epistles. As soon as she has enriched the storehouse of her mind with these treasures, let her commit to memory the prophets, the Heptateuch, the books of Kings and of Chronicles, the rolls also of Ezra and Esther.

When she has done all these she may safely read the Song of Songs, but not before: for, were she to read it at the beginning, she would fail to understand that, though it is written in fleshly words, it is a marriage song of a spiritual bridal. Let her avoid all apocryphal writings . . . It requires infinite discretion to look for gold in the midst of dirt.

Jerome, *Letter 107, 4, 9, 12.*

---

baptized and made bishop. Ambrose gave his possessions to the poor, and required social justice from Christians: 'The world belongs to everyone, not just to the rich.' He exacted a penance from the Emperor Theodosius after he had massacred 700 Thessalonians. Ambrose carried out all the duties of a pastor, and his work has preserved the evidence of this for us: *Sermons, Baptismal Homilies, Treatise on Virginity*. He introduced hymn singing to the Western churches, and wrote both words and music himself.

Jerome (347–397), who came from Dalmatia (present-day Yugoslavia), led the life of a vagrant in his youth. In Rome, he was a dissipated student; in the East, he tried out the monastic life and came reluctantly to the priesthood. In Rome again (382–385), he put himself at the disposal of Pope Damasus and several circles of pious women. In the end, he went off to Bethlehem, where with his friends he founded several monasteries for men and women. A versatile and difficult man, Jerome made a number of enemies through his outspoken language and his often unfair accusations. He applied himself most industriously to the scriptures. Pope Damasus had given him the task of revising the Latin text of the Bible, and he undertook a new translation of the Old Testament into Latin from the original Hebrew and Aramaic texts. This revised Latin version of the Bible is known as the

Catechizing with joy

A deacon from Carthage, Deogratias, had difficulties in teaching the rudiments of faith to adults who were not envisaging baptism in the immediate future. He talked about this to Augustine, who gave him some advice in *On Catechizing the Uninstructed*.

Remember that we are listened to with much greater satisfaction when we ourselves are enjoying our work; for what we say is affected by the very joy of which we ourselves are aware, and it proceeds from us with greater ease and with more acceptance. Consequently, in respect of teaching those things which are commended to us as articles of faith, it is not hard to give instructions as to where to begin from and where to end a narration, or how it is to be varied, so that at one time it may be briefer and at another longer, yet at all times full and perfect: and again the times when it may be right to use the shorter form and those when it will be better to use the longer. The important thing is that everyone should enjoy catechizing; for the better we succeed in this the more attractive we shall be.

The rule which is to be our guide is not difficult to find. For if in material matters God loves a cheerful giver (I Cor. 9.7), how much more will he in spiritual matters? But the certainty that this joy will be with us at the right time

is something that depends on the mercy of the one who has given us this teaching.

The teaching is complete when it has begun from the text 'In the beginning God created the heaven and the earth' and ends with the present times of the church. This does not imply, however, that we ought to repeat by memory the

St Augustine. Lateran basilica (sixth century)

entire Pentateuch . . . the Gospels and Acts of the Apostles. What we ought to do is to give an overall summary, so that certain of the more wonderful facts may be selected which are listened to with uncommon pleasure and which have been ranked so remarkably among the exact turning points of history.

I must tell you how to acquire the joyfulness I have mentioned . . . It is a serious demand to make upon us to continue discoursing on to the appointed end when we fail to see our hearers in any way moved . . . We have to try anything that may be some use in stirring them up and drawing them forth as it were from their place of concealment. We must speak gently, and by reminding them that we are brothers, we should temper their reverence for us, and by questioning them we should ascertain whether they understand what is addressed to them. We must refresh their minds by saying something seasoned with an honest joy and adapted to the matter that is being discussed, or something of a very wonderful and amazing order, or even something of a painful and mournful nature.

Augustine, *On Catechizing the Uninstructed*, 4,5, 14,18.

Vulgate, and is the official text in the Roman Catholic church. We also owe to Jerome commentaries on the scriptures, polemical writings and letters that are full of interest.

Augustine (354–430) is the Father who has had the deepest influence on religious thought in the West. He was born in Thagaste in Numidia

(Souk-Ahras, Algeria), and his mother was the pious Monica. He was first a student and then a professor in Carthage, before going on to Rome and Milan. For a long time he searched for truth in various philosophies and in Manichaeism, but his association with a woman, who bore him a child, Adeodatus, seemed to get in the way of this. At last he found the light under the influence of Ambrose, by whom he was baptized in 387. He had decided upon a monastic life when the Christians of Hippo (Bône-Annaba) chose him as their priest and then as their bishop (395). Throughout his long episcopacy, Augustine was confronted with many burdens of ministry. He preached, travelled all over North Africa to meet with colleagues and take part in local councils, and spent long hours in the law courts. But he was also troubled by wrangles with the Donatists, who were setting up a rival church, and by a dispute on the question of grace with the monk Pelagius. Augustine's last years were clouded by the invasion of the Vandals, and he died in a town that was under siege.

Of all the Fathers, Augustine is the one of whose writings we still have the most. He was a pastor and a teacher through sermons and catechisms; he also wrote learned commentaries

58

86

87

Vincent of Lérins (first half of the fifth century)

Is there a universal criterion for distinguishing religious truth from error?

As often, then, as I have made earnest and diligent inquiries of men outstanding for their holiness and learning, seeking to distinguish, by some sure and as it were universal rule, between the truth of the catholic faith and the falsity of heretical perversity, I would get from almost everyone some such answer: we must doubly fortify our own faith, first, of course, by the authority of the divine law, and second, by the tradition of the catholic church.

Here someone may possibly ask: since the canon of the scriptures is complete, and is abundantly sufficient for every purpose, what need is there to add to it the authority of the church's interpretation? The reason is, of course, that by its very depth the holy scripture is not received by all in one and the same sense, but its declarations are subject to
interpretation, now in one way, now in another, so that it would appear, we can find almost as many interpretations as there are men . . .

In the Catholic church itself, especial care must be taken that we hold to that which has been believed everywhere, always and by all men. For that is truly and rightly 'catholic', as the very etymology of the word shows, which includes almost all universally. This result will be reached if we follow ecumenicity, antiquity, consensus. We shall follow ecumenicity if we acknowledge as the one true faith what the whole church throughout the world confesses. So also we shall follow antiquity if we retreat not one inch from those interpretations which, it is clear, the holy men of old and our own fathers proclaimed. Likewise, we shall follow
consensus if in antiquity itself we earnestly strive after the pronouncements and opinions of all, or certainly almost all, the priests and teachers alike . . .

If a new question arises on which no pertinent decree can be found, the catholic Christian will undertake to examine and investigate the views of the forefathers and to compare them with each other, yet only of those who, though living in different times and places, yet steadfastly remained in communion and faith with the one catholic church, and stand out as teachers worthy of acceptance. Whatever he discovers that not one or two alone, but all together, with one and the same agreement, openly, often, and continually have held, have written, have taught, let him also understand that he must believe this without any hesitation.

Vincent of Lérins,
The Commonitory, III, IV (434).

on the scriptures, and treatises on philosophy and theology, some of which sought to combat errors. Among his most famous works, the best known are the *Confessions*, a long thanksgiving for his conversion; *The City of God*, a historical reflection to help Christians who were disturbed over the capture of Rome by Alaric in 410; and the treatise *On the Trinity*. All the theologians who came after him, right up to Luther, Calvin and Jansen, owed much to Augustine.

One could point to dozens of Latin Fathers, not much of whose work still remains. However, certain writings, like the *Commonitoria* (Memoranda) of Vincent of Lérins, enjoyed a huge success. We have already come across Leo the Great, pope from 440 to 461, in connection with the Council of Chalcedon (see pp.97f). The fourth great figure among the Latin Fathers is considered to be Pope Gregory (590–604), who was also called The Great. The Middle Ages had already begun. His writings often merely reproduce the ideas of his predecessors, in particular those of St Augustine.

For further reading

H. Bettenson (ed.), *The Early Christian Fathers*, Oxford University Press 1969

H. Bettenson (ed.), *The Later Christian Fathers*, Oxford University Press 1973

Peter Brown, *Augustine of Hippo*, Faber and Faber 1967

G. L. Prestige, *Fathers and Heretics*, SCM Press 1977

Maurice Wiles, *The Christian Fathers*, SCM Press 1977

Engraving on a tomb. Lyons (fifth century)

7
The Middle Ages

The Disintegration and Rebuilding of the Christian World from the Fifth to the Eleventh Centuries

Byzantine copyist

It took three centuries for the church to be accepted in the Roman empire, but by the end of the fourth century Christians had come to believe that the church could not continue to exist outside this framework. Civil and religious departments became coterminous; bishops were turned into high officials; it was the emperor who convened councils, and so on.

However, the empire was very sick. On the death of the Emperor Theodosius it was finally divided into two parts, and during the fifth century it disintegrated under the onslaughts of the Barbarians in the West. In the East it kept going for another ten centuries, although its area became smaller and smaller. The church survived all these fluctuations and underwent a deep change.

The ten centuries which separated the age of antiquity from the Renaissance of the sixteenth century have been called the Middle Ages. Originally the term was somewhat pejorative. The humanists of the sixteenth century wanted to signify their contempt for the intervening period which separated them from the ancient civilization that they intended to resurrect.

A great deal happened in a thousand years! For us the Middle Ages call to mind cathedrals, the crusades, monasteries – in other words, Christendom. But to reach that time we have to travel through half a dozen centuries of obscurity, which saw the painful evolution of a European civilization founded on Christianity.

I · Invasions, and a Redrawing of the Religious Map

1. Invasions by Germanic tribes

During the early years of the fifth century, many Germanic tribes, pressed on by the Huns, crossed the Danube and the Rhine and broke in waves on the Roman empire. In 410, Rome was captured and sacked by the Visigoths under Alaric, who proceeded to settle in southern Gaul and Spain. The Vandals conquered North Africa, where St Augustine died in 430 in the besieged town of Hippo. Carthage fell in 439. Attila's Huns invaded the West. The holy alliance of the Germanic Barbarians and the last Roman troops stopped Attila near Troyes (451), while Pope Leo the Great succeeded in negotiating for the departure of the Barbarians (452). Rome was sacked again by the Vandal Genseric in 455. At last, in 476, the last Roman emperor, a beardless adolescent named Romulus Augustulus, was dethroned by the hairy Barbarian Odoacer. The ancient world, both Roman and Christian, had ceased to be. A new era had begun. The empire continued to exist in the East, but the Latin West had disintegrated into a multitude of Barbarian kingdoms: Ostrogoths, Visigoths, Burgundians, Vandals, Alans, and so on.

The end of the world?

Many Christians believed that the end of the world had come: they thought the church could not survive the collapse of the empire. The capture of Rome in 410 was a traumatic experience for believers. Pagans saw it as the gods'

88

In his monastery in Bethlehem, Jerome learns of the capture of Rome

Alas, news was suddenly brought to me of the death of Pammachius and Marcella, the siege of Rome, and the falling asleep of many of my brothers and sisters. I was so stupefied and dismayed that day and night I could think of nothing but the welfare of the community; it seemed as though I was sharing the captivity of the saints, and I could not open my lips until I knew something more definite; and all the while, full of anxiety, I was quavering between hope and despair, and was torturing myself with the misfortunes of other people. But when the bright light of all the world was put out, or rather, when the Roman empire was decapitated and, to speak more correctly, the whole world perished in one city, 'I became dumb and humbled myself, and kept silence from good words, but my grief broke out afresh, my heart glowed within me, and while I meditated the fire was kindled . . .'

Everything, however long, has its end; the centuries that have passed never return, and it is true to say that all that begins must perish, and all that grows undergoes decay and death. There is no created work which is not attacked by old age and consequently disappears. But Rome! Who would believe that Rome, built up by the conquest of the whole world, had collapsed, that the mother of nations had become also their tomb; that the shores of the whole East, of Egypt, of Africa, which once belonged to the imperial city, were filled with the hosts of her menservants and maidservants, that we should every day be receiving in this holy Bethlehem men and women who once were noble and abounding in every kind of wealth but are now reduced to poverty? We cannot relieve these sufferers: all we can do is to sympathize with them, and unite our tears with theirs.

Jerome, *Preface to Commentary on Ezekiel,*
Books 1 and 3.

The Christian West in the Middle Ages

Uppsala
Riga
Lund
St Andrews
Glasgow
Armagh
Dublin
York
Cashel
Canterbury
Hamburg
Bremen
Magdeburg
Gnierzo
Cologne
Mainz
Prague
Rouen
Trier
Reims
Sens
Tours
Vezelay
Salzburg
Gran
Bourges
Besançon
Kalocsa
Lyons
Tarentaise
Venice
Vienne
Milan
Bordeaux
Le Puy
Genoa
Ravenna
Zara
Conques
Avignon
Split
Santiago de
Compostella
Auch
Arles
Aix
Pisa
Ragusa
Toulouse
Narbonne
Braga
Rome
Bari
Tarragona
Naples
Brindisi
Toledo
Otranto
Lisbon
Valencia
Cagliari
Seville
Palermo
Messina

● Mediaeval Latin arch-dioceses

Chief cities of ecclesiastical provinces

◉ Cities where General Councils were held

☿ Places of pilgrimage

The Barbarians in the churches

Orosius, priest of Braga, north of Portugal, had fled before the Vandals and taken refuge at Hippo, near Augustine. In his *History against the Pagans* he sets forth a Christian vision of universal history from Adam to 417.

Yet if the Barbarians had been let loose upon the Roman lands simply because the churches of Christ throughout the East and the West were filled with Huns, Suebi, Vandals and Burgundians, and with believers belonging to various and innumerable races, it would seem that the mercy of God ought to be praised and glorified in that so many nations would be receiving, even at the cost of our own weakening, a knowledge of the truth which they never could have had but for this opportunity.

Orosius, *Seven Books of History against the Pagans*, ed. W. Raymond, Columbia University Press 1936, VII, 41.

The conversion of Clovis

Gregory of Tours (538–594) was born at Clermont-Ferrand, lived at Lyons and in 573 became Bishop of Tours. In his writings and particularly in his *History of the Franks* he is our main informant on the political and religious life of the fifth and sixth centuries in Gaul: the Soissons vase, the royal massacres among the Merovingians, and so on.

When the two hosts joined battle there was grievous slaughter, and the army of Clovis was being swept to utter ruin. When the king saw this, he lifted up his eyes to heaven, and knew compunction in his heart and, moved to tears, cried aloud: 'Jesus Christ, thou that art proclaimed by Clotilde Son of the living God, thou that art said to give aid to those in stress, and to grant victory to those that hope in thee, I entreat from a devout heart the glory of thy succour. If thou grant me victory over these enemies, and experience confirms the power which the people dedicated to thy name claims to have proved, then will I also believe on thee and be baptized in thy name. I have called upon my own gods but here is proof that they have withdrawn themselves from helping me: I believe that they have no power, since they came not to the succour of their servants. Thee do I now invoke, on thee I fain to believe, if but I may be plucked out of the hands of my adversaries.' And as he said this, lo the Alamanni turned their backs and began to flee.

Gregory of Tours, *History* II, 21 (30), ed. O. M. Dalston, Clarendon Press 1927.

punishment for abandoning the old religion. Christians wondered why the apostles and martyrs whose bodies were buried in Rome had not protected the town. Some said that God wanted to punish Christians for their sins. But why had innocent children perished? In Bethlehem, Jerome gave free rein to his grief, while in Hippo Augustine attempted to attribute some meaning to these events in his *City of God*.

Bishops defend the towns

In this tragic situation, the church was the only organized institution. Many bishops supplemented the work of the collapsing imperial administration. Augustine received refugees at Hippo, and ordered priests and bishops to stay with their people. Quodvultdeus was the driving force behind the resistance in Carthage, while Exsuperius defended Toulouse and Sidonius

Apollinarius defended Clermont. Patient supplied provisions to Lyons and the areas around it, and Geneviève of Nanterre, a holy nun, kept up the courage of the Parisians.

The conversion of the Franks

There was nothing for it but to submit to going along with these Barbarians. Besides, some of them had a great respect for the Roman world, and took the old imperial officials into their service. Orosius thought that perhaps the invasions heralded a new stage in the church's life. There was no doubt that many of the Germans had adopted the Arian Christianity which Ulphilas had preached to them in the fourth century. They were on the whole tolerant as far as the mainstream Christians were concerned, but the Arian Vandals embarked on a cruel persecution of other Christians in Africa. The Franks had remained pagans, but as Constantine had done before him, Clovis, their king, attributed his victory over the Alamanni to the God of Clotilde, his Christian wife. Clovis' conversion to the Christian church had far-reaching consequences. The Franks profited from the good will of the old Gallo-Romans. Clovis got the better of the Arian Germans. The mainstream Christians, with one of their own as sovereign, looked less towards Constantinople. Clovis was their new Constantine.

Justinian

In Constantinople, the Emperor Justinian (527–565) launched a heroic attempt to recapture the territories which had fallen into Barbarian hands, and partially succeeded in Africa and Italy. But his main claims to fame are the building of St Sophia in Constantinople and the publication of the Code of Roman Law, a collection of all the laws of the Empire. The Code is the basis of law in European civil and religious society.

The Offensives of Islam from the Seventh to the Ninth Century

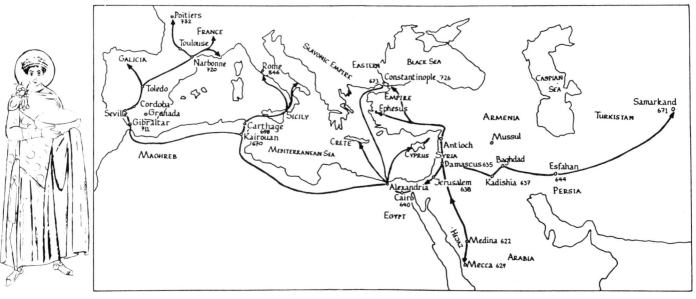

The Emperor Justinian. Mosaic at San Vitale, Ravenna

The Koran

(92) ## Extracts from the surah of the Cow (Koran, Chapter II)

The Koran is divided into surahs or chapters, often named after one of the subjects with which they deal. The name of the second surah comes from vv.63f., which describe the sacrifice of a cow by Moses.

Seventh-century Arabic inscription: 'God is my hope'

(91) ## Opening prayer

In the Name of God, the Merciful, the Compassionate!

Praise belongs to God, the Lord of all Being,
the All-merciful, the All-compass-
ionate,
the Master of the day of Doom.

Thee only we serve; to Thee alone we pray for succour.
Guide us in the straight path,
the path of those whom Thou hast blessed,
not of those against whom Thou art wrathful,
nor of those who are astray.

It is not piety, that you turn your faces
to the East and to the West.
True piety is this:
to believe in God, and the Last Day,
the angels, the Book and the Prophets,
to give of one's substance, however cherished,
to kinsmen, and orphans,
the needy, the traveller, beggars,
and to ransom the slave,
to perform the prayer, to pay the alms.
And they who fulfil their covenant
when they have engaged in a covenant,
and endure with fortitude
misfortune, hardship and peril,
these are they who are true in their faith,
these are the truly godfearing (172).

The people were one nation: then God sent forth
the Prophets, good tidings to bear
and warning, and he sent down with them
the book with the truth, that he might
decide between the people touching their differences;
and only those who had been given it
were at variance upon it, after the
clear signs had come to them being insolent
one to another; then God guided those
who believed to the truth, touching which
they were at variance, by his leave;
and God guides whomsoever he will
to a straight path (209).

God
there is no god but he, the
Living, the everlasting.
Slumber seizes him not, neither sleep;
to him belongs
all that is in the heavens and the earth.
Who is there that shall intercede with him
save by his leave?
He knows what lies before them
and what is after them,
and they comprehend not anything of his knowledge
save such as he wills.
His throne comprises the heavens and earth;
the preserving of them oppresses him not;
he is the All-high, the All-glorious (256).

The Koran, trs. A. J. Arberry, OUP 1964.

2. The birth of Islam and the Arab invasions

A century and a half later, other invaders, from Arabia, caused a much more fundamental upheaval to the geography of the Mediterranean church.

A forgotten Arabia

Seventh-century Arabia was a crossroads of civilizations and religions. According to tradition, the Hanifs held to a primitive monotheism. Jewish and Christian communities had become established along the shore of the Red Sea and in the south (Yemen). However, the larger part of the country was overrun by polytheistic nomadic tribes who were constantly waging war against one another. Arabs were attracted to the town of Mecca, with its black stone (the Ka'bah), because of the fairs held there, and because it was a place of pilgrimage.

The last of the prophets

In about 610, Mohammed, influenced by these various currents, proclaimed a message which he had received from heaven. Divine judgment was at hand. There was only one God, to whom the believer (Moslem) owed absolute submission (Islam). Being the last in a long line of prophets which went through Abraham and Jesus, Mohammed had the mission of restoring monotheism to Arabia and of giving his people, in their own language, the Book (Koran) which would make them equal with other peoples. Rejected by the people of his tribe, in 622 Mohammed fled Mecca for Medina. This is known as the Hijrah, the beginning of the Moslem era. Unable to rally the Christians and the Jews, Mohammed turned against both and began to proclaim his new religion as a world-wide one. After succeeding in unifying the Arab tribes, he returned in triumph to Mecca and died there several months later (632).

The holy war

With only the exhausted remains of the Roman and Persian empires to oppose them, the Arabs, who constituted a new military force, hurled themselves into a series of lightning conquests. They accepted death enthusiastically in their 'striving on the road to God' (*jihad*, often translated 'holy war'). The task of the conquerors, who were sometimes thought of as liberators, was made easier by the passivity of the oriental populations of Syria and Egypt, which were in a permanent state of conflict with Constantinople over questions of dogmatics and ethics (cf. p.99). Jerusalem was captured in 638, at the

Dome of the Rock, Jerusalem (Mosque of Omar)

same time as Syria and Palestine. Alexandria fell in 642, Persia in 651. At the end of the century it was North Africa's turn, though the people there put up more resistance. Kairouan was founded by the Arabs in 670. Carthage was captured in 698. In 711, Arabs and Berbers who had been converted to Islam began to conquer Spain. They were to get as far as the heart of the kingdom of the Franks (Poitiers, 732).

From that time on, Islam appeared as the great Christian enemy. This was the beginning of an endless war. The reconquest of Spain was not completed until 1492. From the eleventh century onwards, the Christians in the West were to organize crusades to win back the places where Christ had lived. However, the Arabs assimilated Greek civilization and made themselves the vehicles for the tradition of this ancient knowledge. Certain areas, such as Spain and Sicily, became centres of cultural exchange between Islam and Christianity.

3. A new religious geography

The church's centre of gravity shifts

The oldest Christian churches in the East and in North Africa collapsed under Arab domination. In spite of being relatively tolerated by the Moslems, these communities were to decline slowly in the East, though they have maintained a presence there up to our own days. The

Christian Copts of Egypt and the Lebanese Maronites are the best known of these. These churches have preserved stable institutions like monasticism and have a cultural distinctiveness which is evident in their liturgical language. On the other hand, the progressive emaciation of the Christian communities in North Africa can easily be seen. There were about forty bishops immediately after the Arab conquest, no more than five in 1053 and two in 1076. The last Christians disappeared at the beginning of the twelfth century. And so the church's centre of gravity was no longer the Mediterranean, with Rome at its centre. It had shifted towards the north. The Arab presence in the Mediterranean made communications and exchanges between West and East by sea more difficult. On the continent, the Slavs settled on the banks of the Danube and came down to the Mediterranean, to the Dalmatian coast, to Macedonia and as far as the Peloponnese by the end of the sixth and beginning of the seventh centuries. They formed a barrier between the Greek East and the Latin West. And so the features of a new Christian geography were drawn.

The Byzantine empire

In the south, the Eastern Roman empire had lost Syria, Palestine and Egypt. It was threatened to the north and east by the Slavs and the Bulgars. It had become a Greek-speaking Asiatic state. From now on it is known as the Byzantine empire, taking its name from Byzantium, the town which had preceded Constantinople on the

---

Two ways of envisaging the conversion of pagans

 93 **Advice given by Pope Gregory the Great to St Augustine on his mission to England**

Destroy as few pagan temples as possible; only destroy their idols, sprinkle them with holy water, build altars and put relics in the buildings, so that, if the temples have been well built, you are simply changing their purpose, which was the cult of demons, in order to make a place where from henceforth the true God will be worshipped. Thus the people, seeing that their places of worship have not been destroyed, will forget their errors and, having attained knowledge of the true God, will come to worship him in the very places where their ancestors assembled. In former times they used to sacrifice a large number of cattle in honour of demons; there is no need to change their customs at festivals. Thus, on the feast of dedication or on the feasts of martyred saints whose relics have been placed in the church, they should build booths out of branches round the church as they used to round pagan temples, and celebrate the festival with religious banquets . . . Allowing them to give outward expression to their joy in the same way, you will more easily lead them to know inner joy, for be assured that it is impossible to rid such deluded souls of all their misconceptions at once. You do not climb a mountain in leaps and bounds, but by taking it slowly.

Gregory the Great, *Letters* XI, 56.

94 **Capitulary of Charlemagne on Saxony (about 785)**

The legislative texts of the Carolingian sovereigns were called *capitularies*.

Anyone who enters a church by violence and, by force or by theft, removes any object from it or sets fire to the building, shall be put to death.

Anyone who, in contempt of Christianity, refuses to respect the holy fast of Lent and eats meat shall be put to death.

Anyone who commits a dead body to the flames, following pagan rites, shall be put to death.

Any unbaptized Saxon who tries to conceal the fact from his fellows and refuses to accept baptism shall be put to death . . .

Bosphorus. The decline of the patriarchates of Alexandria, Jerusalem and Antioch, which were isolated in the Arab world, strengthened the role of the patriarchate of Constantinople, which from then on appeared as the head of the Eastern church and as a rival to the pope, the Bishop of Rome.

The Barbarian West

In the Barbarian kingdoms of the West, the impression given during the centuries which followed the invasions is of a general worsening of the situation. City life disappeared at the same time as trade. The only activity to survive was farming on the big estates. The decadence showed itself in a general decline in moral standards, a lack of interest in study and the arts, and in a religion which was mixed up with pagan superstitions. Yet the apparent decadence was a crucible. Gradually the Christian faith helped to bring to birth a civilization which combined the Graeco-Latin heritage with Germanic contributions.

A religion of the countryside and of nature

During this period, country parishes multiplied on the large estates. Christianity became a peasant religion full of the poetry of the countryside, whose devotion both expressed and

inspired loyalty to the soil which provided nourishment. Mamertus, Bishop of Vienne in the fifth century, instituted Rogations, prayers for a fruitful harvest which were recited in a procession around the fields. These roots in the country, the cult of saints and their relics, and a taste for the miraculous, all combined to produce a popular religion, nostalgia for which is growing up again in our own times.

Monks, upholders and creators of a culture

It was the monks who kept the vital spark of Christianity alive rather than the priests and bishops, whose qualities left much to be desired. The monks were often in the forefront of any evangelization which went on. The Irish monks, who were always on the move, suffered the same hardships as the early Christian travellers. St Columbanus (540–615) left Bangor in Ireland and travelled into Britanny, founding monastries at Luxeuil in the Vosges, Bregenz on Lake Constance, and Bobbio in northern Italy. The Irish monks introduced a new form of penance, consisting of penitential tariffs and private confession. Other monks who followed the Rule of St Benedict were also evangelists, like Augustine of Canterbury (600), or exponents of the scriptures and guardians of the Latin tradition, like the Venerable Bede (seventh-eighth century).

The Emperor Charlemagne. Statue in Metz, France

II · The First Rebuilding of the Christian World

1. The Carolingian renaissance

While the Merovingian kingdoms were collapsing, their kings under the control of the Mayors of the Palace, a family of warriors came gradually into the limelight. It was that of the Mayors of the Palace of Austrasia, the eastern kingdom whose capital was Metz. One of them, Charles Martel, took charge of church affairs: he appointed

bishops and abbots and disposed of the church's lands as he chose. He halted the Arab advance in 732 at Poitiers, and then in 737 at Avignon. Holding on to the main sources of power, Pepin the Short, Charles Martel's son and successor, requested Pope Zacharias to legitimate this state of affairs. Pepin and the papacy came to a mutually acceptable arrangement.

The birth of the papal states

When consulted by Pepin the Short, the pope replied, 'It is better to give the title of king to the one who holds the power.' In 751, therefore, Pepin had himself crowned king by Boniface, the apostle of Germany. Pope Zacharias, who was being threatened in Rome by the Lombards, and could no longer count on the help of the Emperor of Constantinople, sought refuge with Pepin. In 754 the pope reconsecrated Pepin and also his sons, including the future Charlemagne. During an expedition to Italy the new king, God's elect, the new David, re-established the pope in Rome and restored to him full power over the lands which had been recaptured from the Lombards (756). And so the papal states came into being, which were to last until 1870. The pope became ruler over them, but came within the orbit of the kings of France, which put him in a delicate situation over against the Emperor of Constantinople.

A new Western empire

Charlemagne (768–814) carried on his father's policy. He strengthened the unity of Western Europe, pushed the Arabs back into northern Spain and extended his kingdom to the east, converting the Saxons by a campaign of terror. He imposed his opinions on the papacy. On Christmas Day 800, the pope bestowed the imperial crown on him. The new empire, with a marked Germanic stamp, was to succeed the Roman empire. This re-establishment of an empire represented the persistence of an ideal of unity and peace, now realized in both a political institution and in the church. From this time on the two poles of Western society were the pope and the emperor. However, the new emperor was considered to be a usurper by the court of Constantinople, who could not tolerate the imperial title being borne by anyone outside the Byzantine capital. This was another factor in the disputes between the Greek East and the Latin West.

Order is restored

The Carolingian sovereigns considered it their duty to restore order to the church and regain some of its prestige. This has given rise to the term 'the Carolingian Renaissance'. Under Pepin, the monk-bishop Boniface (died 754) restructured the dioceses of Germany. Through many capitularies (legislative texts), often inspired by monks such as Alcuin, Charlemagne undertook a vigorous reform of the Frankish church. He chose his bishops with extreme care, and thought of them as high-ranking officials. As to the secular clergy, he favoured the establishment of communities of canons of the kind inspired by Chrodegang of Metz (died in 766). Benedict, Abbot of Aniane, near Montpellier, extended the Benedictine Rule and reformed a number of monasteries. Without always succeeding, he tried to re-establish the custom of the election of the abbot by the monks.

Liturgical reform

To put a stop to the decadence of the liturgy in what used to be Gaul, Charlemagne introduced and imposed on his kingdom the books of the Roman liturgy. Steeped in the spirit of the Old Testament, reform moved towards ritualism and legalism. The communal aspect of prayer was diminished. For the faithful who no longer understood Latin, the mass had become a mysterious and sacred spectacle. Ordinary bread was replaced by unleavened bread. The priest now celebrated with his back to the people and recited the canon in a low voice. Private masses grew in number. The capitularies sought to halt the successful progress of the penitential tariffs of the Irish and restore to life the old liturgical form of penance.

Intellectual renewal

By calling for the foundation of schools for the clergy, Charlemagne set in motion an intellectual renewal. At the court of Aix-la-Chapelle, the Palatine Academy brought together the great minds of the age, many of whom were monks. An attempt was made to reinstate classical Latin, as well as the study of scripture, the Church Fathers and the liturgy. The copyists' workshops produced many manuscripts remarkable for their calligraphy and their rich illumination. This renewal reached its peak at the beginning of the ninth century. Some great names reappeared in theology, and it recovered its taste for dogmatic controversies. Paschasius Radbertus (died 865), Rabanus Maurus (died 856) and Ratramnus expressed different points of view about the real presence of Christ in the eucharist. Florus (died 860), a deacon of Lyons, tried to improve the texts of scripture in circulation and regarded the reading of the Word of God as the best remedy against superstition or the excessive cult of images.

2. The vicissitudes of the Byzantine empire

For more than a century (726–843), in the midst of all the dynastic and military troubles, an argument over icons (the Greek word for images) held the centre of the stage in the Byzantine empire. The Christians of the first centuries had been strongly opposed to representations of the deity, which they considered to be idols. However, from the third century onwards the catacombs had been decorated with pictures of people and scenes from the scriptures, among which pictures of Christ held pride of place.

The Byzantine tradition gave a role to icons in teaching. They were 'silent sermons', 'books for the illiterate'. They were venerated as though they captured the presence of the person who was represented. Some people were not happy at this and spoke of icons in terms of superstition and even idolatry.

The war over icons

In 726, the Emperor Leo III destroyed a particularly venerated image of Christ which was above the gate to his palace in Constantinople. This was the beginning of the policy of iconoclasm, i.e. the destruction of icons, which the emperor carried out despite popular riots and the resistance of the monks. Was the emperor influenced by the proximity of Islam? It is more likely that he wanted to purify popular religion and limit the influence of the monks, who were the great defenders of icons. Iconoclasm reached its peak during the reign of the Emperor Constantine V (741–775). The monks suffered martyrdom to defend the icons. The Empress Irene restored calm by convening a council at Nicaea in 787, the seventh ecumenical council, which recognized the legitimacy of the veneration of icons.

However, the conflict arose again in 813 and did not finally die down until 843. From then on, the place of icons was no longer disputed. The church and the people had triumphed over imperial desires. Nevertheless, mosaics and paintings had to be executed according to rigorous theological principles: they depicted on the walls of the churches the descending hierarchy which began with Christ the Pantocrator (the all-powerful) on the cupola and ended with the saints low down in the chapels.

The hey-day of Byzantium

Although shadows were falling over the West at the end of the ninth century, the Byzantine

Christ pantocrator. Mosaic from Daphne, Greece

126

empire moved into a particularly brilliant period with the Macedonian dynasty (867–1056) and its great king Basil II (976–1025). Even greater than the military successes and the literary works was the remarkable blossoming of the monastic life. In 963 the monk Athanasius founded the first establishment on Mount Athos, in northern Greece. The Holy Mountain was to become a republic of monks and the high place of Orthodox spirituality.

3. Evangelization continues

In the West

The political and dynastic crises in the East and West did not prevent evangelization from continuing, whether spontaneously or in a more organized way through prince or papacy. Augustine of Canterbury, at the end of the sixth century, had been sent by Pope Gregory the Great to re-establish the church in England. In the first half of the eighth century the great missionary in the West was the English monk

Winthrif, better known under the name of Boniface (680–754). He reorganized the Frankish church and founded a great many bishoprics and abbeys before dying a martyr death among the Frisians (in the Netherlands). At the end of the eighth century, Charlemagne gave the newly-conquered Saxons the choice between baptism and death, but his adviser, the monk Alcuin, expressed certain reservations over this method of conversion. During the ninth century evangelization got as far as Hamburg, Bremen and the Scandinavian countries, thanks to Anskar (801–865).

Among the Slavs

Greeks and Latins co-operated over the evangelization of the Slavonic countries in the plains by the Danube. German missionaries had come to Bohemia and Moravia from Bavaria. At the same time, a Moravian prince had appealed to Constantinople. In 863, the patriarch sent two brothers: Constantine, better known as Cyril, and Methodius, natives of Thessalonica, who

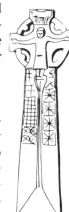

Celtic cross in Ireland

Cyril and Methodius among the Slavs (863)

When the Slavs were baptized along with their prince Rastislav, Sviatopolk and Kotsel (members of the prince's family) sent to the Emperor Michael (of Constantinople, 842–867), saying: 'Our country has been baptized, but we have no master to preach to us, instruct us and explain the holy books to us. We understand neither Greek nor Latin: some teach us one thing and some another, and we do not understand the meaning of the sacred books and their power. So send us masters who are capable of explaining to us the letter of the holy books and their spirit.'

On hearing this, the Emperor Michael assembled all his philosophers and told them all that the Slav princes had said. The philosophers replied: 'At Thessalonica there is a man called Leo: he has sons who know Slavonic well, two trained in the sciences, and philosophers . . .'

As soon as they arrived, Constantine (Cyril) and Methodius established the letters of the Slavonic alphabet and translated the Acts of the Apostles and the Gospel. The Slavs rejoiced at hearing the mighty works of God in their own tongue . . . Now some people

began to find fault with the Slavonic books, saying, 'No people has the right to its alphabet save the Hebrews, the Greeks and the Latins, as is shown by what Pilate wrote on the Saviour's cross.'

The Pope of Rome (John VIII), on hearing that, found fault with those who murmured against the Slavonic books, saying: 'Let the words of Holy Scripture be fulfilled: that all tongues should praise God.'

Nestorian Chronicle XX – an eleventh-century text.

96 Prohibition of the Slavonic liturgy by Pope Stephen V (885)

This text clearly contradicts the previous one.

Methodius brought to those who heard him superstition rather than edification, polemic rather than peace . . . The celebration of the divine offices, the holy mysteries and solemn masses which Methodius claimed to present in Slavonic were not authorized by anyone . . .

In the name of God and with our apostolic authority we therefore prohibit them, and on pain of anathema, save for simple souls who would not understand otherwise, the Gospel and the texts of the apostles shall be read in this Slavonic language by educated people.

were familiar with Slavonic. These two invented an alphabet for the language, which hitherto had been only oral. They translated holy books and liturgical texts into Slavonic. But they then fell foul of the Bavarian bishops who saw them as rivals, and would not allow them to conduct any liturgy other than in Latin. According to them, prayer was permitted only in the three languages in which Pilate had written the inscription on Jesus' cross (John 19.20). The two brothers went off to Rome, where they received a warm welcome. Pope John VIII accepted the Slavonic liturgy. Constantine (Cyril), who had died in the meantime, was buried in a Roman church. Methodius was nominated Archbishop of Greater Moravia at Sirmium (Mitrovica on the Save, not far from its confluence with the Danube). But after his death in 884, the German bishops succeeded in persuading the new pope to condemn the Slavonic liturgy.

The Bulgars and the Russians

Persecuted, the disciples of Methodius took refuge in Bulgaria. The Bulgars, an Asiatic tribe largely influenced by the Slavs, were poised between Rome and Constantinople. In turn they adopted the Cyrillic alphabet and the Slavonic liturgy. In the following century, the Russians used this alphabet and liturgy themselves. However, all this intense evangelizing activity was seriously threatened by new invasions from the north, west and south during the tenth century.

III · New Chaos, and the Slow Return to Equilibrium

1. The Dark Ages in the West (end of the ninth to the tenth century)

Destabilization

The unity of the Frankish empire vanished with the treaty of Verdun in 843, which divided up the heritage of Louis the Pious (814–840) into three parts. The two kingdoms of France and Germany were the forerunners of the two countries we know today. Lotharingia, the long corridor which extended from the North Sea to Southern Italy, quickly broke up in to a myriad of kingdoms. At the beginning of the tenth century, the office of emperor disappeared. In addition to civil wars, the new invasions resulted in complete disorganization in the West. Normans from Scandinavia landed on the northern and Atlantic coasts of the continent. They sailed up the rivers, killing and plundering. Those who could, fled into the interior. Thus we can trace the movement of the relics of St Philibert from Noirmoutier as far as Tournus. In the East, the Magyars or Hungarians, who came from the Urals, invaded Germany and laid areas waste as far as Burgundy. In the south the Saracens, Moslem pirates, left Africa and Spain to raid the coasts of Italy and Provence. For nearly a century (888–975), basing themselves at La Garde-Freinet above St Tropez, they plundered the surrounding areas, even taking hostage Maïeul, the Abbot of Cluny.

The holy empire and the new kingdoms

Stability began to emerge towards the end of the tenth century. In 962, the empire was restored in favour of a German king, Otto I. The holy Romano-Germanic empire was to last until 1806, but in spite of its desire to be universal, it really remained German. In 987 the Capetian dynasty took firm root in France. At the same time, the invaders were establishing and building up new states. The Normans settled in the area which from that time on (911) has been called Normandy after them. In the majority of cases, the birth of a new nation coincided with the baptism

---

Bishops of Le Mans in the tenth century

The Lord Mainard, bishop (from 951 to 971), who was one of the nobility of Maine, was the brother of the Viscount of the city of Le Mans. Having originally led a secular life, he had numerous children, sons and daughters. He was judged so ignorant that he was taken for a layman rather than a clerk. Anyway, since the city of Le Mans had long been without a pontiff, as many wanted to obtain the bishopric for money, but some, astutely demonstrating their learning, set themselves forth as being worthy of the bishopric, the Lord, who has chosen weakness to confound strength, chose a man who was aware of his ignorance and was an unlettered sage, namely the Lord Mainard, in accordance with the word of scripture

according to which modest rusticity is preferable to pride in science. With the consent of the clergy and of the king who ruled over the people at that time, Mainard was consecrated bishop by the will of God because of his great humility and his great innocence.

On the death of Bishop Mainard, the Lord Sifroi, a man of deplorable behaviour and blameworthy in every respect, seized hold of the vacant see. Although he was born of noble parents, he did base deeds during his episcopate. He set himself to tearing down everything that his predecessor had built up.

Sifroi began to be a destroyer of the church even before being consecrated bishop. Specifically, he gave away land known as Coulaines, which belonged to

his predecessors in the see, worth a thousand pounds and more, along with the town of Dissay on the Loir, to the Count of Anjou, Foulque. This was so that he would intervene with the king of France to secure the bishopric for Sifroi.

Then, whereas he should have acknowledged his guilt in respect of the property of the church that he had plundered and should have repented of his sins after having committed such a crime, alas, he capped all his wickedness by taking in his old age a woman called Audeberge who had sexual relations with him, conceived, and bore him daughters. These died, but he had a son Aubri who survived. When this son had grown up, his father heaped on him gifts belonging to the church . . .

of its leader. The Hungarians, beaten in 965 on the Lech, settled in the valley of the Danube. The kingdoms of Hungary came into being with the baptism of its king, Stephen, in 1000. Catholic Poland was born in 966 with the baptism of Duke Mieszko. By allowing himself to be baptized in the Dniepr in 989, the Grand Duke Vladimir extended the church of Constantinople north-wards and brought Russia, centred on its capital, Kiev, into the states of Europe.

Enamelled Gothic fibula

2. The church submerged in the feudal system

The feudal system

Civil war, like invasions, contributed to the breaking up of the state. All that counted were the bonds which people established between themselves by an oath. Land belonged to the warrior who defended it. He put himself under the protection of a more powerful lord who

---

(98)

The three orders of feudal society

Adalbero, Bishop of Laon from 977 to 1030, spent his life in political intrigue, changing sides several times. In his poem he gives the king of France advice on reorganizing the state.

The heavenly people is divided into several bodies, and we are told that it is in its image that the peoples of the earth are disposed . . .
The order of our church is called the kingdom of heaven, and God himself has established ministries without blemish . . .
If the state is to enjoy the tranquil peace of the church, it must be subject to two different laws . . .
One, the divine law, makes no distinction between its ministers: according to it, they are all of equal status . . .
The son of a worker is not inferior to the heir to the throne. To such, this merciful law forbids all common earthly occupations. They do not till the glebe; they do not walk behind herds of cattle . . . God is their sole judge. He has subjected the whole human race by his command-

ments. There is not a prince who is exempt from them . . .
So they must keep vigil, abstain from food, pray without ceasing for the miseries of the people and for their own . . .

The society of the faithful forms but a single body . . . but the state comprises three. For the other law, the human law, distinguishes two other classes: nobles and serfs are not ruled by the same statute. Two figures occupy the chief place: one is the king and the other the emperor; as we can see, it is their rule that ensures the solidity of the state. There are others whose condition is such that no power constrains them, provided that they abstain from crimes punished by the royal justice. These are the warriors, the protectors of the churches; they are the defenders of the people

both great and small – defenders of all, and at the same time ensuring their own security. The other class is that of serfs: this unfortunate breed has to pay for everything with pain. What abacus could calculate the cares which drain the serfs, their long journeys and their harsh travail? Money, clothes, food, the serfs provide everything for all the world; no free man could exist without the serfs . . .

The house of God is thought to be one, but it is divided into three: some pray, some fight and others work. These three parts which co-exist do not suffer from being disjunct: the services rendered by the one are the condition of the work of the two others: each in turn is charged with providing relief for the whole. Thus this threefold assembly is no less one; and so it is that the law has been able to triumph and the world to enjoy peace.

Adalbero, *Poem to King Robert.*

would grant his vassal the possession and administration of a fiefdom or benefice. The social bonds were changed in this way into a hierarchy of warriors and landowners. The church, which owned large areas of land, was caught up in this system. Every holder of an ecclesiastical office had the use of a piece of land or a benefice which provided him with a living. The bishop was a lord and vassal in the same way as the laity. He held jurisdiction over his land and dispensed justice; he maintained an army. This helps us to understand the great desires people had to hold ecclesiastical office. The old rules of election by the clergy and people were forgotten. Not being hereditary titles, like other fiefdoms, bishoprics and abbeys were redistributed on the death of those who held their titles. Lords, the emperor, kings, dukes and so on disposed of them to whoever earned their favour. Since an episcopal fiefdom involved both a spiritual and a temporal jurisdiction, it was granted by a kind of investiture ceremony: the lord bestowed the cross and ring on his candidate. This was lay investiture. Of course, the bishop was always consecrated by another bishop, generally the metropolitan (archbishop).

Mediocre bishops and bad popes

On the whole, the quality of bishops left much to be desired, because the princes were not guided solely by religious considerations when making their choices. They preferred a good military man as bishop; they wanted to provide for their numerous children; and they would even sell the position to whoever would pay the most. The term for this sort of thing is simony, that is to say, selling holy things: Simon Magus was the prime example of this (see Acts 8.20). There were bad priests and bad Christians to match the bad bishops. Many of these priests were accused of Nicolaitism, i.e. keeping concubines (the reference is to Rev. 2.6, 14–15). It is true that ecclesiastical legislation about the marriage and celibacy of priests was not always very clear.

Even the papacy was involved in these abuses. In the tenth century, the womenfolk of a Roman family kept the see of Rome under their thumbs. That explains the papal concubines and the popes aged less than twenty. On moral grounds, the German emperors took their turn in setting their candidate on Peter's throne.

The three orders

However, the feudal system found a certain equilibrium. The writers of the period discerned the will of God in the organization of a tripartite society. This was the famous theory of the three orders: 'Some pray, some fight and some work.' The church tried to restrain violence by peaceful institutions: the Peace of God forbade taking advantage of the weak, the Truce of God forbade fighting on certain days. The religious celebration of chivalry gave its blessing to soldiering.

3. The break between the Latin and Greek churches: the schism of 1054

Politics and religion

From the fifth century on, the gap between the Latin and the Greek churches went on increasing. The reasons for this were at the same time political, cultural and dogmatic. The Greek church was tied up with the power of Byzantium. The emperor made and unmade the patriarchs of Constantinople. In restoring the empire in the West, the papacy seemed to be operating politically against the emperor of Constantinople, and the churches were indirectly caught up in this tension between the two empires.

Cultural differences

The cultural gap was even more serious. The two churches did not understand each other. The East did not know Latin, and the West no longer understood Greek very well. The inheritors of a great culture, the Greeks remained faithful to it in both the secular and the religious spheres. In

131

The reproofs of the monk Nicetas Stethatos to the Latins

Nicetas Stethatos (c.1005–1090), a monk at the monastery of Studios near Constantinople, was not just a controversialist. He was also a good spiritual writer, a representative of hesychasm (*hesychia*, repose in God), that form of contemplation bound up with the incessant repetition of the Jesus prayer to the rhythm of breathing: 'Lord Jesus Christ, Son of God, have mercy on me.'

Those who still participate in the feast of unleavened bread are under the shadow of the law and consume the feast of the Jews, not the spiritual and living food of God . . . How can you enter into communion with Christ, the living God, while eating the dead unleavened dough of the shadow of the law and not the yeast of the new covenant . . . ? And who has taught you to break up the marriage of priests . . . ? Therefore, my brothers, make a serious examination of yourselves on these questions and see if it is not from this source (Judaism) that the four plagues which I have just mentioned and dismissed have come: namely, unleavened bread, fasting on Saturdays, priestly celibacy and the oblation of fast days.

the West, the Carolingian renaissance was quickly extinguished. The tenth century was a cultural desert. In the few contacts which they had, Greeks and Latins heartily despised one another. To the Byzantines, the Latins, people from dark-age countries, were wild and un-cultured savages with huge appetites. To the Latins, the Greeks were degenerate, effeminate hair-splitters. The adjective 'Byzantine' became pejorative.

Liturgy and doctrine

It was still liturgical and doctrinal differences which set the two churches in opposition. For the Greeks, ritual was faith in action. In the West, it was easier to distinguish the doctrine from the rite. For someone in the East, to change the ritual was to change the faith. That is why questions about fasting, unleavened or leavened bread, or whether the celebrants were bearded, assumed great importance. In the East, monks and bishops were celibate, but priests could be married. In the West, celibacy was demanded of all priests, or, at the very least, married men in principle renounced sexual relations after their ordinations.

The Greeks criticized the Latins for having modified the formula of faith by adding the *filioque* to the Niceno-Constantinopolitan creed. 'The Spirit proceeds from the Father,' said the Creed, 'and from the Son,' added the Latins. There was a theological nuance in the under-standing of the role of the Spirit. Not knowing its history, the Latins accused the Greeks of having cut the expression out.

The pope and the patriarch

Although the Greeks had a more collegial view of episcopacy, the pope, as Peter's successor, sometimes claimed power to intervene in the universal church. For those in the East, Rome held only a primacy of honour.

There were a great number of divisions fol-lowed by reconciliations from the fifth to the eleventh century. At the beginning of the events of 1054, there was at first a willingness for reconciliation on the part of Pope Leo IX. The pope and the Byzantine emperor had a common enemy, the Normans, in southern Italy. An alliance would allow them to face up to this enemy. But a religious reconciliation was the preliminary necessity. Unfortunately, the two

Sentence of excommunication delivered by Cardinal Humbert against Michael Cerularius

In 1015 Humbert entered the monastery of Moyenmoutier in the Vosges and became a fervent supporter of reform in the church. Pope Leo IX, who had been Bishop of Toul, brought him to Rome as secretary, made him a cardinal and entrusted several missions to him, including one to Constantinople. He was a man of character but unbending, uncompromising and without pity.

Michael Cerularius (1000–1058), born of a great family in Constantinople, had become a monk following his imprisonment for a plot against the emperor. The friendship of another emperor brought him the status of patriarch in 1043. He proved very hostile to the Latins. In 1058 he was arrested and deported by the Emperor Isaac Comnenus and died before being brought to trial.

As for Michael, who has improperly been given the title patriarch, and those who share in his folly, they sow an abundance of heresies each day in their midst (in the city of Constantinople). Like the Simonians, they sell the gift of God; like the Valesians, they make their hosts eunuchs and then elevate them up not to the priesthood but also to the episcopate. Like the Nicolaitans, they allow ministers of the holy altar to be contracted in marriage . . . Like the Pneumatomachi (those who fought against the Spirit) they have suppressed the procession of the Holy Spirit a filio in the creed. Like the Manichaeans, they declare that fermented bread is alive . . . Moreover, allowing beard and hair to grow, they refuse communion with those who, following the custom of the Roman church, cut their hair and shave their beard . . .

That is why, being unable to bear these unprecedented injuries and these outrages directed against the chief apostolic see . . . we sign against Michael and his supporters the anathema that our most reverend pope has pronounced against them if they do not return to their senses . . .

May Michael the neophyte, who improperly bears the title of patriarch . . . and all those who follow him in the above-mentioned errors, may they all fall under the anathema, Maranatha, with the Simonians . . . and all the heretics, and indeed with the devil and his angels, unless they return to their senses . . . Amen, Amen, Amen!

people charged with achieving an agreement were not the right men for the job. The papal legate, Cardinal Humbert, a man from Lorraine who was anxious for reform, had only a limited acquaintance with Greek culture and was quite inflexible. The patriarch of Constantinople, Michael Cerularius, also proved stubborn. The absence of relations with Rome pleased him, because in this way he remained the only master of the Greek church.

The break

The legation of Cardinal Humbert in Constantinople was the occasion for bringing out well remembered injuries. Not succeeding in finding a basis for discussion, Humbert solemnly excommunicated the patriarch Michael Cerularius in the church of St Sophia. The form of excommunication drawn up by Humbert reveals his deep ignorance. Many of the accusations were without foundation. Again, he found fault with those in the East for leaving out the *filioque*, for the marriage of priests, and so on. He did not know that Maranatha means 'Come, Lord', and is not a condemnation (I Cor. 16.22). The excommunication pronounced by Cerularius against Humbert was not of a very high standard either.

Fruitless efforts at reconciliation

At the time, no one attached much importance to

Joint declaration made by Pope Paul VI and the Patriarch Athenagoras (7 December 1965)

Among the obstacles in the way of the development of these brotherly relationships of trust and esteem (between the Roman Catholic Church and the Orthodox Church) is the memory of painful decisions, acts and incidents which in 1054 came to a climax with the sentence of excommunication pronounced against the patriarch Michael Cerularius and two other figures by the legates of the Roman see, led by Cardinal Humbert, legates who were themselves then the object of a similar sentence passed by the Patriarch and Synod of Constantinople . . .

Pope Paul VI and Patriarch Athenagoras I, in his synod, confident of expressing the common desire for justice and the unanimous feeling of love among their faithful, and recalling the precept of the Lord, 'When you present your offering at the altar . . . ' (Matt. 5.23–24), declare with one accord that they:

(a) Regret the offensive words, the unfounded accusations and the despicable acts which, from one side or the other, marked or accompanied the sad events of this period;

(b) Equally regret and blot out from memory and from the realm of the church the sentences of excommunication which ensued, the memory of which even in our day acts as an obstacle to reconciliation in love, and consign them to oblivion;

(c) Finally, deplore the disturbing precedents and subsequent events which, under the influence of various factors, including a failure to understand and mutual distrust, finally led to the effective schism in communion.

Pope Paul VI and Patriarch Athenagoras I, with his synod, are aware that this reciprocal gesture of justice and pardon is not enough to put an end to the differences, older or more recent, which exist between the Roman Catholic Church and the Orthodox Church and which, by the action of the Holy Spirit, will be surmounted through the purification of hearts, through regret for the wrongs of history, and a positive concern to arrive at a common understanding and expression of the apostolic faith and its demands . . .

these events. They had seen it all before! Besides, as the pope had died before these excommunications, did his legate still have any power? And yet the date of 1054 is still symbolic, because there was no real reconciliation after that. The Crusades made the gap even wider. The Councils of Lyons in 1274 and of Florence in 1438 only achieved ephemeral reconciliations which were badly prepared and rejected by Christians in the East. The capture of Constantinople by the Turks in 1453 emphasized the isolation of Greek Christians.

The joint declaration of Pope Paul VI and Patriarch Athenagoras, by regretting the exchange of insults in 1054 and the excesses of the past, forms one step on the long road to reconciliation.

For further reading

Peter Brown, *The World of Late Antiquity*, Thames and Hudson 1971

Christopher Dawson, *The Making of Europe*, Sheed and Ward 1953

Ferdinand Lot, *The End of the Ancient World and the Beginnings of the Middle Ages*, Harper and Row 1961

Hugh Trevor-Roper, *The Rise of Christian Europe*, Thames and Hudson 1965

A. A. Vasiliev, *A History of the Byzantine Empire. 324–1453*, University of Wisconsin Press and Blackwell 1952

8

Christendom: The Foundations of a Society

End of the Eleventh to the Thirteenth Centuries

The word 'Christendom' indicates a certain kind of relationship between society and the church in the Middle Ages. At that time the people of Europe were part of a large community, and what held them together was the Christian faith. Church and state were the two aspects of the same reality which was both spiritual and temporal, a parallel to soul and body in the human individual. This community only had meaning in its supernatural fulfilment as the kingdom of God. That at least was the ideal vision put forward by certain theologians in the best centuries of the Middle Ages, the twelfth and thirteenth.

One of the dominant features of this Christendom was the increasingly important place acquired by the papacy in the church and in mediaeval Europe, at the expense of often violent battles with the Germanic emperor. But the equilibrium was always fragile. If the first half of the thirteenth century saw the height of papal power, the last years of the century already knew a serious dispute over the claims of Rome and the first cracks in Christendom.

This chapter tries to pick out the most important features of the age of Gregory VII, St Bernard and St Louis, to which Catholics of the nineteenth and twentieth centuries often look back with nostalgia. We have inherited from this era many Catholic doctrines and customs, as well as the most beautiful examples we have of religious art. However, we must beware of idealizing a period which is only one step in the long progress of the church. We shall have occasion to see that Christians of the Middle Ages did not always behave in conformity to the gospel.

I · The Foundations of Mediaeval Christendom

1. The affirmation of the papacy

In the previous chapter, we saw how Europe attained relative equilibrium around the middle of the eleventh century. We have established, too, that the feudal system had certain unfortunate consequences for the life of the church. Many churchmen, especially those from reformed monasteries like the ones dependent on Cluny, founded in 910 – to which we shall be returning later – were concerned to have a more holy church and looked for ways of reform. It was a question of pastors being mindful of their responsibilities. But many were of doubtful quality because they had been given their positions by the princes. Ought not the secular lords to be relieved of the task of appointing bishops, especially the chief one, the Bishop of Rome?

Reform decrees

(102) In 1059, Pope Nicholas II defined the rules for papal elections. The pope would be appointed by the cardinals. The rest of the clergy and the people would have to be satisfied with acclaiming the newly elected man. From that time on, the cardinals had a special role to play in the church. These cardinals were the most important clergy in Rome: the bishops of the areas around Rome, those in charge of the biggest churches in Rome and the seven deacons responsible for administration. The emperor did not take kindly to being displaced from his role as the one who appointed the pope, and in times of crisis he was to put up his own candidate in opposition to the one chosen by the cardinals.

(103) Pope Gregory VII planned an enormous moral reform. The decisions of 1074 attacked simony and those priests who went on living a married life. The pope counted on the collaboration of the princes and bishops, but these reforms often did not go down well. Gregory VII was encouraging

saintliness, but many people thought that in the matter of priests married before their ordination he was changing old-established customs.

Against lay investiture

Temporarily discouraged, Gregory VII thought that all the evil sprang from lay investiture. He wanted to do away with it at all levels. In 1075 he forbade bishops to accept appointment by the laity, and forbade metropolitans (archbishops) to consecrate those who had accepted appointments in this way. Gregory VII made no distinction between the estates attached to a position and the position itself. The question of estates hardly interested him at all. He wanted to see the episcopacy independent of temporal powers. This was a radical measure which in certain respects was also a novelty, since the people no longer took part in the election as they had been accustomed to do. At the same time, the pope justified his right to act in this way in affirming his authority over the world-wide church and over princes by means of *dictatus papae* (papal (10) decrees or affirmations). He sent legates to see that his decisions were carried out.

The investiture dispute

The German emperor, Henry IV, opposed the papal decision which lost him a large measure of his authority in a country where bishops were among the most powerful lords. A long struggle between the popes and the emperors followed. Henry IV proclaimed the deposition of Gregory VII. The latter in turn deposed Henry and released his subjects from their oath of obedience. Henry humbled himself before Gregory at Canossa in 1077 in order to regain his powers. But in the end Gregory VII died in exile in 1085. Several decades passed before things were sorted out. In the meantime, much thought was given to the distinction between spiritual and

Reforming decrees

 The election of the pope: decree of 1059 (Nicholas II)

Instructed by the authority of our predecessors and other holy fathers, we have decided and established that after the death of a pope of the universal church of Rome, first of all the cardinal bishops shall together, and with the most careful attention, seek out the most worthy person, and then present him to the cardinal clergy; finally, the rest of the clergy and the people shall come forward to support the new election.

 Decisions of the Council of Rome (1074 – Gregory VII)

Anyone who has been promoted by simony, that is to say at the price of money, to one of the sacred orders or to a position in the church, shall not be able henceforth to exercise any ministry in the holy church.

Those who obtain churches at the price of money lose these churches.

From henceforth no one can buy or sell churches.

Those who have committed the crime of fornication (married priests) cannot celebrate the mass nor perform in minor orders at the altar.

We also resolve that the people may not attend the offices of those who have scorned our constitutions – which are those of the holy fathers themselves – so that those whom neither the love of God nor the dignity of their functions can correct should be humiliated by lack of human respect and by the reproof of the people.

The *Dictatus* (decrees) of Pope Gregory VII (1073–1085)

2. Only the Roman pontiff is rightly called universal.

3. He alone can depose or absolve bishops.

9. The pope is the only man to whom all princes bend the knee.

12. He is allowed to depose emperors.

16. No general synod (council) can be convened without an order.

18. His sentence cannot be repealed by anyone and he alone can repeal all other sentences.

19. He must not be judged by anyone.

22. The Roman church has never erred; and according to the testimony of scripture it never will err.

27. The pope can absolve subjects from oaths of fidelity made to unjust rulers.

 The two swords (commentary on Luke 22.35–38)

Both swords, the spiritual and the material sword, belong to the church. But one must be drawn for the church and one drawn by the church: the first by the hand of the priest, the second by that of the knight, but assuredly on the order of the priest and the command of the emperor.

St Bernard (1090–1153), *Letter* 256.

(106) The pontifical conscience of Pope Innocent III (1198–1216)

The church has brought me one particularly precious dowry, namely the fullness of spiritual power and broad temporal possessions with a mass of riches. For the other apostles have been called to share the power, but Peter is the only one who has been called to enjoy the plentitude. I have received from him the mitre for my priesthood and the crown for my royal state; he has established me vicar of him on whose robes it is written:

'King of kings and Lord of lords, priest for ever after the order of Melchizedek.'

Just as the moon receives its light from the sun, so the royal power receives the splendour of its dignity from pontifical authority.

We mean to use the fullness of power that we have received from the one who is the Father of mercy primarily on behalf of those with whom one must deal mercifully.

Pope Innocent III (1198–1216)

---

temporal power in the episcopal office. The Concordat of Worms (1122) and the Lateran Council (1123) saw a return to peace. The emperor gave up spiritual investiture by cross and ring, but the pope allowed the emperor to invest the bishop with his temporal powers by means of a sceptre. In this latter sphere, the bishop owed obedience to his sovereign. At the same time, the reforming work of Gregory VII and his successors was confirmed.

The triumph of papal law

From this time on, the popes who had led the way over reform had the upper hand in Christendom. It was they who now took the initiative in calling councils in which only the Latin church was involved (the Lateran Councils of 1123, 1139 and 1179). The collected letters of popes on various matters (decretals) had the same authority as holy scripture. That explains the success of the 'forged decretals' composed in the ninth century in order to reinforce the pope's power; they retained their authority all through the Middle Ages. Canon law became omnipresent in the government of the Roman church. Popes had

to interfere more and more in church affairs. St Bernard was worried about Eugenius III; 'When (10 do we pray? When do we teach the people? When do we enlighten the church? Every day the papal palace resounds to the laws of Justinian and not to those of the Lord.'

Theocracy

The confrontations between the emperors and the pope arose no less frequently. The German king utilized Roman law, study of which had revived in the twelfth century. After an indecisive struggle, the Emperor Frederick Barbarossa had to make submission to Pope Alexander III at Venice in 1177. With Innocent III (1198–1216) the papacy attained the height of its powers. The pope appeared in the position of supreme arbiter of Europe. He appointed his candidate as emperor, made the king of England bow to his will. On the basis of his interventions, he developed the theory of papal power. This has sometimes been described as 'theocracy'. Innocent III affirmed that he held the fullness of (10 power in Christendom. In the spiritual sphere, all the churches were under his control. The temporal sphere retained its autonomy, but because of the pre-eminence of the spiritual, the pope intervened in political affairs when the salvation of Christians was at stake because of the sinfulness of the world. He also intervened in cases of emergency when the princes did not have feudal powers. The Fourth Lateran Council (1215) bears witness to papal self-assessment and papal power: the assembly legislated in all areas of Christian life.

Crisis, and a desire for reform

The aspirations of the pope once more came up against imperial ambitions in the time of Frederick II (1212–1250). The struggle reached its climax when Pope Innocent IV deposed the emperor at the Council of Lyons in 1245 and reaffirmed theocratic principles in the most uncompromising way. The empire was weakened by this, but so was the papacy. It was too much tied up in political affairs and lost some of its moral authority.

By the end of the thirteenth century many were demanding that the church should be reformed. The institutions were manifestly suffering decay: there was a lessening of enthusiasm in the monasteries, and increasing difficulties at each papal election because of the disagreements between cardinals. Once again division in the church was claiming attention.

The Second Council of Lyons in 1274 set out to find the solutions to these problems. The results were scanty. The reconciliation between the Latin and the Greek churches was a brief one, because the ground had been badly prepared. Reform made scarcely any progress. In 1294 the cardinals thought that they were obeying the Holy Spirit when they dragged an eighty-year-old hermit from his cell to make him pope (Celestine V). It was a fiasco.

The priest and marriage

The New Testament

Paul chose not to be married so as to be more available for the service of the gospel (I Cor. 7.7; 9.5), but he did not make this a general rule. The only prescription in scripture about the marriage of a minister of the church is in I Tim. 3.2; Titus 1.6: 'The *episkopos* must be the husband of one woman.' The patristic tradition interpreted this passage as a prohibition against conferring ordination on a man who had married twice, and a prohibition against a widowed priest remarrying. Some fathers also thought that it was an obligation on bishops to marry.

The first three centuries

No law in West or East prohibited the ordination of married men, nor required married priests to abstain from sexual intercourse. Similarly, there seemed to be no objection to a priest who was celibate at the time of his ordination subsequently marrying. However, the importance attached to asceticism and virginity suggested that it was more perfect for a priest to remain celibate, or to abstain from sexual intercourse if he was married.

The fourth century

In both East and West marriage was

→

prohibited after ordination. Anyone who was married remained so after ordination. The celibate remained celibate. Each had to be faithful to the first bond he contracted, marriage or ordination.

At the beginning of the century, the majority of clergy exercised their marital rights. At the end of the century, the clergy who abstained from sexual intercourse were in the majority. We find two explanations for this: greater availability to God, and the incompatibility of engaging in sex, which was thought to be impure, with the daily celebration of the eucharist.

In the West (Spain and Rome), councils required the conjugal abstinence of bishops, priests and deacons.

The fifth century

In the East, bishops, priests and deacons could still marry. In the West, the Bishop of Rome required all the churches to demand conjugal abstinence of bishops, priests and deacons, but they could continue to cohabit with their spouses.

The sixth century

In the East, the church finally fixed its discipline concerning clergy and marriage (692). It is still the same today.

A married man who is chosen as bishop must separate from his wife. He must leave his home and go to live in a distant monastery. The bishop must provide for the needs of his spouse. However, increasingly bishops were chosen from among monks.

Those priests and deacons who were married at the time of their ordination did not change their married life in any way. Practice to the contrary was even condemned.

In the West, marital abstinence by the clergy was reinforced: one council wanted to introduce a watchman into the bedrooms of clergy. Sanctions were taken against those who had a child after ordination.

From Charlemagne to the eleventh century

Married men who practised conjugal abstinence while living with their wives were still ordained. However, young celibate clergy trained in the schools were ordained without having been married. Despite the prohibition, some married after ordination. That is the situation which Gregory VII found in 1073.

The Gregorian reform

In 1074 Gregory VII no longer dis-

tinguished between priests who were married before ordination and priests who were married afterwards. All cohabitation was proscribed on pain of being banned from the ministry. There was resistance to the pontifical decision: 'This law is intolerable and unreasonable.' 'Without the aid of women's hands we shall die of cold and nakedness . . . ' Some regarded this law a novelty as compared with tradition. However, although it was illegal, the marriage of priests was considered valid.

The Second Lateran Council (1139) decided that the marriage of priests is invalid. In 1170, Pope Alexander III required that the wife of a married man ordained priest should first give her consent and should herself take a vow of chastity.

In law it was still possible to ordain a married man who had left his wife. In practice, it was very difficult; the priesthood was in effect restricted to celibates and widowers. However, it was not until the Code of Canon Law of 1917 that it was said that marriage is an impediment to orders and thus that the law of ecclesiastical celibacy was explicitly imposed.

After M. Dortel-Claudot,
État de vie et rôle du prêtre,
Paris 1971, 43–90.

2. The monastic church

The monks played a determinative role in reform and in the life of the mediaeval church. For a long time, the monk represented the Christian ideal.

Cluny

The abbey of Cluny, founded in 910, restored the main principles of the Benedictine Rule: the free election of the abbot, independence from princes and bishops. Moreover, the abbey affirmed its

The abbey of Cluny (after an eighteenth-century engraving)

direct allegiance to the pope. During the eleventh and twelfth centuries it became the head of an Order which multiplied throughout Europe. In fact, unlike the old monasteries, all the new ones that were founded remained under the authority of the abbot of Cluny. In its heyday, the 'state of Cluny' comprised 50,000 monks.

Cluny stressed liturgy and continuous prayer, but at the expense of manual work in the fields. The personality and longevity of its first abbots – Majolus (948–994), Odilo (994–1049), Hugh (1049–1109) and Peter the Venerable (1122–1156) – contributed to Cluny's influence in the eleventh and twelfth centuries. Cluny played a part in the reform of the other monasteries and in the general reform of the church. With no lay attachments, the Order championed the role of the papacy and provided bishops and popes. The abbey was generous in its charity to the poor. It contributed to the spread of romanesque art and architecture: the church of Cluny was for a long time the biggest in Europe. The Cluny establishments attracted groups of other buildings around them. Other Benedictine abbeys contemporary with Cluny exercised an influence

in their areas: La Chaise-Dieu in the Auvergne; Saint Victor in Marseilles; Camaldoli, founded by St Romuald in Tuscany.

Hermits

At the end of the eleventh century a strong movement of hermits grew up. Seized with the desire for penitence and poverty, men and women took themselves off into 'dreadful' places – forests, caves, ravines, islands – to expiate their sins. But the fame of their saintliness attracted crowds, and they often became popular preachers. If Peter the Hermit was the best known, the deeds of Robert of Arbrissel (1045–1116) had the most far-reaching consequences. He ended up by settling his disciples at Fontevrault, in the Loire valley, as a community of women and a community of men. However, it was the abbess who had authority over everyone.

The Middle Ages witnessed that strange form of religious life, the life of the recluse or anchorite. Men and women shut themselves up for the rest of their lives in cells built against the sides of churches. Small windows allowed them to hear the offices and receive food.

Monastic Europe

▲ Cluny and its foundations

In 1109 the Cluny Order comprised 1184 houses, 883 of which were in France

■ Citeaux and its foundations

It had 694 abbeys in the thirteenth century

● Other abbeys

Rievaulx
Fountains
Canterbury
Lewes
Prémontré
Fulda
Savigny
Gorze
La Trappe
Clairvaux
Melk
Fontevrault
Cîteaux
Einsiedeln
Cluny
Chiaravalle
Fruttuaria
La Chaise-Dieu
Grande Chartreuse
Moissac
Lerins
Camaldoli
Sahagun
Cuxa
Vallombrosa
Fontfroide
St Victor
Marseilles
Tre
Farfa
Silos
Fontana
Moreruela
Fossanova

La Chartreuse

108 In founding La Chartreuse in 1084, Bruno sought to bring together the eremitic life and the communal life. He gave pride of place to solitude and simplicity in relation to God.

The regular canons

Regular canons adopted the Rule of St Augustine, combining monastic asceticism with the exercise of the ministry. The best known are the Praemonstratensians, founded in 1126 by Norbert.

Citeaux

109 In founding the abbey of Citeaux in 1098, Robert of Molesmes sought to recapture the Benedictine austerity which Cluny seemed to have forgotten.

There was a return to poverty in clothing, food and buildings, to a simple liturgy and to solitude in the middle of forests. The Cistercians were great ones for clearing land. In this new Order, in contrast to Cluny, the abbot did not have authority over all the other foundations. He had to be content with presiding over the general chapter, i.e. the annual gathering of abbots.

Clairvaux and St Bernard

From the abbey of Clairvaux, which he founded in 1115, Bernard (1090–1153) added considerably to the development of the Cistercian Order. He himself founded sixty-six abbeys. St Bernard's activity went well beyond the boundary of Clairvaux. During the middle of the twelfth century he was the most important person in the church.

Letter B. Initial from the Clairvaux Psalter

108

The foundation of La Grande Chartreuse (1084)

Bruno, having left the city of Rheims, planned also to break with the world and, fleeing from all dealings with his fellows, which he found distasteful, he went to the district of Grenoble. There he chose for his dwelling place a mountainous peak, with great precipices, and utterly terrifying, which one reached by a very difficult and rarely used path. Below it was a valley situated at the foot of a sheer cliff. It was there that he founded his rule and it is there that his followers live today.

The church is not very far from the foot of the mountain. It has a somewhat undulating roof. Thirteen monks live there; they have a cloister which would suit the cenobitic rule very well; but

they do not lead a communal life in the cloister like other monks. What happens is that each has his own cell around the cloister: they work, sleep and eat there. On Sunday each of them receives his food from the steward, namely bread and vegetables, and they cook this remarkable diet in their cells.

The water that they use to drink and for other purposes comes from a spring by a conduit which goes round the cells and runs into each room through special openings. They have fish and cheese on Sunday and also on feast days . . .

They do not go into their church at the times to which we are accustomed, but only at certain hours. They hear mass on Sundays and on solemn feast days.

They hardly ever speak, for if they need anything they ask for it by sign language . . .

They are under the direction of a prior: however, the Bishop of Grenoble, who is a very religious man, exercises the functions of abbot and superior.

Though they condemn themselves to poverty, by contrast they accumulate books in their very rich library . . .

The place is called La Chartreuse. They do not cultivate the land much to produce grain, but they have the custom of obtaining the cereal they need in exchange for the fleeces of sheep which they rear in large numbers.

Guibert of Nogent, monk (1053–1124),
History of his Life.

Cîteaux, or the 'new monastery'

Abbot Aubri[1] and his brothers, not forgetting their promise, decided unanimously to institute in this place the Rule of St Benedict and to apply it, rejecting all that went against this Rule, cloaks and fur-lined coats, shirts and cowls, bed coverings and varied dishes in the refectory, fat too and all that was contrary to the purity of the Rule . . .

And since, on reading the Rule of the life of St Benedict, they noted that this doctor had not had either churches or altars or offerings or burial places or offerings from other people, or ovens or mills or villages or men to till the land; that women did not enter his monastery and that he did not bury anyone other than his sister, they renounced all these things . . .

Filled with scorn for the riches of this age, the new soldiers of Christ, poor like the poor Christ, began to examine by what means, by what system, by what practice they could assure their own existence in this life and that of the guests, rich and poor, who came to them and whom their Rule required them to welcome as though they were Christ. They then resolved to accept bearded lay brothers, with the authorization of their bishop, and to treat them as themselves in life and in death, save only in the monastic state; they also employed workers for hire because without

the help of these people they did not think that they could completely fulfil day and night the prescriptions of the Rule.

As these holy men knew that the blessed Benedict had built his monasteries not in the cities, strongholds or villages but in places remote from the throng, they set about imitating him. And just as this holy man required that in monasteries there should be twelve monks and an abbot, so they set about doing the same thing.

The Charter of Love,
the first legislation for Citeaux,
dating from about 1118.

[1] Aubri was the second abbot of Citeaux (1098–1108)

Letter Q. Initial from a twelfth-century Cistercian manuscript

Often far from his abbey, he was involved in many different matters. He worked for the reform of the clergy. He raged at Cluny's slackness. He encouraged bishops to practise poverty and to be concerned for the poor. He ended a schism in the church of Rome and drew up a rule of life for a monk of Clairvaux who had been made pope, Eugenius III, in 1145. Bernard tried to Christianize feudal society: he censured the sumptuous living of the lords and proclaimed the sanctity of marriage. As preacher on the second crusade, at Vézelay and Spire (1146), he tried to put an end to the massacres of Jews, which some fanatics made part of their crusade.

However, stamped as he was by the ideal of feudal chivalry and monastic life, Bernard did not always grasp how his age was developing. The claims of the inhabitants of the growing towns against the lords and bishops seemed to him to be a blow directed at traditional feudal order. To a greater and greater extent, Bernard defended the faith against a growing number of heretical doctrines, but in persecuting and condemning Abelard (1140) he managed to put a brake on theological thinking.

Without doubt, Bernard was first and foremost a spiritual master. He was the last of the Fathers, a man for whom meditation on the scriptures was the starting point for everything else. Rather than stressing asceticism and spiritual exercises, Bernard stressed union with God, and taught that all religion should lead to the practice of charity. He suggested a way of returning to God which led from self-knowledge to discovery of God. His sermons on the Song of Songs are most representative of his spiritual work.

II · The Works of Faith

1. Monastic religion and popular religion

The omnipotence and humanity of God

Mediaeval religion took on many of the aspects of rural and feudal society. At the top of the feudal hierarchy was God, as the Supreme Lord whose vassals and serfs the earthy lords were. This all-powerful Being was loved, but even more he was feared. He was the dispenser of pain and pleasure, life and death. Successes and failures, famines and epidemics were attributed to Providence. However, evangelical movements came to stress more and more the humanity of God in Jesus. Pilgrimages to the Holy Land and the Franciscan way of life bear witness to this.

The Christian ideal: the monk

In an era when clergy were the only people to express themselves through the written word, the monk was the Christian ideal. The calendar of saints scarcely acknowledged anyone but

Cloisters of the abbey of Fontenay (Côte d'Or, twelfth century)

bishops, monks and other religious, or, in extreme cases, the odd princess, widowed early in life, who spent the rest of her days in penitence and doing good works for the poor. St Bernard compared the world to a huge sea which had to be crossed before salvation was gained. Monks did not get wet because they crossed over on a bridge. The secular clergy made use of St Peter's boat. As for unfortunate married people, they had to swim across, and many were drowned in the process. Instead of actually becoming monks, pious laity tried to reproduce the monastic life. St Louis recited the office hours, got up in the night for matins, and practised many mortifications. Many of the laity directed that, when they died, they should be buried in a monk's habit.

Religion at it was lived

However, it would give a false impression to suggest that these illuminating examples depicted the Christian life of ordinary people. En masse, the people of Europe were Christian, but it was a different kind of Christianity from ours. Dissenting movements which rippled across the surface of the Middle Ages contradicted the idyllic unanimity of which historians of the last century spoke. There was a big difference between the fine systems of the theologians and the religion of the frustrated and illiterate country people who struggled for survival against epidemics and bad weather.

Christianity fully abosrbed a religious past going back into the mists of time, a pre-Christian religion linked to the life of nature and the cycle of the seasons. As the liturgical year unfolded, the Christian relived the main stages of his salvation and at the same time celebrated the death and rebirth of nature. At a stroke, the old customs had been Christianized and the Christian festivals taken into folklore.

2. Daily life

In the twelfth and thirteenth centuries the church centred its theological doctrine upon the seven sacraments and tried, often with difficulty, to impose a universal discipline, certain aspects of which still remain.

Baptism

Almost everywhere, children were baptized within a few days of their birth, and not just at Easter or Pentecost, as in former times. Baptism by infusion, that is to say the rite that we now practise of pouring water on the head, gradually replaced baptism by immersion. Communion was no longer given to the newborn in the form of wine, as it once was, since this custom had been dropped from the mass in the West. Baptism was so important that stillborn children were taken to sanctuaries, where, it was said, they came to life again for a long enough time to receive baptism.

The evolution of penitential practice in the church over six centuries

Canonical penance (see chapter 3, pp.52ff.; chapter 4, pp.77f.) fell into disuse from the sixth century on. The Irish monks suggested that Christians should adopt the practice current in their monasteries: tariffs for penance. The Penitentials indicate an appropriate penance for every fault. It was possible to resort to it on more than one occasion in a lifetime.

Some seventh- and eighth- century tariffs

We recommend that each priest should learn all the tariffs that he reads here and should consider with care the sex, the age, the social condition, the state and the person of each penitent. He should take into consideration inner feelings and judge according to circumstances . . . Anyone who kills a monk or a cleric shall leave armed service and enter the service of God or do seven years penance. Anyone who kills a lay person through hate or cupidity shall do four years penance. The soldier who kills in the course of a war shall fast for forty days. The mother who kills the child she is carrying in her womb before the fortieth day following conception shall fast for one year; if it is after the fortieth day she shall fast three years. However, there is a great difference between the poor woman who has killed her child because she cannot feed it and the profligate . . . Anyone who gets so drunk as to vomit shall fast forty days if he is a priest or deacon; thirty days if he is a religious; twelve days if he is a lay person.

Penitential of Bede
(Great Britain).

Commutations

A mass is equivalent to three days fasting . . . sixty-six psalms recited during the night, plus three hundred blows, is equivalent to two days of fasting. One hundred and twenty masses plus three psalters plus three hundred blows is equivalent to one hundred gold sous . . .

The powerful man shall take twelve men who will fast in his stead for three days, on bread, water and green vegetables. He shall then go in search of seven times one hundred and twenty men, each of whom shall fast in his place for three days. The fast days thus obtained will be equal to the number of days contained in seven years.

Penitentials of the seventh-eighth
and tenth centuries.

Confession and communion

In 1215, the Fourth Lateran Council imposed on Christians the obligation to confess their sins and communicate at least once a year, at Easter, in their own parishes. The sacrament of penance had come to the end of its development and from this time on is known as 'confession'.

Even the most ardent only took communion two or three times a year. In spite of his piety, St Louis only communicated six times in his life. We might say that this was a mark of respect for the eucharist, but equally it was a sign of limited understanding of the sacrament. The mass had become a sacred and mysterious spectacle. Even more important than communicating was seeing – hence the disproportionate importance attached to the elevation, the exposition of the blessed sacrament, and the feast of Corpus Christi, a festival instituted during the thirteenth century. Seeing the host was supposed to have special virtues: prayer was automatically granted and protection given against sudden death on a

The Last Judgment. Tympanum of Autun

Pilgrimage was a special penance. The pilgrimage to Jerusalem became a crusade. This carried with it an indulgence which had penitential value and could also apply to the dead.

The penitential tariff fell into discredit, and confession of sins took pride of place.

Various eleventh-century confessions

We must confess our secret sins to the clergy of all orders. As to public faults, it is fitting for them to be confessed only to priests through whom the church binds and looses acts which it knows by reason of their public nature.

If you do not find any clergy at all to whom to make your confession, choose an honourable man from your locality . . . In the absence of all clergy a pure man can purify a guilty man . . .

And if someone cannot find anybody to confess to, he should not despair, for the Fathers are agreed in saying that it is enough to confess to God: John Chrysostom, Cassian, Ambrose . . .

Lanfranc, Archbishop of Canterbury (1005–1089).

During the course of the twelfth century a close association was gradually established between confession, contrition and absolution by the priest.

The confession of grave sins must be made to a priest, and in detail, for he is the only one who has the power to bind and loose . . . Confession made to anyone else does not procure absolution from sins; here we are absolved by self-abasement and by the prayers of our brothers. That is why in this case we do not say, 'I forgive your sins' (the first trace of the formula of absolution) but only, 'May almighty God have mercy on you.'

Compulsory confession and annual communion: the Lateran Council (1215)

All the faithful of either sex who have reached the age of discretion must faithfully confess all their sins at least once a year to their own parish priest, carefully perform, as far as they are able, the penance which he imposes on them, and reverently receive the sacrament of the eucharist at Easter. Save in the case where, on the advice of their parish priest, for some reasonable cause, they think that they should abstain from receiving it for the moment. Otherwise, they are to be forbidden to enter the church, if they are alive, and to be deprived of burial by the church, if they are dead.

journey. This was not far removed from magic. The host could act as a talisman in love, and as a guarantee of a good crop. Bloody hosts were the divine response to the sacrilegious.

Marriage

During the early Middle Ages, the theology of marriage was not clear. There was uncertainty, part of it harking back to tradition and part of it deriving from the church. By the thirteenth century, marriage, clearly defined as one of the seven sacraments, had become the sole prerogative of the church, which determined the obstacles and the conditions under which it was valid. Free consent was the essential criterion for marriage. The liturgical texts, often very beautiful, could vary according to regions. Recited in Latin, they were mostly incomprehensible to those being married. The important thing was to go to church in order to be able to celebrate the occasion joyfully afterwards.

Growing up in the faith and passing it on

There was nothing that could be understood as a catechism. The community passed on the faith by osmosis. It was the duty of parents and godparents to teach children the Our Father and the Ten Commandments. The number seven served as a mnemonic in religious education: seven deadly sins, seven cardinal virtues, seven gifts of the Spirit, seven petitions of the Lord's Prayer, seven sacraments, and so on. Those who learned to read did so from the psalter.

The sermon given on Sundays and festivals was intended to educate young and old. The thirteenth century witnessed a major effort at preaching the gospel. Those who preached were more accessible and more willing to use the language of the people. We can see here the influence of the Mendicant Orders. Dominic's disciples took the name of preachers. Heretics had learned how to use plain words; it was necessary to reply to them in the same way. The pulpit came down to where the people were, in the nave, replacing the ambo near the altar. Today, acoustics have made us revert to the ambo. Some churches had an outside pulpit for those days when there was an enormous crowd. Dominic used to preach near mills. Preachers used many examples drawn from daily life. Those who were listening showed what they thought, asked questions, applauded or contradicted while the sermon was going on. The preacher interrogated anyone who had been asleep or had left the church before the sermon began.

3. The sacred and the profane

What characterized the Middle Ages was the omnipresence of a religion which belonged to everyday life, a blending of the profane and the sacred. Daily life permeated religious places and times on an equal footing. There was no partitioning off of religion, as there is today.

The church, the people's house

Churches and cathedrals were public places and were used for far more than worship. People took refuge there in wartime, often with their furniture and cattle. Some people practically lived in the holy place. As there were no chairs or benches, the faithful sat on straw in the winter and fresh grass in the summer. Weekly mass might be an obligation in principle, but participation in it was often of a dubious nature. Some people waited in public houses and only went in at the time of the elevation. Others left the church immediately after the elevation. People chatted, went out during the sermon, arranged to meet their lovers, and so on.

Popular festivals

The unfolding of the liturgical year strikes us by its mixture of rituals that were truly religious in the sense we mean today with customs whose origin and significance is obscure. There were many different customs, depending on the areas of Christendom. The Yule log was kept and relit on gloomy days. On Holy Innocents Day (28 December) children took over the church; the order of things was reversed, and everything gave way to buffoonery. On 1 January the Feast of Fools was often celebrated: there was dancing on the church pavement and card-playing inside. A bishop and a pope were elected from among the fools. Deacons and subdeacons ate sausages and black puddings on the altar . . . Every now and then the bishops would ban this festival, but it kept going for a long time. There was a feast of asses, when Balaam's ass was celebrated in church. On Shrove Tuesday in Rheims, after the solemn office of Tenebrae, the canons went in procession, each pulling behind him a herring on a piece of string. Each canon tried to protect his own herring from the canon behind him, who was trying to tread on it . . . These were by no means all the customs practised, some of which have lasted to our own day in spite of the opposition of the clergy.

Touching the sacred

Christians wanted to touch the sacred; this was sometimes the consequence of devotion to the humanity of Christ. Pilgrims and crusaders wanted to see and touch the places where Christ and the saints had lived. Francis of Assisi celebrated Christmas with a real live crib. This desire to touch the divine explains the extraordinary development of the cult of relics. They were bought and sold and cut into tiny pieces. St Louis had great devotion to a holy nail from the cross. He caused La Sainte Chapelle in Paris to be built as a magnificent reliquary for the Crown of Thorns, which he had acquired in the East. If there were no suitable prestigious relics, one could always venerate those of a local saint who watched over the fields and flocks or over a guild of craftsmen.

(111)

How the faith was lived in daily life

Are religious practices and festivals enough to describe Christian life? Christians of today

Discoveries of Relics

The *Histories* of Ralph Glaber (the Bald or the Beardless), a restless monk (985–1050), are among the best evidence of his time.

When the whole world was, as we have said, shining bright with new churches, a moment came in the eighth year after the millennium of the incarnation of the Saviour when various indications made it possible to discover numerous relics of saints in places where they had long been hidden. As if they had been waiting for the moment of some glorious resurrection, at a sign from God they were presented to the contemplation of the faithful and produced great comfort in

their hearts. It is known that these discoveries first began in a city of the Gauls, at Sens, in the church of the blessed martyr Stephen. The archbishop of the city at that time was Lierri, who made an amazing discovery there of objects from the ancient cult: among other discoveries he is said to have set hands on a piece of Moses' staff. When news of these discoveries was noised abroad, innumerable faithful came, not only from the country of Gaul but even

from all over Italy and countries beyond the sea; and it was not rare to see sick people return from there cured by the intercession of the saints. However, it all too often happens that if something begins by being useful to human beings, their guilty greed soon makes it a stumbling block. This city to which, as I have said, people rushed in crowds, amassed great riches as a result of their piety, and its inhabitants became excessively insolent as a result of so great a benefit.

Ralph Glaber, *Histories*, III, 6.

would hardly want to define themselves by reference to worship alone. What were the major characteristics of mediaeval Christian behaviour? Historians have taught us to distinguish between what was laid down as the rule, and how life was actually lived. Theologians, preachers, synodical statutes and councils laid down a great number of rules. That is not to say that they were adhered to. The clergy preached an inflexible sexual morality, but in practice they were more indulgent, even among themselves. Public opinion often judged greed more harshly than fornication.

There are not many documents in which the laity speak about their faith. Wills tell us a little about the religious life of at least those who had goods to bequeath. The testators were first of all concerned with having fine funerals and with having masses said for the repose of their souls.

At the same time, they showed a concern for the poor. In fact, during the thirteenth century, poor people and vagrants were not yet considered a public nuisance. The living, real Christ was seen in them. To give alms was to heap blessings on oneself and to obtain people to intercede. Many of the testators requested that on the day of their funeral money and food should be given to the poor. Some of them similarly left money to maintain hospices and leper hospitals. A hospital was more often than not a small establishment of around a dozen beds for the sick among the poor and poor travellers. The latter were often pilgrims, who travelled along all the roads of Europe in great numbers. Undoubtedly, vanity figured largely in the establishment of these foundations, which perpetuated the memory of the dead person.

Conques. Tympanum of the Last Judgment

Vezelay. The Christ of the tympanum

III · Faith as an Inspiration to Intellect and the Arts

1. A culture based on faith

Monastic and episcopal schools

We have seen that, during the peak of the Middle Ages, intellectual activity was almost entirely confined to the monasteries. They looked after the ancient texts of classical literature and of the Church Fathers. Within this framework, intellectual study could only have a religious goal: to be able to read scripture and the traditional texts, but also to comment on them and in this way to nourish the spiritual life of the monk. Bishops had a small episcopal school near their cathedral in which clergy were given a basic education. Charlemagne had encouraged the foundation of these schools. The bishops entrusted them to the charge of a theological teacher or chancellor, who was allowed to recruit assistants.

New intellectual requirements

The flourishing of Christendom in the twelfth and thirteenth centuries entailed intellectual requirements. The Gregorian reform encouraged legal studies: a return to Roman law and an elaboration of canon law, especially at Bologna. With the movement of the population and the growth of cities, a new social class wanted access to the intellectual life. The episcopal schools established in the cities grew more important at the expense of the monastic schools, but even these were no longer sufficient. Independent teachers founded their own schools, like that of La Montagne Sainte-Geneviève in Paris. All this was the beginning of a series of difficulties and conflicts.

Claims of the intellectuals

The bishop reserved the right to grant teachers a licence to teach. That enabled him to hold on to his authority over the teachers and students and to keep control of what was taught. However, in towns such as Paris, students came in greater and greater numbers and proved increasingly restive, and their teachers wanted to escape the narrow tutelage of the bishop and his chancellor. They wanted an autonomy comparable to that of

Isaiah and St Matthew. The Old Testament bearing the New Testament. Stained glass window, Chartres

---

(112)

Reason and faith

Honorius Augustodunensis is a mysterious monk who has no connection with Autun, though his name might suggest that. He probably lived in Regensburg in the middle of the twelfth century. He was interested in all kinds of subjects and among other works composed an encyclopaedia of the science of his time.

There is no other authority than truth proved by reason; what authority teaches us to believe, reason confirms for us by its proofs. What the evident authority of scripture proclaims, discursive reason proves; even if all the angels had remained in heaven, man and all his posterity would nevertheless have been created. For this world has been made for man, and by world I understand the heaven and earth and all that is contained in the universe. Man's exile is his ignorance, his homeland is science.

113

The recognition of the University of Paris by Pope Gregory IX (1231)

Paris, mother of sciences, shines with a precious splendour, thanks to those who learn there and those who teach. There they prepare for the army of Christ the armour of faith, the sword of the Spirit and the other arms which proclaim the praise of Christ . . .

We grant to the masters and students the power to make wise regulations about the methods and times of courses and discussions and about a suitable form of dress; who should give the lectures, at what hour, and what author to choose; about the fixing of wages and

the power to expel those who break these rules.

If, by chance, wages are withheld or if you are offended and done serious wrong, you will be allowed to suspend courses until you have obtained appropriate recompense . . .

the communities or the trade guilds. Besides, in the monastic tradition, still exemplified by St Bernard, intellectual work consisted essentially in commenting on the scriptures. However, during the twelfth century, new texts had been made available to scholars, for example translations of Aristotle from Greek or Arabic. Teachers like Abelard (1079–1142) developed a theological method which sought to deepen theological truth with the aid of reason. Many were disturbed by it.

112

The birth of the universities

After a period of often bloody conflicts, the universities came into being. These were associations of teachers and pupils or sometimes just of pupils. The universities obtained autonomy to organize their own courses and administration. They escaped lay jurisdiction and partially that of the bishop and depended directly on the papacy. In 1231 Pope Gregory IX solemnly conferred privileges on the University of Paris.

114

The beginnings of romanesque art in the eleventh century

When the third year after the year 1000 approached, you could see churches being rebuilt almost everywhere, and above all in Italy and Gaul; although most of them had been very well constructed and did not really need this, keen rivalry moved each Christian com-

munity to have a more sumptuous church than that of its neighbours. One could have said that the very world was shaking itself, stripping off its old raiment and reclothing itself everywhere with a white robe of churches. At that time almost all the churches in the

episcopal sees, those of the monasteries dedicated to all kinds of saints, and even the little village chapels, were rebuilt by the faithful to make them more beautiful.

Ralph Glaber, *Histories*, III,4.

The harmonious encounter of reason and faith

And so Scholasticism came into being, that method of mediaeval teaching at which a number of mediaeval masters, like Thomas Aquinas (1225–1274), shone. More than ever before, the church took on the culture of the age. In his *Summa theologica*, Thomas Aquinas put forward a harmonious synthesis between ancient science and Christian revelation. Speculative research was made subordinate to man's final destiny: philosophy, which embraced science, was the servant of theology.

2. Popular Christian art

Religious theatre

Christians still expressed their faith by means of the popular religious theatre. The liturgical dramas presented the Old and New Testaments either right inside the churches or on their pavements. The miracle plays illustrated the intervention of the Virgin and the saints. One of the most famous, the thirteenth-century miracle play of Theophilus, tells the story of a clerk who made a pact with the devil in order to attain wealth, and called upon the Virgin to get him out

Virgin and child. Abbey of Fontenay (Côte d'Or)

---

(115)

The enthusiasm of the inhabitants of Le Mans for their cathedral

After the rebuilding of the choir of the cathedral, all the inhabitants began the task of cleaning and decorating the building with a view to a solemn transfer of the relics of St Julian (April 1254).

The day after the Solemn Feast of Easter, there was a great crowd from the whole city of Le Mans, of both sexes and of every age, in the church of the blessed Confessor. In order to clear the church, they removed the debris, vying to see who could clean the best. Among the other women working were matrons who, contrary to feminine ways, took no heed of their fine dresses and carried sand outside the church in their multi-coloured dresses, their cloaks of scarlet, green or other bright colours. Many of those who carried out the dirt from the church in their elegant clothes were happy to soil these garments with the dust.

Others, with babes at their breasts, filled their laps with sand and in this way carried it outside the church. It was fitting that the praise of children should play its part in the divine work . . . Their more robust older brothers carried great pieces of wood and blocks of stone outside the church . . .

There was such fervour among the population, such faith, such ardent devotion, that all those who saw it were full of admiration and, on seeing such dedication, could not hold back their tears of joy.

The inhabitants were also concerned that the light shut up in their hearts should be manifested to outsiders. They

decided and ordained that members of each guild should carry candles the size of which would be proportionate to the resources of the individual, and that they should be lit on the solemn feast day.

It must be added that the owners of vineyards and the vintners, on seeing the candles of others, because they had not done the like themselves, came to an agreement and said: 'The others have made a temporary light; let us make windows which will light the church in the future.' So they made a whole window which contained five medallions in which they had themselves painted in the exercise of their craft . . .

of the demon's clutches. Later on, the mystery plays were long and complicated representations by the guilds of biblical episodes such as the passion.

A Bible in stone

(114) Although these texts might not be very accessible to us today, mediaeval art and architecture is more familiar. Romanesque, which began in the monasteries and on the Mediterranean, blossomed at the end of the eleventh and during the twelfth century; it was characterized by vaulted

(115) roofs, sculptures on the spandrels and capitals, and frescoes. Gothic, born in the Ile-de-France, enjoyed an upsurge. It was the art of the towns and bears witness to the stability of the thirteenth century. Stained glass and statuary developed. Sculptures, stained-glass windows and frescoes provided a Bible and a catechism in pictures. This art illustrated numerous biblical episodes, the great mysteries of the faith, virtues and vices.

Artists depicted in stone the anguish and hopes of believers: expectation of paradise and fear of hell. The devil is to be seen there, accompanied by his messenger, the sorceress. On the other hand, never had art been so associated with daily life, with the fantasies of the imagination and with preoccupations that were truly religious. It is through what we see in cathedrals that we discover the trades, the leisure pursuits, the clothing of our ancestors.

For further reading

Rosalind and Christopher Brooke, *Popular Religion in the Middle Ages*, Thames and Hudson 1984

M. Deanesley, *A History of the Mediaeval Church*, Methuen 1969

David Knowles, *The Evolution of Medieval Thought*, Longmans 1965

O. von Simpson, *The Gothic Cathedral*, Routledge 1956

R. W. Southern, *St Anselm and His Biographer*, Cambridge University Press 1963

Cathedral builders   Amiens cathedral (thirteenth century)   Cimabue. Virgin in majesty. Florence (end of thirteenth century)

9
Christendom: Expansion, Challenge and Defence

End of the Eleventh to the Thirteenth Centuries

Templar charging during the second crusade

Christendom was a temporal and spiritual reality, a society totally founded on Christianity, and it had to fight against the enemies of the faith because they threatened its whole structure. Outside it, there were the Moslems; within, heretics. So Christendom began to arm itself, in the form of crusades, and to organize repressive justice, in the form of the Inquisition.

But this was not a full solution. The gospel cannot be spread by force. A concern for mission arose as a result of doubt about the crusades. Because of certain ways in which the institutional church behaved, new forms of religious life came into being.

I · Crusade and Mission

1. Armed Christianity

In coming together and arming against a common enemy, Islam, which was wrongfully occupying the places where Christ had lived and was threatening Christians in the East, Christendom showed itself aware of its own identity and unity. Such were the crusades, an indispensable feature in any account of the Middle Ages.

The pilgrimage to Jerusalem

The origin of the crusades lay in the pilgrimage to Jerusalem. This was first of all a ritual of purification and penitence. By going to Palestine, pilgrims sought to share in the earthly life of Christ and his sufferings. They could even die where Jesus died in order to rise again with him on Judgment Day. The dangers that were encountered gave people the idea of armed pilgrimages. Moreover, in Spain, it was claimed that those who died fighting the infidels (Moslems) were assured of salvation. In the eleventh century, a new Moslem power, the Turks, who had come from the steppes of Central Asia, threatened the balance of power in the East and particularly in Constantinople after the Byzantine defeat at the battle of Manzikert in 1071. It looked as if pilgrimages would become more difficult and the Greek emperor appealed for help.

---

(116)

The Council of Clermont (1095)

. . . Pope Urban II gave a moving description, with many details, of the desolation of Christianity in the East and expounded the atrocious suffering and oppression which the Saracens were inflicting on the Christians. In his pious allocution the orator, who was moved almost to tears, equally stressed the way in which Jerusalem and the Holy Places where the Son of God had lived in the flesh, with his most holy companions, were trampled underfoot. He also reduced many of his audience to tears; they shared his deep emotion and his pious compassion for their brothers. With the eloquence of the one who sows the word of truth, he delivered to the assembly a long and very persuasive discourse. He called on the great men of the West and their companions-at-arms to respect the peace scrupulously in all their dealings, to hang the sign of the saving cross from their right shoulder and to prove themselves the élite and famous soldiers that they were by military valour against the pagans.

There was a prodigious desire among rich and poor, women, monks and clergy, countrydwellers and city folk, to go to Jerusalem or to help those who were going. The husbands decided to leave their dear wives at home; however, these, with tears, wanted to follow their husbands on pilgrimage and abandon their children and all their riches. Lands which hitherto had been costly were now sold cheaply, and arms were bought so that divine vengeance should be exacted on the friends of Allah. Thieves, pirates and other criminals rose from the depths of wickedness; touched by the Spirit of God, they confessed their crimes and, repudiating them, took part in the crusade to make satisfaction to God for their sins.

However, the pope, a prudent man, summoned to war against the enemy of God all those who were capable of bearing arms and, by virtue of the authority which he holds from God, absolved from all their sins all the penitents from the moment that they took up the cross of Christ, mercifully also dispensing them from all the troubles that arise from fasts and other macerations of the flesh . . .

Ordericus Vitalis, a Norman monk,
History of the Church, (1135).

The capture of Jerusalem at the time of the first crusade (15 July 1099)

. . . On the Friday (15 July), very early in the morning, we launched a general assault on the city without being able to harm it, and we were stupefied and struck with great fear. Then when the hour approached at which Our Lord Jesus Christ consented to suffer for us the torment of the cross, our knights posted on the siege engine fought fiercely, among others Duke Godfrey and Count Eustace his brother. At that moment one of our knights, called Lietaud, scaled the wall of the city. As soon as he reached the top, all the defenders of the city fled from the walls across the city. Our men pursued them; they chased after them, killing them and smiting them with their swords, as far as the temple of Solomon, where there was such carnage that our men walked in blood up to their ankles . . .

Having broken through the pagans, our soldiers seized a large number of men and women in the temple, and they killed them or spared them alive, depending on what seemed good to them. A large group of pagans of both sexes to whom Tancred and Gaston of Bearn had given their banners as safe conduct had taken refuge on top of the temple of Solomon. The crusaders soon ran through the city, seizing gold, silver, horses, and mules, and pillaging the houses, which were bulging with riches.

Then, happy and weeping for joy, our men went to adore the sepulchre of our Saviour Jesus and paid their debt to him (their vow to go on crusade). The next morning, our men climbed on to the roof of the temple, attacked the Saracens, men and women and, having drawn sword, beheaded them. Some threw themselves down from the temple. When he saw this, Tancred was filled with indignation . . .

Anonymous History of the First Crusade, written by a knight who took part in the crusade.

The call to the crusade

At the Council of Clermont in 1095, Pope Urban II asked the knights of the West to go to the aid of the Christians in the East and win back the holy places. In this way he fulfilled his role as Christian leader and heir to the countries of the empire, which he assigned as rewards to those who responded to his call. At the same time, the departure of the poor knights lessened the risk of war on Christian territory. They went to fight somewhere else and to find the fiefs which they had not been able to gain in the West. The church which, hitherto, had always had a horror of blood, herself organized the holy war, which was given the name 'crusade'. The pope granted plenary indulgence to those who took up the cross from the moment of their departure: they were given a dispensation from all the penances required for the pardon of their sins.

Rivers of blood and naive piety

Enthusiasm was great amongst the unfortunate people led by Peter the Hermit: they were decimated all along the journey. The knights followed them and captured Jerusalem in 1099 to the accompaniment of dreadful massacres and naive manifestations of piety. Several Latin feudal Christian states were founded, including the kingdom of Jerusalem. Although religious military orders were organized to defend them (Knights Templar, Knights Hospitaller, and so on), these states disappeared one after the other. Jerusalem was recaptured by the Sultan of Egypt, Saladin, in 1187. By 1291 there were no longer any crusaders left in Palestine.

The taking of Constantinople by the crusaders in 1204

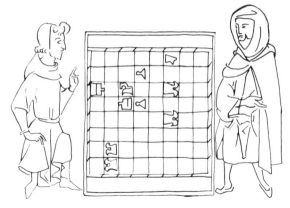

Chess game between a Christian knight and a Moslem
(thirteenth century)

Scanty results

The crusaders had helped to bind Christendom
together and affirm the power of the papacy. But
they had widened the gap between Christians in
the East and Christians in the West. At the time
of the Fourth Crusade in 1204, for example, the
crusaders seized Constantinople and plundered
it. In spite of St Louis' efforts to give a religious
meaning to the seventh (1249–1254) and eighth
(1270) crusades (he died on the latter), the
crusades ended in failure. They were to have
further economic results. However, the idea of
crusades persisted for a long time, into the
sixteenth and even the seventeenth century.
Nostalgia for a Christendom united in the face of
a common enemy lingered on.

2. From crusade to mission

The completion of evangelization in Europe

Christianity did not just have violent conflicts
with those who did not share its faith. During the
twelfth century the evangelization of Europe
was completed by the conversion of the Scandinavian peoples and other populations in the
north-east, like the Prussians.

Persuasion and knowledge of others

The failure of the crusades caused people's
minds to change. Rather than exterminating the
Moslems, would it not be better to persuade
them? In the course of the fifth crusade (1218),
Francis of Assisi met the Sultan of Egypt. Raymond Lull (1235–1316), a Spanish Franciscan,
thought that conversion was a work of love
achieved by the intellect. The preacher had to
understand the languages and doctrines of the
peoples he met. Raymond called for the foundation of foreign-language schools.

The first church in China

During the thirteenth century, the pagan Mongols sowed terror as far as Europe. The rumour

went round that there were Christians among them. This was the legend of Prester John. With their help, would it not be possible to attack Islam in the rear? Ambassadors were sent by Pope Innocent IV and St Louis, under the leadership of the Franciscans John of Plancarpin (1245–1247) and William Rubrouk (1253–1255). Then there were missionaries in the proper sense

---

(118)

The first Archbishop of Pekin

Letter from Khanbalik (Pekin), 8 January 1305

In the year of our Lord 1291, I, Brother John of Monte Corvino, of the Order of Friars Minor, left the city of Tauris, in Persia, and penetrated into India. For thirteen months I sojourned in that country and in the church of the Apostle St Thomas, here and there, and baptized about a hundred people . . . Resuming my journey, I arrived at Cathay, the kingdom of the emperor of the Tartars, who is called the great Khan. In delivering to the said emperor the letters of the Lord Pope, I preached to him the law of our Lord Jesus Christ. The emperor is too rooted in his idolatry, but he is full of good will to Christians. And I have been twelve years with him . . .

Isolated in this distant pilgrimage, I was eleven years without making my confession until the arrival of Brother Arnold, a German from the province of Cologne, who has been here for two years.

In the city of Khanbalik I built a church which has been finished six years. I added a campanile with three bells. I have baptized, I think, almost six thousand people in the church, and had there not been the campaign of calumny of which I spoke earlier, I would have baptized more than thirty thousand. I am often busy administering baptism. I have also bought, one by one, forty children of pagans below seven and twelve years of age. As yet they know no faith: I have baptized them and educated them in Latin letters and in our worship.

Through me, a king in this region, of the sect of Nestorian Christians, who was of the race of that great king called Prester John of India, adopted the true faith; he received minor orders and, robed in consecrated vestments, served me at mass. The Nestorians even accused him of apostasy: nevertheless, he brought the majority of his people to the Catholic faith. He built a fine church, worthy of his royal munificence.

I beg you, brothers whom this letter may reach, to have a care that its content comes to the knowledge of the Lord Pope, the cardinals and the Procurator of our Order at the Roman court. Of our Minister-General I ask alms of an antiphonary and readings from the lives of the saints, a gradual and a psalter to serve as a model for us, since here I have only a portable breviary and a small missal. If I have a model, the children will copy it.

At present I am in process of building a new church so that the children can be distributed in several areas. I am getting old and my hair is quite white, less from age – I am only fifty-eight years old – than from weariness and care. I have learned the Tartar language and script reasonably well; that is, the language customarily used by the Mongols. I have translated the whole of the New Testament and the Psalter into this language. I had it transcribed in superb calligraphy and I show it, I read it, I preach it and I make it known publicly as a testimony to the law of Christ.

And I had made an agreement with King George, mentioned below, had he lived, to translate the whole of the Latin office, so that it could be sung through all the territories of his state; during his lifetime the Latin rite was celebrated in his church in the language and scripture of his country, both the words of the canon and the prefaces . . .

Text quoted in de Ghellinck,
Revue d'Histoire des Missions,
1 December 1928.

The letter reached Europe. Pope Clement V sent several bishops to the Far East. Those who reached Khanbalik consecrated John of Monte Corvino bishop and in this way he became the first Archbishop of Pekin. A bishop was installed at Zayton (Ts'iuan-Tcheou) in the south of China. However, despite reinforcements the mission gradually grew weaker, and disappeared completely when the Mongols were replaced by a new Chinese dynasty.

of the word, Franciscans and Dominicans who organized themselves appropriately for expeditions to distant countries, taking the name of Pilgrim Friars. These were to be found in Central Asia, in the Persian Gulf, in India and as far as China. On their travels they encountered Nestorian Christian communities founded by Persian missionaries. There was not much understanding between Latin religious and these Eastern Christians. Through the mediation of the Polo brothers, the father and uncle of Marco, the Mongol Khan who had become emperor of China asked the pope for missionaries. The Franciscan John of Monte Corvino arrived at Khanbalik (Pekin) around 1294, and from there sent a moving letter to Europe. He became the first Archbishop of Pekin. The length of the

The Polo brothers presenting the cross and the Gospels to the Great Khan, 1265

journey and political difficulties eventually resulted in the disappearance of this first Chinese church.

II · Christendom Challenged

It must not be supposed that Christendom was a perfect society, where there was always unanimity. To the degree that it had met with too much success, the institutional church now encountered opposition, even in the name of the gospel. Moreover, mediaeval Europe was not a closed world. Doctrines circulated freely, and some of them were older than Christianity and alien to it. But since faith was the cement of society, those who did not share the official faith were accused of undermining the foundations of society and were tolerated less and less.

1. The Jews

Popular violence

We shall first of all look at the situation of the Jews, communities of whom were scattered from Spain to the area of the Rhine. From the early days of the church, anti-Jewish polemic had been plentiful. Even if it claimed to be theological, it was often lacking in Christian charity! Barely tolerated in Spain, where they were forcibly converted after the recapture of the country from the Moslems, the Jews were better accepted elsewhere. But matters worsened when the crusades got under way. Since the issue of the day was going to fight the enemies of Christ, the crowds attacked those whom they held responsible for Christ's death and who were much nearer to hand than the Saracens or Turks. Massacres took place along the Rhine, though St Bernard tried to stop them.

Discriminatory legislation

The Third and Fourth Lateran Councils (1179 and 1215) increased discriminatory measures against the Jews: they had to wear distinctive dress (a piece of yellow material and a pointed hat); certain trades, and marriage with Christians, were forbidden them; they had special areas to live in and were expelled from certain countries. Sometimes there were also insulting customs: for instance, in Toulouse in the thirteenth century a Jew had to present himself at the church on Good Friday to have his ears boxed. Since they were not allowed to work on the land, Jews gathered in towns and often devoted themselves to commercial and financial activities. Christians refused to deal in loans involving interest, which was considered to be usury, but they often resorted to Jews in this respect so that others incurred the sin. The papacy played a curious role in all this. At the very time it was working out discriminatory legislation for fear that the faith would be contaminated, it was seeking to hold violence in check and treated Jews far better than other princes did.

2. Gospel and dissent

Mediaeval religious dissidents were very quickly lumped together under the category of heretics. Often we know of them only through official ecclesiastical sources, particularly through the

---

(119) The Waldenses, or the Poor Men of Lyons

A large number of internal documents from dissident groups were destroyed by the inquisitors charged with repressing these groups. We often have to resort to the inquisitors to get to know their victims. Clearly their presentation is always malicious.

The sect or heresy of the Waldenses or Poor Men of Lyons emerged about the year of Our Lord 1170. The person responsible for it was an inhabitant of Lyons, Valdes or Waldo, hence the name of these sectarians. He was rich; but having given away all his possessions, he planned to observe poverty and gospel perfection, in imitation of the apostles. He had the Gospels and some other books of the Bible translated into the vernacular for his use along with some sayings of Saint Augustine, Saint Jerome, Saint Ambrose and Saint Gregory, arranged under titles, which he and his supporters called Sentences. They read them very often, but did not have

much understanding of them; however, in their infatuation, although they were barely literate, they usurped the function of the apostles and dared to teach the gospel on the streets and in public places. The aforesaid Valdes or Waldo drew into this presumptuous way of behaving numerous accomplices of both sexes whom he sent out to preach as disciples.

Sent word by the Archbishop of Lyons, Lord John of the Fair Hands, who forbade them to be so presumptuous, they refused to obey him, arguing in mitigation of their folly that they had to obey God rather than men. God ordained that the apostles should

preach the gospel to every creature, they repeated, applying to themselves what had been said of the apostles. They even rashly declared themselves to be the imitators and successors of the apostles, by a false profession of poverty and under the veiled image of sanctity. In fact they scorned prelates and clergy because they said that these had abundant riches and lived in luxury.

Called on to give up speaking publicly, they disobeyed and were declared contumacious, subsequently being excommunicated and expelled from their city and homeland.

Contempt of ecclesiastical power had been and still is the main heresy of the Waldenses . . . They argue that all oaths, whether in law or elsewhere, are forbidden by God without exception or explanation . . .

Bernard Gui, 1260–1331,
Inquisitor's Manual, II.1f.

investigations of the Inquisition, which do not present them in a very good light. The majority of their writings have been lost, and hearsay is never to be trusted. As had once happened with the first Christians, gossip about minority groups ran riot, and it was easy to think that they were all the same.

An evangelical protest

To begin with, many of these dissident groups were an evangelical protest against a church which had become too prosperous. Gregorian reform had borne some fruit. The more conscientious Christians spoke up against priests who were too greedy or who took concubines. Many of them, wanting to be faithful to the poverty of Christ as in the gospel, levelled their demands at the institutional church. These opposition movements often arose in the towns, which were experiencing even more of a boom in the twelfth century. The middle class reacted against a church which was too feudal and too powerful. Secular clergy and monks, shut up in their monasteries, no longer provided for the spiritual and intellectual needs of the townspeople, some of whom formed their own groups outside the established framework.

Valdes and the Poor Men of Lyons

One of the best known of the evangelical movements is that of the Poor Men of Lyons, started by Peter Valdes, or Waldo, in about 1173. A rich merchant, uneasy about the source of his wealth, Valdes abandoned all his possessions and preached poverty to his fellow citizens. Men and women joined him; they prayed, read the scriptures in the vernacular, and proclaimed in the market places, 'You cannot serve two masters, God and mammon.' The authorities were unhappy because members of the movement preached without being priests and questioned the wealth of the church. The pope, whom they had consulted in Rome in 1179, delegated the decision on their preaching activities to the Archbishop of Lyons. He came down against them and the Waldensians went to swell the growing list of heretics. They spread through the Languedoc, Provence and northern Italy. Valdes only wanted to arouse people's consciences to the demands made by the Word of God. Marginalized, the Waldensians met up with other groups and associated with them. Rejected by the church, they denied the need for an institution. They maintained that life-style determined who was the true minister, and recognized only universal priesthood. They were against work when this was a matter of acquiring wealth, along with oaths and the death penalty.

The hope of a better world

Other movements, which also wanted a return to the gospel and the early church, drew upon Revelation or the writings of the prophets when speculating on the future of humankind. These are known as apocalyptic or millenarian movements (see Rev. 20.4f.). In a tough society where injustices were rife, some people were waiting for the advent of a just kingdom where positions would be reversed. This was perhaps the starting point for the revolutions sparked off by people who claimed to be inspired by the Holy Spirit. The writings of a holy monk from Calabria, Joachim of Fiore (1130–1202), helped to fuel these dreams. After the age of the Father (associated with the Old Testament) and that of the Son (associated with the Church), the eternal age of the Holy Spirit would begin, and would put the church in its proper place.

The Cathari

Finally, doctrines contrary to Christianity arose in some groups, as for instance in the case of the Cathari, who had spread through Languedoc and northern Italy. They were thought of as the successors of the ancient Manichees, but the connection is not very easy to establish. Pilgrimages and crusades had undoubtedly contributed to the spread of their doctrines. The Cathari (the

The New Manichaeans or Cathari

The same comments can be made here as on the previous text. The doctrines of those who were called Cathari were not always so extreme.

The sect, the heresy and the deluded adherents of the Manichaeans acknowledge and confess two Gods or two Lords, namely a good God and an evil God. They affirm that the creation of all things visible and material is not the work of God the heavenly Father – whom they call the good God – but the work of the devil and Satan, the evil God. They thus distinguish two creators, God and the devil, and two creations, one of invisible and immaterial beings, and the other of visible and material things.

Likewise, they imagine two churches: one, the good church, which they say is their sect; this they claim to be the church of Jesus Christ. In their view the other, the evil church, is the Roman church; they impudently call it the mother of fornications, great Babylon, harlot and basilica of the devil, synagogue of Satan.

For baptisms with water they substitute another baptism, a spiritual one, called consolamentum *of the Holy Spirit, when for example they receive a person, well or ill, into their sect or their order, laying on hands according to their execrable rite . . .*

They deny the incarnation of our Lord Jesus Christ in the womb of Mary Ever Virgin and argue that he did not take a true human body nor true human flesh like other men by virtue of human nature, that he did not suffer and die on the cross, that he was not raised from the dead, and that he did not ascend to heaven with human body and flesh. All this, they say, is figurative.

They call imperfect heretics those who have in truth the faith of heretics but do not follow them in their life-style and do not observe the rites; they are called believers in the lying language of the heretics.

Montségur castle, Ariège, a refuge of the Cathari until 1244

By contrast, they call perfect the heretics who have professed the faith of the heretics and live their life in conformity to it, fulfilling and observing the rites involved; these are they who dogmatize the others . . .

Bernard Gui, op.cit., I, 1.

pure) professed a dualism which was not always so extreme as Bernard Gui would have it. They were concerned with an answer to the question which mankind has been asking from earliest times: where does evil come from? Dualism had the advantage of being simple. It must be said that the Cathari thought of themselves as Christians, and sometimes even referred to themselves as the 'good Christians'. Some of their rituals perhaps go back to Christian antiquity. But since they regarded the material world and the body as wicked, they denied the incarnation of Christ and condemned marriage. It is understandable that the church saw them as being a grave danger to the faith. How can the success of this strange doctrine be explained? In contrast to the laxity of the clergy of the Languedoc, the poverty and discipline of the 'perfect', the Cathari equivalent of ministers, aroused admiration. To choose Catharism was a way of protesting against the church as it was. While the 'perfect', the 'good men', led an austere life, demands were considerably reduced for ordinary believers. They had to extinguish all sexual desire, and above all contribute to the livelihood of the 'perfect'. The doctrine of reincarnation also had its attractions. A future life could redress the balance in favour of those who had been unfortunate in a first life, and vice versa.

2. The rise of the Mendicant Orders

The ideal of returning to the gospel was not the monopoly of dissident groups. It inspired a new form of religious life, the Mendicant Orders. Their founders wanted to respond to the appeal of the gospel, and the needs of people in their times. In particular, they were aware of the growth of heresy, of the development of the towns and the intellectual ferment. However, to begin with the responses of Dominic and Francis of Assisi were quite different.

Dominic and the Friars Preachers

Dominic, who was born in Spain about 1170, was originally a regular canon of Osma. He would have liked to have gone to preach to the peoples of Eastern Europe, but a meeting with the Cistercians charged with combatting heresy in Languedoc decided his future course. He could see why the monks had failed. Since they were the pope's envoys, they believed that they were obliged to maintain the splendour expected of official personages. But it was the austerity of the Cathar preachers that had brought them success. Dominic concluded from this that the practical poverty of preachers was the only effective remedy. With several companions, he went out to meet heretics in the Toulouse area, 'imitating the poverty of the poor Christ', and entered into dogmatic arguments with them. In 1215, the Bishop of Toulouse gave official approval to the small band of preachers: 'We recognize Brother Dominic and his companions as preachers in our diocese, with the aim of stamping out corruption and heresies, of pursuing vice, and teaching the rule of faith and instilling saintly habits in the people. Their way of life is to live like religious, travel around on foot, in the poverty enjoined by the gospel, while preaching the word of truth.' In 1216 the pope himself recognized the Order of Friars Preachers, who adopted the rule of St Augustine. Dominic died in Bologna in 1221.

Presence in the world

The Friars Preachers were priests who lived frugally in small urban communities. They divided their time between preaching and study. In deference to the spirit of the communities, the organization of the Order was democratic. Positions were held as a result of elections and were temporary; only the Master General was elected for life. They had no revenue from large abbeys, but depended on charity for their upkeep. That is why they are referred to as a Mendicant Order. They appealed particularly to people in towns and members of guilds. The pope also charged them with repressing heresy by making the Inquisition their responsibility.

Francis and the Friars Minor

The course of the early life of Francis of Assisi was similar to that of Valdes. In his Testament of 1226, Francis sketched out the main stages of his career. Born in about 1181, the son of a rich (121) merchant, in 1205 he abandoned his dreams of chivalry to dedicate himself to Lady Poverty. He met Christ the poor man in a leper. He believed first of all that Christ was ordering him to rebuild churches, like that of St Damian. Having given his father all his possessions, even his clothes, he begged for food and whatever else he needed. His life was that of a hermit, but the gospel message which he heard in the church of the Portiuncula in 1208 came as a revelation to him: 'Go and proclaim that the kingdom of heaven is at hand. Take with you neither gold nor silver . . . ' With several companions, he set off along the highways and byways, joyfully proclaiming the good news of peace. He either worked for food, or begged it, and did what Valdes and many others had done before him.

Testament of Francis (1226)

The Lord has given me, Brother Francis, grace to begin thus to do penance; for when I was in sin, it was very bitter to me to see lepers; but the Lord himself led me into the midst of them and I practised mercy towards them. And when I left their presence, what had before seemed bitter to me was changed into sweetness of soul and body. And after that I remained a little, and I came out from this world. And the Lord gave me such great faith in the churches that I thus adored him with simplicity and said, 'We adore you, Lord Jesus Christ, here and in all our churches which are upon the earth, and we bless you for having redeemed the world by your holy cross.'

Afterwards the Lord gave and still gives me so great faith in the priests who live according to the rule of the Holy Roman Church, because of their character, that, even if they persecute me, to them I shall have recourse. And if I had as much wisdom as Solomon, and if I found some poor priests of this world, I would not preach against their will in the parishes where they live . . .

And when the Lord gave me brothers, no one showed me what I must do, and the Most High revealed to me that I must live according to the rule of the Holy Gospel. And I caused it to be written in a few and simple words, and the Lord Pope confirmed it. And those who came to embrace this life gave as much as they could to the poor; they were content with a single tunic patched within and without at will, with a girdle and breeches. And we wished for no more. We clerks say the office like other clerks, the lay-brothers say the Pater

St Francis preaching to the birds. English manuscript of 1255

noster and willingly enough we remained in the churches, And we were simple and submissive to all. And I worked with my hands, and I will work still, and I strongly desire that all other friars shall labour at some work in conformity with honesty. Let those who know not how, learn, not with the desire of receiving payment for their work, but for a good example and to drive away idleness. And when they do not give us payment for work, let us betake ourselves to the table of the Lord begging alms from door to door. The Lord has revealed to me this salutation which we must utter; 'The Lord give you peace.'

The brothers must not receive churches, poor dwellings, nor any other places built for them, unless conformable to the holy poverty which we have promised in the rule, dwelling here below like strangers and pilgrims. I strictly forbid all the brothers under obedience, wherever they may be, to dare to ask for letters at the court of Rome for themselves or for any interposed person, for a church or for any other place, under the pretext of preaching, or because of persecution against themselves; but wherever they are not received, let them pass on elsewhere to do penance with the blessing of God.

And I firmly desire to obey the Minister General of this fraternity and the guardian it shall please him to give me.

And let not the friars say, 'This is another rule.' For it is a remembrance, a warning, an exhortation; it is my testament, that I, little Brother Francis, leave to you, my blessed brothers, in order that we may observe in a more catholic way the rule that we have promised to the Lord. And the Minister General and all the other ministers and guardians are bound by obedience to add nothing and take nothing away from these words. And in all the chapters they hold, when they read the rule, let them also read these words . . .

And whoever shall observe these things, let him be filled from heaven with the blessing of the most high Celestial Father, and on earth let him be filled with the blessing of his well-beloved Son, and of the Holy Spirit, Paraclete, and with all the powers of heaven and from all the saints. And I, brother Francis, your little servant, as far as I can, confirm within and without this very holy benediction.

He preached without being a priest. However, Francis had no wish to sit in judgment on either priests or the church. He only asked for freedom to live according to the gospel, as Jesus had done before in Palestine. In 1209 Pope Innocent III recognized the way of life of those who saw themselves as 'minors', on the lowest rung of the social ladder. They confined themselves to moral preaching.

Peace and joy

In 1209, Francis had a dozen companions; ten years later, they numbered 3000. In 1212, Clare and her companions followed Francis's example. The brothers dispersed into several countries. In 1219 Francis went off to the Holy Land and tried to convert the Sultan of Egypt. Some of the brothers wanted to have a strict organization with convents and study houses, but Francis did not care for this. However, although the gospel was their only rule of life, he had to draw up a rule (1223). But he continued his joyful preaching. In 1223 he celebrated Christmas with a real live crib. The next year, the marks of the stigmata appeared on his body. He expressed his love of nature and the creator God in his Canticle of Brother Sun. He acted as mediator between local lords. His Testament of 1226 shows some nostalgic longing for his early years. On 3 October 1226 he calmly welcomed 'our sister, bodily death', and two years later he was canonized.

The Order of Friars Minor may have had a difficult existence, even being divided over what constitutes faith to its founder, but Francis has always been the most popular saint of the Middle Ages, perhaps even in history. He is the supreme witness of the return to the gospel, overthrowing mediaeval sensitivity by his imitation of the life of Christ, by his love of nature, and by his rejection of wealth which distorts human relations.

III · The Repression of Heresy

The Inquisition does not represent the universal attitude of the church towards religious dissidents during the Middle Ages. There were many hesitations for several centuries, and it was the thirteenth century before a systematic scheme of repression was organized for the whole of Christendom.

1. Hesitations and reservations

As we have seen, anti-heretical legislation was worked out under the Christian empire. Bishops such as Augustine or John Chrysostom had accepted it, while totally rejecting the death penalty for heretics. In spite of the existence of repressive laws, the church had shown herself generally unwilling to use violence against heretics up until the eleventh century. There is no known instance of the death penalty against heretics during the early Middle Ages. Only imprisonments have been mentioned.

Popular movements and a progressive hardening

A change came about during the eleventh and twelfth centuries. The number of dissidents seemed to be increasing. Christendom was becoming aware of itself. Unity of faith was the basis of society, and it had to be safeguarded at all costs. The value of Roman law was recognized

The escalation of repression

(122) A bishop cannot demand the death of heretics

We have not received power to cut off from this life by the secular sword those whom our creator and redeemer wills to live so that they may extricate themselves from the snares of the devil . . . Those who today are our adversaries in the way of the Lord can, by the grace of God, become our betters in the heavenly country . . . We who are called bishops did not receive unction from the Lord to give death but to bring life.

Wason, Bishop of Liège,
letter to the Bishop of Châlons,
about 1045.

(123) Legislation of Frederick II against the heretics

Anyone who has been manifestly convicted of heresy by the bishop of his diocese shall on the bishop's request be seized immediately by the secular authorities of the place and delivered to the stake. If the judges think his life should be preserved, particularly to convict other heretics, they shall cut out the tongue of the one who has not hesitated to blaspheme against the Catholic faith and the name of God.

(124) The birth of the episcopal Inquisition: decisions of the Council of Toulouse (1229)

In every parish in the city and outside the city the bishops shall designate a priest and two or three laymen, or even more if necessary, of unsullied reputation, who shall be committed on oath to search out assidously and faithfully the heretics living in the parish. They shall be assiduous in visiting suspected houses, rooms and cellars and the most hidden nooks of places which are about to be demolished. If they discover heretics or people giving credence or favour, sanctuary or protection to heretics, they shall take steps to prevent their flight and denounce them as soon as possible to the bishop and to the lord of the place or his bailiff.

The temporal lords shall carefully search out the heretics in the villas, the houses and the forests where they meet and destroy their lairs.

Interrogation under torture (fifteenth century)

(125) Letter of Pope Gregory IX to the Bishops of France, 13 April 1233

Seeing that you are caught up in the whirlwind of your many occupations, and have hardly time to breathe because of the difficulty of having too much work to do, and therefore thinking it reasonable that you should share your activities with others, we are sending you the aforesaid Friars Preachers, to the kingdom of France and neighbouring regions. Their mission is to combat the heretics. We ask you to receive them with kindness and to give them their due, to offer them your advice, help and goodwill, in these matters and in others, so that they can fulfil the mission that has been entrusted to them.

again. People discovered anti-heretical legislation in it without bothering to find out how it had been applied originally. There was a slow escalation in its use. In 1022 some heretics, perhaps Manichaeans, were accused of debauchery and condemned to the stake by the king, under pressure from the mob. However, in similar cases, bishops rejected the death penalty – like Wason of Liège in 1045. Bernard of Clairvaux, confronted with the heretics of Cologne in 1144, insisted first of all on the necessity of converting them. But if excommunication was not enough, it was necessary to resort to violence in order to preserve the Lord's vineyard from the foxes who were laying it waste.

2. The working out of legislation against heretics

The decree of Gratian (1140), which brought together the traditional legal texts (Roman law, decretals, etc.), envisaged three stages in the procedure to be adopted against heretics: attempts at persuasion, canonical sanctions (pronounced by the church) and finally appeal to the secular arm, i.e. to justice as dispensed by the princes. These would act by confiscating possessions and by corporal punishment, but the death penalty was not explicitly laid down. The Third Lateran Council of 1179 distinguished between the heretics who were experiencing spiritual difficulties and those who had to be opposed because they had formed groups. In 1184 Pope Lucius III and the Emperor Frederick Barbarossa organized a joint campaign of repression. The 'suitable punishment' was not defined precisely. In 1197 King Peter of Aragon classed heresy as a crime of high treason, punishable by death at the stake. In 1199 Innocent III also spoke of heresy as high treason.

The Albigensian crusade

When the legate he had sent to carry on the fight against the heresy was assassinated in Lan-guedoc, Innocent III appealed for a crusade against the Albigensians (1208). Albi was at the centre of an area where there were numerous heretics. The name Albigensians is used primarily to denote Cathari, but it is sometimes also extended to Waldensians. The crusade was to become a war between the lords of the north and those of the south. The former used it as an excuse to regain their fiefdoms. The most infamous episode of this crusade is the massacre in 1209 of the people of Béziers, who had taken refuge in their cathedral.

3. The Inquisition

The Inquisition, in the strict sense of the word, came into being in the years 1220–1230, when the civil and religious powers were systematically joining forces to search out and punish heretics and when papal rulings made such action general throughout the church. It was then, when the question of suitable punishment was being decided on, that death at the stake became the norm. Vindictiveness triumphed over attempts at a remedy. But there is no doubt that death was not the most frequent punishment: there were many others, like imprisonment, fines, pilgrimages, and so on.

Inquisitions and inquisitors

Three different types of Inquisition are usually distinguished, according to their origins. There was the secular Inquisition of Frederic II (1224) and Louis IX (1229); the episcopal Inquisition (Toulouse, 1229) and the papal Inquisition. In 1233 Pope Gregory IX revived earlier legislation and made the Inquisition a special tribunal directly responsible to the papacy. He entrusted it to the Friars Preachers, the Dominicans, but also to the Friars Minor. A complex procedure evolved which in 1252 authorized torture. It was the church which took direct responsibility for meting out punishments, only leaving the civil powers the task of carrying out the sentences. All

Theological justification for the repression of heretics

With regard to heretics, two considerations are to be kept in mind: 1. on their side, 2. on the side of the church.

1. There is the sin, whereby they deserve not only to be separated from the church by excommunication, but also to be shut off from the world by death. For it is a much more serious matter to corrupt faith, through which comes the soul's life, than to forge money, through which temporal life is supported. Hence if forgers of money or other malefactors are straightway justly put to death by secular princes, with much more justice can heretics, immediately upon conviction, be not only excommunicated but also put to death.

2. But on the side of the church there is mercy, with a view to the conversion of them that are in error; and therefore the church does not straightway condemn, but after a first and second admonition, as the apostle tells us. After that, if he be found still stubborn, the church gives up hope of his conversion and takes thought for the safety of others, by separating him from the church by sentence of excommunication, and further, leaves him to the secular court, to be exterminated from the world by death.

Thomas Aquinas, *Summa Theologica*, IIa, IIae, 11, art.3.

---

that was needed then was a theological justification, which was produced by Thomas Aquinas.

It is hard to explain how the church, in the name of the gospel, could burn alive those who did not accept its teaching. In some aspects Christendom was a régime which was, if not totalitarian, at least authoritarian, and not above using force. In order to ensure its survival, it made use of the methods of its time, torture and death.

For further reading

J. R. H. Moorman, *Francis of Assisi*, SPCK 1963

E. LeRoy Ladurie, *Montaillou*, Penguin Books 1980

Steven Runciman, *History of the Crusades* (three volumes), Penguin Books 1971

The Krak of the knights in Syria (twelfth century)

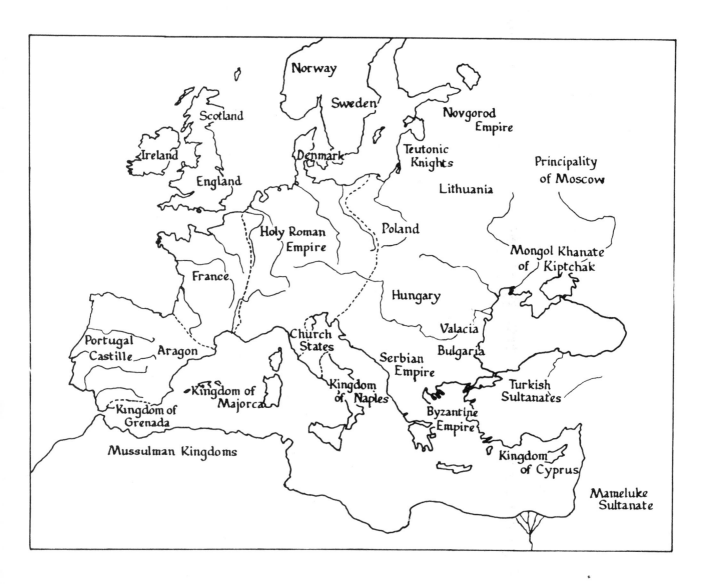

Political Europe at the Beginning of the Fourteenth Century

10

The Autumn of Christendom

Fourteenth and Fifteenth Centuries

Danse macabre from La Chaise-Dieu (Haute Loire), painted about 1460

It is customary to speak of the decline of Christendom during the fourteenth and fifteenth centuries. However, we must look further at this word 'decline'. It refers in the first place to the whole system of Christendom. That, as we have seen, was based on the supremacy of the papacy, which came to play the role of universal arbiter in Europe at the time of Innocent III. This equilibrium was fragile, even in the thirteenth century. It was gradually shattered during the following centuries in the course of several crises, some of which were very serious. The sovereigns disputed the pope's role in the political sphere. Even within the church, divisions resulted in a schism and in an argument over the basis of papal powers. The difficulties of the age and the confusion in people's thinking brought about an eruption in religious thought and marked the end of unanimity. However, this picture of decadence was not the whole of the church's life during this period. Changes were at work which heralded a new era. These centuries were also a time of a great deepening of the faith for many Christians.

I · The Birth of the Lay Spirit

1. The rise of national monarchies

We have seen earlier that the popes' struggles against the Germanic emperors resulted in the weakening of imperial power. During the Great Interregnum (1254–1273) there was no longer even an emperor. But the papacy did not seem to make the most of this. The popes abused the spiritual weapons like excommunication by using them for a temporal end. On the other hand, the decline of the empire was advantageous to Western monarchies. They confirmed this by making feudal laws work in their favour. We have all learned early on at school how the kings of France and England increased their domains. The Spanish kings regained their peninsula by conquest from the Moslems; the final stage of this, the capture of Granada in 1492, saw the unification of Spain. All the Western kingdoms gradually became states in the modern sense of the word, setting up the core of a centralized administration in spheres of finance and justice. From this more powerful position they came into confrontation in the first national conflicts, such as the Hundred Years War between England and France (1337–1453). At the same time, in their desire to strengthen and develop their authority, these monarchies were to come up against the obstacle of papal power, and therein lay a fresh source of conflict.

2. A significant conflict: Philip the Fair against Boniface VIII

To an ever increasing extent, the princes would not tolerate papal intervention in the church in their kingdoms, and at the same time they asserted their own authority in the ecclesiastical affairs of their territories. On two occasions (1296 and 1301–1303), the king of France, Philip the Fair (1285–1314), and Pope Boniface VIII (1294–1303) came to violent blows. A grandson of St Louis, pious and prim in moral matters, the king had few scruples when it came to means of getting hold of money. Besides, his advisers, the canonists, influenced by Roman law, glorified royal power. The pope was himself an obtuse and headstrong man, steeped in papal prerogatives which he asserted without discernment. The first conflict centred on the fiscal immunity of the church: Boniface VIII would not allow the king to levy taxes on the wealth of the church. The canonization of Louis IX in 1297 poured oil on the troubled waters of the dispute. The subject of the second conflict was the legal immunity of the clergy. Philip had hauled up before the royal tribunal the Bishop of Pamers, a protégé of Boniface. There was an outburst of fiery words, but also of downright violence. When the pope threatened to depose the king, invoking precedents in his support, the canonists in the royal entourage went on the offensive. Stirring up national and religious feeling against a pope accused of all kinds of vices, William of Nogaret went to threaten Boniface in his very palace, at Anagni, on 7 September 1303. Badly shocked, the pope, already well advanced in years, died a month later.

Besides the act which led to the setting up of the papacy in France, the conflict provoked a debate. In the Bull *Unam Sanctam* (1302), Boniface VIII took up all the theocratic affirmations of his predecessors: the superiority of spiritual power to which temporal power had to be subject. On the face of it, the king proclaimed himself sole master in his kingdom. There was no one above him in the temporal sphere. Moreover, the idea emerged that a defaulting pope could be judged by a general council.

Philip the Fair versus Boniface VIII

 King Philip the Fair defines his power (1297)

The government of the temporality of the kingdom belongs to the king alone and to no one else, and he does not have, nor recognize, any superior. Nor does he intend to submit himself to or be ruled by anyone in any matter concerning things temporal in his kingdom.

 Boniface VIII at the consistory of 1302

Our predecessors have deposed three kings of France: the French have all that in their chronicles and we have it in ours; since the king of France has committed all the errors committed by his ancestors, who were smitten, and more, we shall have the sorry task of deposing him like a naughty boy unless he comes to his senses.

 The bull *Unam Sanctam* (1302)

Of the one and only church there is one body and one head, not two heads, like a monster – namely Christ, and Christ's vicar is Peter, and Peter's successor . . .

The temporal authority must be subject to spiritual authority . . . If therefore the earthly power err, it can only be judged by the spiritual power; and if a lesser power err, it shall be judged by a greater. But if the supreme power err, it can only be judged by God, not by man . . . For this authority, although given to a man and exercised by a man, is not human, but rather divine, given at God's mouth to Peter and established on a rock for him . . . furthermore we declare, state, define and pronounce that it is altogether necessary to salvation for every human creature to be subject to the Roman pontiff.

Bettenson, *Documents of the Christian Church*, pp. 115f.

 Accusation by Nogaret, lawyer of Philip the Fair, against Boniface VIII (1303)

I claim that the individual in question, surnamed Boniface, is not a pope. He has not entered by the door and must be considered a thief and a robber. I claim that the aforesaid Boniface is a manifest heretic and a horrible simonist, such as there has never been since the beginning of the world. Finally, I claim that the aforesaid Boniface has committed manifest crimes, of great enormity and infinite in number, and that he is incorrigible. It is the duty of a General Council to judge him and condemn him.

3. The lay spirit

Another conflict in 1324 between Pope John XXII and Ludwig of Bavaria, whom the pope would not recognize as emperor, again resulted in the appointment of an antipope and the multiplication of works on the respective rights of popes and kings. Quite apart from polemics and insults, these writings suggested a thorough consideration of the respective natures of church and state. This is what is understood by the 'birth of the lay spirit'. At that time the term 'lay' did not have any anti-religious connotations. It could sometimes be a synonym for anti-clerical, but

Birth of the lay spirit

Marsilius of Padua (1275–1342) had been Rector of the University of Paris in 1313. He entered the service of King Ludwig IV of Bavaria and clashed with Pope John XXII of Avignon. The *Defensor Pacis*, written with John of Jandun, puts forward a theory of the relationship between church and state which is completely opposed to the theocratic theories of the popes of Christendom.

Men gather together in order to live in a satisfying way, which allows them to seek and share among themselves the various products that they need. This gathering together, thus accomplished, with the aim of providing satisfaction, is called a city.

We say that the prince, by his action in accordance with the law and the authority conferred on him, is the rule and the measure of every civil act.

Of all the definitions given to the word church, the truest and most appropriate, in conformity with the first use of this name and the intention of the first people to adopt it, although it is not the current meaning in modern usage, is that which makes it the totality of those who believe in and call on the name of Christ, the different parts of this whole being found in each community . . . The ministers, bishops, priests and deacons are not of themselves the church.

Christ said, 'Tell it to the church', and not, 'To the apostle or the bishop or the priest or to one of their colleagues'. By this he meant the church as the multitude of the faithful, judged to be constituted to this end under his authority . . . Judicially to declare someone guilty, to cite, enquire, judge, acquit or condemn . . . is the role of the whole of the faithful forming the community where a judgment must be given, or for the General Council.

It appertains to the authority of the sole human legislator – who has no superior – either to him or to those on whom this power has been conferred by him, to convoke the General Council, to designate the persons who must form part of it.

If with the aim of temporal utility it is for the legislator to designate people who are to be promoted to diverse offices in the city . . . it seems all the more right that the same human legislator, namely the totality of the faithful, should decide on both the promotion of the priestly office and the institution of priests in their functions.

Marsilius of Padua, *Defensor Pacis*, 1324.

only if the second word was understood in its etymological sense: against clerics.

Two main ideas characterized the lay spirit: the independence of the state in the temporal sphere and the insistence on speaking of the church as the whole body of believers, not limiting it to a clerical institution. The consequences drawn from this vary depending on the writer. Some affirm that the church and state are each relatively autonomous, each forming a society with its own sovereignty. We are quite ready to accept that today. Marsilius of Padua went much further. Only the state was sovereign. The church was not a society; it existed within the state, which endowed clergy with their powers and convened councils. This was theocracy in reverse, a totalitarian system in embryo.

The Golden Bull of 1356 was a symbol of this lay spirit, since it excluded all intervention of the pope in the nomination of the emperor of Germany.

II · The Tribulations of the Papacy

Papal palace at Avignon (fourteenth century)

1. The popes in Avignon

In June 1305, after a vacancy of nearly a year, the divided cardinals elected the Archbishop of Bordeaux, Bertrand de Got, as pope. He had proved conciliatory in the quarrel between the king of France and the pope. Philip the Fair was present at his coronation in Lyons in November 1305. He asked for the pope's help in settling the dispute between the French and the English over Gascony. In addition, the papal states were disturbed by troubles. All these things, and others, kept Clement V in or near France, and he never reached Rome. Until 1377, the popes preferred to live in the Comtat-Venaissin, which wa a papal property, or in Avignon, which they had acquired. This was not the first time the popes had left Rome, but they had never been away from Italy for so long. The Romans spoke of the 'Babylonian captivity'. However, the situation in Avignon was only slightly inconvenient for the governing of the church. The town was quiet and well placed. It was easy to communicate with the whole of Christendom. Besides, the popes of the time had a lively concern for the welfare of the whole church. They were very interested in missions to distant places, and in crusades.

All-consuming taxation

However, the installation of the papacy so close to the kingdom of France could be detrimental in many areas. Just as the cardinals chosen were almost exclusively French, so all the popes of

---

Petrarch's invectives against Avignon

Petrarch (1304–1374) spent part of his life in Avignon, where he had become enamoured of Laura, whom he celebrates in his poems. Despite his indignation, he did not despise the favours of the popes of Avignon.

Avignon is impious Babylon, a living hell, a sink of iniquity. There one finds neither faith nor charity nor religion nor fear of God nor shame; nothing is true, nothing is holy; although the residence of the sovereign pontiff should have made it the sanctuary and stronghold of religion . . . Of all the cities that I know, it is the most corrupt. How shameful to see it suddenly become the capital of the world, when it should only occupy the last place.

The cardinals! . . . Whereas the apostles went barefoot, we now see satraps mounted on horses caparisoned with gold; already they eat with gold and soon they will have gold roads, unless God represses their insolent luxury. One would take them for kings of Persia, or Parthians who had to be revered, and whom one would not dare to approach with empty hands.

Catherine of Siena asks Gregory XI to return to Rome

Caterina di Benincasa (1347–1380), twenty-third in a family of twenty-five children, had extraordinary mystical experiences from a very early age. Though she had chosen to be dedicated to the religious life, she played an active part in the struggles that were going on in Siena, where she had been born, and also in Tuscany, Avignon and Rome, where she died. Three concerns dominated her life: the conversion of sinners, the relaunching of the crusades and the return of the pope to Rome.

Be the true successor to St Gregory; love God, have no attachments either to kinsfolk, or friends, or temporal necessity. Do not fear the present storm, nor the spoilt members who have rebelled against your authority. God's help is near: attach yourself only to the good shepherds, for it is the bad ones who have provoked the rebellion. Bring a remedy for these evils and act in Jesus Christ. Go forward! Finish what you have begun. Do not delay, for delay has caused numerous ills, and the devil is at work devising hindrances for you. Raise the standard of the true cross, for by it you will have peace. You will console the poor of Jesus who await you with longing. Come, and you will see the wolves become sheep. Peace, that war may cease. No longer resist the will of God, for the starving sheep wait for you to return to the see of St Peter. You are the Vicar of Jesus; you must resume your proper seat. Come without fear, for God will be with you. Do not wait, for time does not wait. Respond to the Holy Spirit. Come like the lamb who, unarmed, lays low his enemies, making use of the arms of love. Be bold; save the church from division and iniquity; the wolves will come into your fold and you will cry pity . . . Come as a bold man without fear; but above all, for the love of life, do not come with a military escort, but come with the cross in your hand like a gentle lamb.

Avignon were to be French and gave the impression of being in the service of the king of France. We see this in the matters of the Templars (1307–1314), whose suppression Philip the Fair organized through Clement V, and the Council of Vienne (1311–1312). The popes of Avignon, particularly from John XXII onwards, considerably developed pontifical administration and were surrounded by a court which numbered three or four thousand people. The upkeep of the court and the building of the palace by Benedict XII and Clement VI required substantial resources and taxation as a result; this gave a bad name to the popes of Avignon.

The progress of centralization

The papacy found itself caught up in a kind of vicious circle. Central administration required extra resources. But it had in part relinquished the means of obtaining these resources. The popes appeared increasingly concerned to rule the church directly. Their intervention in the appointment of bishops grew. Beyond question, the holding of elections had undoubtedly been contested by the pope who had put his foot down. But what was once rare became the done thing. The custom of holding elections gradually faded out, and it became an established rule that the pope appointed all bishops, a rule which is still adhered to today. From then on men were made 'bishop by the grace of God and the apostolic see'. Anyone appointed bishop by the pope had to hand over a year's revenue to the papal finances. There was therefore a concern to make any nomination by the pope a matter of more widespread discussion. It is in fact the case that the pope and the princes often arranged such appointments together.

The complaint of Lady Church, by the theologian Jean Petit in 1393, during the Great Schism

So we are in 1393

*Two popes, only one of which is legitimate

*Pope Clement VII, residing in Avignon

*Jean Petit is a theologian at the University of Paris

*Pope Urban VI in Rome

Clement VII and Boniface IX

Alas, what shall I do in the midst of my suffderings,
when for more than fifteen years
a sickness has tormented me,
so severely that all my limbs are broken.
My head and my body are divided,
split into several parts.
For the love of God, Christians,
See how I could be soon cured . . .

For this reason those who have made this storm
around me are the servants of the Antichrist.
It seems that they want to make me
wife of two husbands*
and a widow at the same time;
Many people are afflicted by this . . .
I am wife of Robert of Geneva.*
The others cry, 'No, no,
It is not true, by Saint Geneviève,*
but she is the true wife
of the successor of Bartholomew of Bari*.
The third say, 'No, by God,
in justice neither the one nor the other is her husband,
for neither the one nor the other is the Holy Father.
And so they say that I am a widow . . .

This affair must be settled
first by the greatest
who are not doing their duty.
Neither Pope Clement nor Boniface.
The two of them leave me here to rot
they do not care if I trespass . . .

So without delay take steps
for me to be cured
and pray God with a sincere heart
that this shall be so
and that he will grant it. Amen.

Praying Virgin.
San Marco, Venice
(fourteenth century)

The popes of Avignon undoubtedly did not deserve all the opprobrium that the Italians heaped on them: in 1870 Urban V (1362–1370) was beatified by Pius IX. But above all else they were legalistic men, and their successes were confined to the temporal sphere. They did not enjoy any real religious success. In their failings lay the origins of the great Western schism.

2. The Great Schism (1378–1417)

Two popes

The weight of Christian opinion was behind a return of the papacy to Rome; the appeals of Bridget of Sweden and Catherine of Siena are particularly moving. After three years in Rome (1367–1370), Urban V went back to Avignon. In 1377, Gregory XI made up his mind to re-establish the papacy once and for all in Rome, but his return was made in unpromising conditions. A battle between the papal troops and the townspeople of Cesene, who were in revolt, left four thousand dead on the field. The French cardinals, who appreciated the situation in Avignon, returned to Rome with some reluctance. Hardly re-established in Rome, Gregory XI died in 1378. The Romans, who did not want to let the pope slip out of their hands, became threatening. They wanted an Italian pope. The cardinals made all speed to elect the Archbishop of Bari, Bartolomeo Prignano, who took the name of Urban VI (April 1378). The new pope proved too much for the French cardinals to take, and they left Rome. Claiming that Urban VI had only been elected by popular support, in September 1378 they proceeded to elect another candidate, Robert of Geneva, who took the name of Clement VII. In the confusion within Christianity, the decision of Charles V, king of France, to recognize Clement VII confirmed a schism that was to last forty years. Unsuccessful in seizing Rome, Clement VII established himself in Avignon in June 1379. Christendom was split in two, both geographically and politically, with the 'Clementines' drawn up against the 'Urbanists'. Each side had its holy figures: St Colette and St Vincent Ferrier for Avignon, and St Catherine of Siena for Rome. On both sides, the death of one or other of the popes gave rise to fresh elections: Boniface IX in Rome in 1389 and Benedict XIII in Avignon in 1394. The two popes excommunicated each other, and issued bulls calling for crusades against each other. Christian people suffered as a consequence, and it was at this time that the mass for Christian unity was composed. Such anarchy allowed rulers to interfere more easily in the life of their churches.

Three popes

The cardinals of the two parties tried to find a way out of the situation by convoking a Council at Pisa in 1409. The two existing popes were deposed and a new one appointed, Alexander V. Christendom now had three popes, because Benedict XIII and Gregory XII had refused to abdicate. Then the Emperor Sigismund charged John XXIII,[1] successor to Alexander V, to call a new Council at Constance, which was to last four years (1414–1418). John XXIII, fearful of being judged, fled the Council. By the decree *Sacrosancta* of 6 April 1415, the assembly affirmed the Council's authority over the whole church, including the pope. This was the only way of getting out of the crisis. Failing to establish unity immediately, the Council found a scapegoat in the person of John Hus, and condemned him to the stake in July 1415 (see p.183). The abdication of John XXIII and Gregory XII and the deposition of Benedict XIII allowed the election of Martin V in November 1417. The schism was over. The council also proposed a general reform of the church. This turned out to be just wishful thinking, but it was decided to convene regular councils.

[1]It was because John XXIII was not considered a legitimate pope that the name was adopted in 1958 by Angelo Roncalli.

The decree *Sacrosancta* (6 April 1415) of the Council of Constance

This Holy Synod of Constance, forming a General Council, lawfully assembled in the Holy Spirit to the praise of Almighty God, for the abolition of the present schism, for the union and reform of the Church of God in its head and members, so as to arrive more easily, surely and freely at the union and reform of the Church of God, ordains, defines and declares the following: First, that this same Council, lawfuly assembled in the Holy Spirit, constitutes a General Council, representing the Catholic church militant and that therefore it has its authority immediately from Christ; and that all men, of every rank and condition, including the pope himself, is bound to obey it in matters concerning the Faith, the abolition of the schism, and the reformation of the Church of God in its head and members.

Quoted in Bettenson,
Documents of the Christian Church, p.135.

Bakers and their mobile oven supplying the participants in the Council of Constance (1414–1418)

The decree *Frequens* (9 October 1417) of the Council of Constance

The frequent celebration of General Councils is one of the best means of cultivating the field of the Lord . . .

That is why by the present perpetual edict we resolve, decree and ordain that General Councils shall be celebrated henceforth as follows. The first to follow the end of the present Council shall take place five years later, the second after the one which follows the present Council seven years later, and then every ten years, in a place which the pope or, failing him the Council itself, shall fix and designate in the month preceding the end of the Council . . .

3. The conciliar crisis

The Council of Basle

According to the schedule provided for, Martin V convened a Council at Pavia in 1423 and then at Basle in 1431. This last one brought few bishops together, but many ecclesiastical figures from all the Orders and the universities, including lay prople. Reform was the order of the day. For the most part, this consisted in the lowering of taxes.

Most of the Council affirmed their growing opposition to the pope, in particular over the choice of a place for meeting with representatives of the Greek church with a view to reconciliation. In September 1437, Eugenius IV decided to transfer the Council from Basle to Ferrara, and then to Florence. The pope's supporters left Basle. Those who remained – about a dozen bishops including the saintly Cardinal Aleman (who was to be beatified) and three hundred clergy – deposed Eugenius IV in June 1439 and elected as pope Amédée VIII, Duke of Savoy, who took the name of Felix V. The schism collapsed in ridicule. The Council exhausted itself in a form of parliamentarism which was full of good intentions but proved to be totally ineffective.

The Council of Florence (1439)

The Council transferred to Florence produced far more brilliant results, at least in appearance. The emperors of Constantinople, at bay before the advancing Ottoman Turks, wanted military aid from the West, but this presupposed religious unity. The Council of Florence responded with this aim in view. A Byzantine delegation of several hundred people, including the emperor and the patriarch of Constantinople, arrived in Italy. The theological discussions were conducted much more seriously than at Lyons in 1274: the main points of difference were touched on. The parties were able to sign a decree of union on 6 July 1439, and the pope expressed his joy. (137)

---

(137) Council of Florence: union with the Greeks (6 July 1439)

Eugenius, bishop, servant of the servants of God, that remembrance may be kept for ever.

In agreement over everything that follows with our most dear son John Paleologus, illustrious emperor of the Romans, with the representatives of our venerable brethren the patriarchs and with the other members who represent the Eastern church.

'Let the heavens rejoice and the earth exult' (Ps. 95.11). Here, indeed, the wall which separated the Eastern Church and the Western Church has been destroyed, and peace and concord have returned through 'Christ the corner-stone who has made the two one' (Eph. 2.20,14), the most powerful bond of peace joining them and attaching them by a treaty of perpetual unity; behold, after a prolonged cloud of sadness and the black and odious darkness of a long separation, the serene rays of a union so long desired have at last shone for all . . . !

Here indeed, after a very long period of dissension and discord, the fathers of West and East, exposing themselves to the dangers of sea and land and coming to the end of all difficulties, arrived joyfully and with good cheer at this holy ecumenical council, impelled by the desire of most holy union and with the intent of restoring the ancient bond of charity. Nor have their purposes been frustrated. Indeed, after long and laborious searching, by the mercy of the Holy Spirit, they have at last arrived at this union, so holy and so desired . . .

Latins and Greeks, meeting in this holy ecumenical synod, have shown great zeal one with another so that, among other points, the article which deals with the divine procession of the Holy Spirit has been discussed with great care and after prolonged examinations . . . (there follows a long account of the discussions of the filioque).

Our definition is that the body of

Christ is truly consecrated in bread made of grain, whether it is unleavened or leavened, and that priests may consecrate this same Body of Christ using one kind of bread or the other depending on the custom of their church, whether Western or Eastern . . . (There follow the positions taken on purgatory and hell.)

We also define that the Holy Apostolic See and the Roman pontiff have primacy over all the earth: that this Roman pontiff is the successor of the blessed Peter . . .

We confirm the order to be observed among the other venerable patriarchs which has been transmitted to us by the canons, so that the Patriarch of Constantinople is the second after the most holy Pontiff of Rome, that of Alexandria the third, that of Antioch the fourth and that of Jerusalem the fifth, all their privileges and rights being safeguarded.

Once more, a Council had been truly ecumenical. However, the union did not come about. Some of those from the East, like Isidore of Kiev, had accepted the Council's conclusions in all sincerity, but their clergy and people did not follow their lead. Other bishops, like Mark of Ephesus, who had not signed the decree of union, organized opposition when they returned. What was more serious was that those in the West were hardly interested in the fate of Constantinople. The city and the remainder of the Roman empire fell to the Turks in 1453. Given time, the union might have been achieved, but the Turkish victory severed all relations between East and West. Differences grew, and each side continued to ignore the other.

The pitfalls of Italian politics

The conciliar crisis ended in victory for the papacy. Felix V, who had never had many supporters, abdicated in 1449. All the same, the church's biggest problems were not solved. The much-heralded reform had not got very far. With their authority restored and strengthened, the popes should have set about it, but, caught up in the turmoil of Italian politics and the Renaissance, they were more concerned to marry off their illegitimate children and adorn Rome with prestigious buildings.

III · Human Problems

1. The evils of the age

War, plague and death

There was a trail of calamities throughout the fourteenth and fifteenth centuries, the most terrible of them being the Great Plague or the Black Death, an epidemic originating in Asia which ravaged the whole of Europe from 1347 onwards and returned several times at the end of the century. A third of the population of Europe died – more in some areas. War raged as another endemic hazard: the Hundred Years War is well known. Its victims were not so much those of the battlefield – those who actually fought were relatively few in number – but the civil population, which was plundered and starved by licentious troops who spread throughout the countryside. The written reports of pastoral visitations have endless lists of churches without roofs, ruined clergy houses, the disappearance of objects used in worship. Death became an obsession. Texts and pictures emphasized its horrible side: naked and rotten corpses, with gaping mouths and entrails eaten by worms. The Dance of Death brought home the equality of all mankind in the face of death. People did not so much mourn the dead as fear their own death: they tried to get used to the idea, and the 'arts of dying' multiplied. In Paris the dead were buried in a graveyard which contained a skeleton of one of the Holy Innocents. It was one of the most popular burial grounds.

The Black Death (1347–1348)

There was current at this time a common and general mortality, throughout the world, from a sickness which was called the plague, which took some on the left arm and others in the groin. They died within three days, and when it struck a street or a lodging, one caught it from another, which is why few people dared to help or visit the sick. Nor could they make their confessions, for it was almost impossible to find a priest who would hear them, nor did they dare to clothe or touch the sick . . .

People could not think what to make of the affliction or what remedy to offer for it, but many believed that this was a miracle and divine vengeance on the

Flagellant procession (fourteenth century)

God holds out his hand to Adam and Eve to draw them out of hell. Fresco from the church of St Maurice de Gourans, Ain (fifteenth century)

sins of the world. Hence it came about that some began thenceforward to do great penance in diverse ways by way of devotion. Among others, the people of Germany began to go through the country on the main roads in companies, carrying crucifixes, standards and great banners, as in processions; they went through the streets, two by two, singing loudly hymns to God and our Lady, rhymed and with music; then they assembled together and stripped to their chemises twice a day and beat themselves as hard as they could with knotted lashes embedded with needles, so that the blood flowed down from their shoulders on all sides, while all the time they were singing their songs. Then they threw themselves to the earth three times in devotion and went about among one another with great humility.

When people saw that this mortality and pestilence did not cease as a result of the penitence that they did, a rumour

was heard that this mortality came from the Jews and that the Jews had thrown poison into wells and fountains throughout the world to poison all Christianity, so as to have lordship and control over all the world. Therefore everyone, great and small, was so aroused against them that they were all burned and put to death in the market places where the flagellants went, by the lords and justices of those places. And they went to their deaths dancing and singing as joyfully as if they were going to a wedding. They did not want to become Christians nor would they allow their children to receive baptism . . . They said that they had found in the books of their prophets that when this sect of flagellants ran through the world all Jewry would be destroyed by fire, and the souls of those who died joyously in their firm faith would go to paradise.

Jean le Bel, Canon of Liège (1290–1370), *Vrayes Chroniques* (1326–1361).

Satan in the midst

The all-pervading presence of death encouraged people to examine their consciences. God punished the sins of mankind, and they had to be expiated. That is the origin of the processions of flagellants who travelled through the towns, striking themselves until the blood flowed. Even then, they did not stop their lashing. Someone had to be found to take responsibility, and Jews became the scapegoats. However, the great past master of evil was Satan, and there was a far greater obsession with him than in the preceding centuries. A satanic fervour ran through Europe and did not die down until the seventeenth century. Satan intervened by means of his agents, sorcerers and sorceresses. It was a sign of the times that there were far more sorceresses than sorcerers! Torture extracted confessions, and repression fed the flames at the stakes of thousands of victims. A defective theology and poor psychology interpreted every pathological phenomenon as supernatural and satanic.

2. The intellectual crisis

The church's troubles, the clashes between popes and rulers, and the Great Schism – all these added to the evils of the times to sow doubt in people's minds. Philosophy and theology lost the happy balance and assurance that they had achieved in the thirteenth century.

Ockham

William of Ockham (1290–1350), an English Franciscan who had migrated to the continent, supported Ludwig of Bavaria against John XXII and questioned the pope's conception of the church, championing the role of the laity. Furthermore, he made a radical distinction between the sphere of reason, that is to say philosophy and science, and the sphere of theology. According to him, one cannot reach God through reason. Theological concepts are only verbal constructions. He therefore went back to reading the Bible and the example of the saints. The almighty power of this inaccessible God was arbitrary. He meted out punishment and reward as he saw fit.

Wyclif

John Wyclif (1324–1384), a theologian from Oxford, accorded a privileged place to scripture as over against tradition, and refused in the name of his philosophy to recognize eucharistic transubstantiation. Above all, however, the Great Schism made him reject the traditional theology of the church. When two popes squabbled over the tiara like two dogs fighting for a bone or two crows over a carcass, it was impossible to identify the church with prelates who lived against the laws of God and of scripture. The church was the whole body of the chosen people who have Christ as their head. Wyclif died in his bed. All his enemies could do, a long time after his death, was to throw his bones in the river.

Hus

The same fate was not enjoyed by John Hus (1369–1415), a theologian from Prague, who took up certain of Wyclif's ideas on the church. During the confusion and drama of the Great Schism – when there were three popes – Hus could not see any resemblance between the true church and the institution calling itself the church. The church was the community of the elect. John Hus set out to reform this sinning church and to make it return to the poverty of the gospel. An increasingly impassioned preacher, he came up against the rich clergy of Czechoslovakia and Pope John XXIII. He went to Constance to defend himself and proved to have only a one-way passport! The fathers who condemned him for his ideas did not have a better doctrine. The execution of John Hus sparked off a revolution in Bohemia which lasted for several decades.

John Hus (1369–1415)

Reply to the Synod of Prague in 1413

To understand this text it is necessary to recall that from 1409 there had been three popes in the church. Here John Hus has particularly in mind John XXIII, the pope of Pisa.

Ah, if only the disciples of Antichrist could declare themselves in accord on the true Holy Roman Church, that is to say all the faithful Christians and saints militant in the faith of Christ, obedient to the teaching of Peter, the Bishop of Rome, and even more to those of Christ! If it came about that Rome were destroyed like Sodom, with its pope and its cardinals – and that is not impossible – the holy church would still exist.

This is what I wish to hold to: I hold the pope to be the vicar of Christ in the Roman Church. But I do not consider this to be a matter of faith . . . I also hold the following: if the pope is predestined, and exercises his pastoral office in imitation of Jesus Christ, then he is the head of the portion of the church militant that he governs. And if he governs in this way as head of all the church militant according to the law of Jesus Christ, then he is its true head under the arch-head, Our Saviour Jesus Christ. But if his life is contrary to Christ, then he is a thief, a robber, who introduces himself surreptitiously, a ravening wolf, a hypocrite and of all mortals the chief Antichrist. The Lord has warned us sufficiently to guard against false Christs and their miracles. And I also hold this: I am ready to accept with respect and reverence, as befits a faithful Christian, all that the Roman Church or the pope and his cardinals define and command to believe and to practise according to the law of Christ, but not all that the pope and his cardinals define and command in general. For nothing is more certain than that the pope and all the Curia can be deceived as to the truth as in their customs.

The last words of John Hus on the stake at Constance

God is my witness that I have never taught nor preached what is attributed to me on the testimony of false witnesses. My prime intention in my preaching and all my actions has been to extricate men from sin. I am ready to die with joy in the truth of the gospel, which I have written, taught and preached in accordance with the tradition of the holy doctors.

Execution of John Hus (1415)

3. Changes in the Christian life

Anxiety about death, disquiet over salvation and a loss of confidence in the church as an institution brought changes in the Christian way of life. Personal experience took preference over consultation with the hierarchy. That is partly the explanation of the condemnation of Joan of Arc in 1431: she had more confidence in her voices than in the bishops, monks and theologians who were in the pay of the English and the Burgundians. However, this individualism manifested itself in very different ways: in a growth of superstition and in a true deepening of the Christian life.

Quantitative piety

For some, disquiet led to a discovery of all the minor means to salvation. Some of the features described earlier on were given even greater emphasis. The cult of the saints and their relics was more flourishing than ever before, often in a familiar and irreverent way. Charles VI of France – admittedly not a very stable character – distributed the ribs of his ancestor St Louis to his relations. They in turn chopped them up into little pieces. The practice of indulgences grew; in Flanders they could be won in lotteries. Piety was measured quantitatively: masses were piled up, and 'altar' priests spent their time saying masses in order to earn their living. The piety of some, especially the rulers, was spasmodic. Moves towards devotion came after bursts of debauchery.

A deepening in religion and mysticism

There was also an emotional piety centred on the humanity of Jesus and Mary. One writer said that Christendom had received the gift of tears.

Deposition. Avigon (1455)

A good Christian had to suffer with Christ, and feel with him the anguish of his passion. The end of the Middle Ages was a period of deepening awareness of the inner life, at least for the most committed Christians. The beginning of the fourteenth century saw a flowering of mysticism, founded on theology. The Dominicans Eckhart (140)

---

(140)

Meister Eckhart

Meister Eckhart (1260–1327), born at Erfurt, a Dominican, lived in Paris, Strasbourg and Cologne. The chief representative of the Rhenish movement of mysticism, he was accused of propagating erroneous doctrines about the divine nature. He left for Avignon to defend himself, and there he died. In 1320 John XXII condemned a certain number of propositions drawn from his works, essentially sermons noted down by his disciples.

God has no name, for no one can say or understand anything about him . . . Thus if I say 'God is good', that is not true; I am good but God is not good . . . And if I also say 'God is wise', that is not true. I am wiser than he. If I say yet again, 'God is a being', that is not true; he is a being above being . . . a master says, 'If I had a God whom I could know, I would not regard him as God . . .' You must love him as he is: neither God, nor spirit, nor image; even more, the One without commingling, pure, luminous . . .

The *Devotio Moderna*: The Imitation of Christ

Whoever desires to understand and take delight in the words of Christ must strive to conform his whole life to him. Of what use is it to discourse learnedly on the Trinity, if you lack humility and therefore displease the Trinity? Lofty words do not make a man just or holy; but a good life makes him dear to God.

If you knew the whole Bible by heart, and all the teachings of the philosophers, how would this help you without the grace and love of God? 'Vanity of vanities, and all is vanity,' except to love God and serve him alone. And this is supreme wisdom – to despise the world, and draw daily nearer to the kingdom of heaven (I,1).

A humble countryman who serves God is more pleasing to him than a conceited intellectual who knows the course of the stars, but neglects his own soul . . . Restrain an inordinate desire for knowledge, in which is found much anxiety and deception . . . If it seems to you that you know a great deal and have wide experience in many fields, yet remember that there are many matters of which you are ignorant. A true understanding and humble estimate of oneself is the highest and most valuable of all lessons (I,2).

No motive, even that of affection for anyone, can justify the doing of evil. But to help someone in need, a good word may sometimes be left, or a better undertaken in its place (I,15).

'The kingdom of God is within you,' says Our Lord. Turn to the Lord with all your heart, forsake this sorry world, and your soul shall find rest. Learn to turn from worldly things, and give yourself to spiritual things, and you will see the kingdom of God come within you (II,1).

My son, you cannot always burn with zeal for virtue, nor remain constantly in high contemplation; the weakness of sinful human nature will at times compel you to descend to lesser things, and bear with sorrow the burdens of this present life (III,51).

(1260–1327), Tauler (1300–1361) and Suso (1295–1366), and then the Flemish priest Ruysbroek (1293–1381) are the best representatives of this Rhenish mysticism: the quest for union with God, surpassing all attempts to depict it, is known as negative theology. At the turn of the fourteenth and fifteenth centuries, the desire for a deep spiritual life took hold of men and women outside the convents and monasteries. They sometimes formed small suspect groups, like the Beguines and the Beghards, or a third order[1], like that of Catherine of Siena (1347–1380). More involved in the world of their day, these latter set great store on religious psychology and ways of making progress in the spiritual life. In works increasingly accessible to a wider audience, they suggested spiritual exercises. It is in this connection that we talk of the movement of 'modern devotion', of which the *Imitation of Christ*, often attributed to Thomas à Kempis (1380–1471), is the best-known example. Some of them, keeping a safe distance from a mysticism which seemed to them to be too speculative, dedicated themselves to educating the Christian people. Jean Gerson (1363–1429), Chancellor of the University of Paris and a theologian at the Council of Constance, devoted much of his time to preaching, to spiritual direction and to the religious education of children. It was in this atmosphere of 'modern devotion' that the men of the Renaissance and the Reformation, including Erasmus and Luther, were steeped.

[1]The third order is so-called with reference to the first order (men) and the second order (women). The third order is an association of laity attached to an Order: Dominican, Franciscan, Carmelite and so on.

IV · Meanwhile, in the East . . .

The Council of Florence in 1439 directed our attention back towards the Greek church and its offshoot, the Russian church, and also towards several Eastern churches which signed ephemeral acts of union with Rome. Often these churches are only remembered in terms of their ambiguous relations with the Latin world: on the Greek side, the hope of military assistance, and on the Latin side, the reaffirmation of Roman primacy over all the churches. We in the West often tend to be ignorant of the rich history and spiritual tradition of the Christians of the East.

1. Churches in the Slavonic world

The Bulgarian and Serbian churches wavered between allegiance to Constantinople and Rome. However, as descendants of Cyril and Methodius, they drew their inspiration primarily from Constantinople when working out their liturgy, their monastic life and their ecclesiastical law. The two churches became autocephalous (with their own head) during the thirteenth century. The Bulgarians had their patriarch in Tarnovo and the Serbians theirs in Pec. When the two states fell to the Turks, their churches went into the shadows.

The principality of Kiev was the heart of the first Russian church until 1240, the date of the destruction of Kiev by the Mongols. Constantinople appointed the Metropolitan of Kiev and passed on its liturgy and its artistic standards to the Russians (e.g. the church of St Sophia in Kiev). The princes of Kiev kept up good relations with the Latin West, through commercial dealings and intermarriage. After 1240, the Russian principalities of the north, especially that of Moscow, undertook the rebuilding of Kiev and fought against the occupying Mongol forces. Relations had never been good between these Russians of the north and the Latins. In 1242, St

Alexander Nevsky, prince of Novgorod, repelled the attacks of the Teutonic Knights, a military and religious Order which was reconverted after the loss of the Holy Land. In 1325, the Metropolitan of All Russia was installed in Moscow.

After the rejection of the union of Florence, a Russian council proclaimed the autonomy of the Russian church by electing the Metropolitan of Moscow in 1448.

2. The end of the Byzantine empire

The Byzantine empire, which was reconstituted in 1261, after the interlude of the Latin empire of Constantinople, struggled hopelessly for survival for two centuries. It was soon reduced to two small 'islets' around Constantinople on the Bosphorus and Mystra in the Peloponnese. In April 1453, Constantinople was besieged by the Turks. On 28 May, processions wended their way around the city, and a last office was celebrated in St Sophia. The Emperor Constantine received the last rites. On the morning of 29 May, the Turks took the city by storm. The emperor died on the battlements. The Sultan Mahomet II rode on horseback into St Sophia, which was strewn with corpses. The second Rome had fallen. Moscow carried on the heritage as the 'third Rome' (1461).

3. Eastern spirituality

Several common factors held together the churches of Bulgaria, Serbia, Russia and Greece: their monastically inspired spirituality and their artistic tradition, which is summed up in icons.

The holy mountain of Athos was covered with monasteries representing all the Orthodox nationalities. After a stay on Athos the monks often went back to their own countries, and it was quite usual for bishops and patriarchs to be

Legend:
- Patriarchate or Eastern autocephalous church
- Eastern monastery
- Latin archdiocese
- Eastern diocese
- - - Dividing line between the Eastern churches and the Latin church

Uppsala

Novgorod

Jaroslav

Trinity

Riga

Moscow
1325

Lund

Riazan

Smolensk

Gnierzo

POLAND

Kiev

Prague

BOHEMIA

Gran

HUNGARY

Venice

Peć

Tarnovo

SERBIA

Rome

Ochrida

BULGARIA

Constantinople

Athos

Meteores

Athens

Antioch

Alexandria

Eastern Churches in the Fourteenth Century

Mohammed II, Conqueror of Constantinople
(1453)

The church of St Peter and St Paul in
Jaroslav (Russia?)

chosen from amongst them. We still have the names of St Gregory of Sinai and of St Theodosius (fourteenth century) for Bulgaria; of St Sava for Serbia; of St Sergius (1314–1392), founder of the monastery of the Holy Trinity in the heart of the forests north of Moscow, of Gregory Palamas (1296–1359), monk of Athos, and later Archbishop of Thessalonica, and many others. Gregory was the exponent of the great spiritual current of Orthodox monasticism known as hesychasm, both a theory and a practice of contemplation which can be defined as the quest for repose (Greek *hesychia*) in God.

Many of the monastery churches have preserved mosaics, frescoes and icons from this period. Perhaps the best known of all is the icon of the Holy Trinity painted by the Russian monk Andrei Rublev in 1411.

For further reading

G. Barraclough, *The Medieval Papacy*, Thames and Hudson 1968

J. Huizinga, *The Waning of the Middle Ages*, Penguin Books 1955

H. Obermann, *Forerunners of the Reformation*, Fortress Press 1981

Steven Runciman, *The Fall of Constantintople*, Cambridge University Press 1965

The Jesus Prayer

Nicephorus the Solitary (second half of the thirteenth century), who came from Calabria, was a monk at Constantinople and then on Mount Athos. He composed a treatise *On Keeping the Heart*. He put forward a method of prayer which involved psychological and physiological techniques.

First of all let your life be tranquil, free from all care, and at peace with all. Then enter your room, shut yourself in, and, sitting in a corner, say what I shall tell you:

'You know that we only exhale our breath, the air that we inhale, because of our heart . . . Sit down, recollect your spirit, introduce it – I mean your spirit – into your nostrils; that is the route your breath takes to reach the heart.

Push it, force it to descend to your heart at the same time as the air is breathed in. When it is there, you will see the joy that follows; you will have nothing to regret. Just as the man who returns home after an absence can no longer contain his joy at being able to see his wife and children again, so the spirit, when it is united to the soul overflows with joy and ineffable delight. So, my brother, accustom your spirit not to be hasty to emerge.

While your spirit is there, you must neither be silent nor remain idle. But do not have any occupation or meditation other than the cry, 'Lord Jesus Christ, Son of God, have mercy on me!' No truce, not at any price. This practice, by keeping your spirit protected from wandering, makes it inpregnable and beyond the reach of suggestions from the enemy; each day it raises it in the love and the desire of God.

Little Philokalia of the Prayer of the Heart. The Philokalia ('love of beauty') is a collection of Eastern spiritual texts published in the eighteenth century.

After Fifteen Centuries . . .

By the middle of the fifteenth century, the papacy seemed to have recovered its glory and its prestige. The last antipope in history had abdicated in 1449. A huge crowd had come to Rome for the jubilee of the Holy Year in 1450. Once again, a pope was able to affirm that 'the Roman pontiffs are the masters of mankind and of all that appertains to humanity'. Was Christendom going to relive the glorious hours of the thirteenth century?

But was it still possible to speak of Christendom? Europe had become a Europe of princes. The Hundred Years War, which ended in 1453, had revealed national antagonisms which were only to grow worse in the future. Disillusioned, Pope Pius II (1458–1464) declared: 'Christendom no longer has a head whom it respects nor one to whom it owes obedience; the titles of emperor and supreme pontiff are only empty names, and those who bear them are only vain images in the eyes of Christendom.' The popes of the late fifteenth century behaved more like Italian princes than like world-wide pontiffs.

However, the people of Europe had good reasons for wanting to unite in the name of a common ideal. The Roman empire had disappeared with Constantinople, now renamed Istanbul, and the Turks were advancing with rapid strides towards the heart of Europe. It there was to be a crusade, it was now or never. Pius II decided to go at the head of the expedition himself. But only a few adventurers turned up at the meeting place, Ancona, and the pope died, embittered, in 1464.

An epoch had come to an end. Another age was dawning. With the rediscovery of ancient sources, literature and works of art, a new culture was beginning to develop. The church was no longer the spearhead of intellectual life, as it had been in past centuries. The invention of printing was going to revolutionize communication. Who would have control?

In spite of its squabbles and divisions, Latin Christendom had always succeded in regaining its unity through the Middle Ages. In the early years of the sixteenth century, the division caused by the Reformation was to be final.

To the west of the continent of Europe, Islam was to be banished from Spain in 1492. The Portuguese had already gained a foothold in Africa, at Ceuta, in 1415. It was the beginning of the discovery of new worlds. Restricted and blocked as it was in the East, did the church suspect that its future lay not with the restoration of Christendom in Europe, but with preaching the gospel to the whole world?

A second volume of *How to Read Church History* will take us from these radical changes at the end of the fifteenth century to the last decades of the twentieth century in which we are now living.

CHRONOLOGICAL TABLES

POLITICAL AND RELIGIOUS EVENTS		EMPERORS
Death and resurrection of Jesus/Pentecost	30	TIBERIUS (14–37)
Martyrdom of Stephen	36	
Conversion of Paul	37	CALIGULA (37–41)
Paul's first mission	45	CLAUDIUS (41–54)
'Council' of Jerusalem	49	
Expulsion of the Jews from Rome/Paul's second mission	50	
Paul at Corinth	51	
Paul's third mission	53	NERO (54–68)
Paul's arrest in Jerusalem and imprisonment in Caesarea	58	
Paul transferred to Rome as a prisoner	60	
Nero's persecution; Martyrdom of Peter (?)	64	
Martyrdom of Paul in Rome (?)	67	
Destruction of Jerusalem and the temple by Titus	70	VESPASIAN (69–79)
Eruption of Vesuvius; destruction of Pompeii	79	TITUS (79–81)
Exile of John to Patmos; Clement Bishop of Rome	95	DOMITIAN (81–96)
Death of John (?)	100	TRAJAN (98–117)
Persecution in Bithynia: Pliny's letter to Trajan	111	
New Jewish revolt	132	HADRIAN (117–138)
Martyrdom of Polycarp at Smyrna (or 169)	161	ANTONINUS (138–162)
Martyrdom of Justin in Rome	163	MARCUS AURELIUS (162–180)
Beginnings of Montanism	170	
The martyrs of Lyons; Irenaeus Bishop of Lyons	177	
Conversion of Abgar king of Edessa (?)	179	COMMODUS (180–192)
The paschal dispute at the time of Victor, Bishop of Rome	190	SEPTIMUS SEVERUS (193–211)
Civil war: Lyons sacked by Septimus Severus	197	
Persecution: prohibition of Jewish and Christian proselytism	202	
All freemen in the empire are Roman citizens	212	CARACALLA (211–217)
Callixtus, Bishop of Rome, and the schism of Hippolytus	217	
Beginning of the Sassanid dynasty in Persia	226	ALEXANDER SEVERUS (222–235)
Persecution: the Bishop of Rome, Pontian and Hippolytus deported	235	MAXIMIN (235–238)
Shapur, king of kings in Persia	241	
Beginning of the preaching of Mani	242	
Cyprian Bishop of Carthage	249	DECIUS (249–251)
General persecution: martyrdom of Fabian Bishop of Rome	250	
Cornelius, Bishop of Rome; Novatian schism	251	VALERIAN (253–260)
Synod of Carthage on the baptism of heretics	256	
General persecution: arrest of the heads of the church	257	
Martyrdom of Cyprian, Sixtus Bishop of Rome, Laurence	258	
The Emperor Valerian prisoner of Shapur	259	
Edict of tolerance for Christians	260	GALLIENUS (260–268)
Condemnation of Paul of Samosata at the Synod of Antioch	268	
Antony in the desert (?)	270	AURELIAN (270–275)
Barbarian invasions; martyrdom of Mani	277	
Conversion of Tiridates king of Armenia	280	
Diocletian emperor; beginning of the Later Empire	284	DIOCLETIAN (284–305)
Maximian given rank of Augustus	285	MAXIMIAN
The emperors Constantius Chlorus and Galerius made Caesar	293	Tetrarchy
Edict of persecution of the Manichaeans	297	
Edict of persecution against the Christians	303	
New edicts	304	
Abdication of Diocletian; new tetrarchy	305	
Constantine emperor in Gaul; anarchy and civil war	306	
Edict of tolerance by Galerius	311	
Constantine's victory at the Milvian Bridge; the Labarum	312	
General peace in the church	313	CONSTANTINE-LICINIUS

WRITERS (by region, approximate date ranges shown by vertical lines in the original)

- **Italy:** SENECA, TACITUS, CLEMENT OF ROME, HERMAS, HIPOPOLYTUS
- **Gaul:** IRENAEUS
- **Africa:** TERTULLIAN, CYPRIAN, LACTANTIUS
- **Greece:** PLUTARCH, EPICTETUS, CELSUS
- **Egypt:** Letter of Barnabas, To Diognetus, CLEMENT OF ALEX., ORIGEN, PLOTINUS, PORPHYRY
- **Syria Palest.:** JOSEPHUS, Didache, IGNATIUS, JUSTIN, LUCIAN, EUSEBIUS
- **Asia Minor:** POLYCARP, MELITO
- **Mesopotamia:** MANI

The names in italics indicate non-Christian authors; the names in lower-case letters indicate the titles of works by unknown authors. The names of Latin writers are in bold. The others wrote in Greek.

193

POLITICAL AND RELIGIOUS EVENTS		WRITERS AND FATHERS OF THE CHURCH							BISHOPS OF ROME	EMPERORS	
		Italy	Gaul Spain	Africa	Greece Egypt Const.	Syria Palest.	Asia Minor	Mesopotamia		West	East
Council of Arles (Donatist Affair)	314		HILARY		ATHANASIUS / EUSEBIUS / CYRIL of Jerusalem			EPHRAEM	SYLVESTER (314–335)	CONSTANTINE (306–	LICINIUS 313–324
Condemnation of Arius at Alexandria	318										
COUNCIL OF NICAEA	325										
Athanasius Bishop of Alexandria	328									CONSTANTINE 337)	
Foundation of Constantinople	330										
Deposition of Athanasius and death of Arius	335								JULIUS (337–352)	CONSTANT (337–350)	CONSTANTIUS (337–
Ulphilas Bishop (Arian) of the Goths	340										
Council of Sardica (Sophia)	343					EPIPHANIUS of Cyprus					
Death of St Pachomius	346										
Hilary Bishop of Poitiers	350						BASIL				
Exile of the Nicene bishops Liberius and Hilary	355						GREGORY of Nazianzus		LIBERIUS (352–366)	CONSTANTIUS 361)	
Death of St Antony	356						GREGORY of Nyssa				
Compromise councils with Arianism	359										
General amnesty by the Emperor Julian	361		AMBROSE							JULIAN (361–363)	
Death of Julian in the Persian war	363										
First national council of Armenia	365	JEROME			CYRIL of Alexandria				DAMASUS (366–384)		
Martin Bishop of Tours, Basil Bishop of Caesarea	370									VALENTINIAN I (364–375)	VALENS (364–378)
Ambrose Bishop of Milan	374										
Disaster at Adrianopolis (death of Valens)	378									GRATIAN (375–383)	THEODOSIUS 378–
Christianity a state religion	380			AUGUSTINE							
COUNCILS OF CONSTANTINOPLE and Aquileia	381								VALENTINIAN II (383–392)		
Jerome at Rome with Bishop Damasus	382				JOHN CHRYSOSTOM				SIRICIUS (384–399)		
Priscillian executed as a heretic	385					THEODORET of Cyr					
Conversion of Augustine	386				SOCRATES						
Jerome at Bethlehem	389										
Massacre of Thessalonica/Latin the official liturgical language	390									THEODOSIUS 395)	
Complete prohibition of pagan worship	391										
Definitive division of the empire	395									HONORIUS (395–423)	ARCADIUS (395–408)
Augustine Bishop of Hippo	396										
Deaths of Ambrose and Martin of Tours	397										
John Chrysostom Bishop of Constantinople	398										
The Confessions of St Augustine	400								INNOCENT (401–417)		
Death of John Chrysostom/Great Germanic invasions	407										THEODOSIUS (408–450)
Rome taken and pillaged by Alaric	410										
Condemnation of Pelagius	411		VINCENT of Lerins								
Persecution of Christians in Persia	420								CELESTINE (422–432)	VALENTINIAN III (425–455)	
Augustine finishes The City of God	427										
Death of Augustine in besieged Hippo	430										
COUNCIL OF EPHESUS	431										
Beginning of the apostolate of St Patrick	432										
Robber Synod of Ephesus	449								LEO (440–461)		
COUNCIL OF CHALCEDON/Attila in Gaul	451	LEO									MARCIAN (450–457)
Capture of Rome by Genseric	455										LEO I
End of Roman Empire in West	476										
Persecution of Christians by Vandals	478									ROMULUS AUGUSTULUS (475–476)	
Clovis King of the Franks	482		CAESARIUS of Arles								ZENO (474–491)
Persian church opts for Nestorianism	486										
Armenian church opts for Monophysitism	491		GREGORY of Tours						SYMMACHUS (498–514)	CLOVIS (482–511)	ANASTASIUS 491–518
Baptism of Clovis (?)	500									THEODORIC (493–526)	
Caesarius Bishop of Arles	503									CLOTAIRE (511–561)	JUSTIN (518–527)
Benedict at Monte Cassino	529										
Justinian Code/Justinian's reconquests	534										
Dedication of St Sophia in Constantinople	537	GREGORY							VIGILIUS (537–555)		JUSTINIAN (527–565)
Rule of St Benedict	540										
Condemnation of Origen	544										
SECOND COUNCIL OF CONSTANTINOPLE	553										
Slav invasion in the East	587										
Evangelization of the Angles by Augustine of Canterbury	596								GREGORY (590–614)		
		Latin			Greek		Syriac				

POLITICAL AND RELIGIOUS EVENTS		WRITERS/FOUNDERS	POPES	FRANCE	GERMANY	ENGLAND	BYZAN-TIUM	EAST
Hegirah, birth of Islam	622						HERACLIUS	OMEYAD
Jerusalem in the hands of Moslem Arabs	638						(610–641)	Caliphs of
Third Council of Constantinople (Sixth								Damascus
ecumenical)	681							(650–750)
Spain conquered by Arabs	711						LEO III	
Charles Martel halts Arabs at Poitiers	732	BONIFACE	STEPHEN II				(717–741)	ABASSID
Rise of the Papal States	756		(752–757)		CHARLEMAGNE			Caliphs of
Second Council of Nicaea (Seventh ecumenical)	767		LEO III		(768–814)			Baghdad
Charlemagne Emperor of the West	800		(795–816)					(750-1258)
Treaty of Verdun (France/Germany/Lotharingia)	843	AL HALLAJ (Iran–Baghdad)	JOHN VIII					
Cyril and Methodius among the Slavs	864	(858–922)	(872–882)					
Foundation of abbey of Cluny	910				OTHO THE			
Otho emperor of Holy Roman Empire	962				GREAT			
Monastic foundation of Mount Athos	963				(936–973)			
Baptism of Polish Duke Miesco	967			HUGH			BASIL II	
Baptism of Vladimir, Prince of Kiev	989			CAPET			(976–1025)	
Stephen King of Hungary	1001		SYLVESTER	(987–996)				
Schism between Greek and Roman churches	1054	ANSELM (1033–1109)	II (999–1003)					
Decree on election of pope by cardinals	1059				HENRY IV			
Byzantines beaten by Turks at Manzilert	1071		GREGORY		(1056–1106)	WILLIAM		SELDJUCID
Reform decrees of Gregory VII	1075		VII			THE CON-		Turks
Submission of Henry IV at Canossa	1077	BRUNO (1035–1101)	(1073–1085)			QUEROR	ALEXIS	
Foundation of La Chartreuse by Bruno	1084		URBAN II			(1066–1087)	COMNENUS	
Clermont: Urban II preaches the crusade	1095		(1088–1099)				(1081–1118)	
Foundation of Citeaux	1098	NORBERT (1098–1134)						
Jerusalem taken by the crusaders	1099							
Concordat of Worms (end of investiture dispute)	1122	ABELARD (1079–1142)						
First Lateran Council	1123	BERNARD OF CLAIRVAUX						
Second Lateran Council	1139	(1090–1153)						
Condemnation of Abelard/Decree of Gratian	1140		ALEX-		FREDERIC	HENRY		
Bernard of Clairvaux preaches the second crusade	1146		ANDER III		BARBA-	PLAN-		
Assassination of Thomas à Becket at Canterbury	1170		(1159–1181)		ROSSA	TAGENET		
Valdo preaches poverty in Lyons	1173	VALDO			(1152–1190)	(1154–1189)		
Submission of Frederick Barbarossa at Venice	1177	JOACHIM OF FIORE		PHILIP				
Third Lateran Council	1179	(1130–1202)		AUGUSTUS				GENGHIS
Loss of Jerusalem by the crusaders	1187			(1180–1223)		RICHARD		KHAN
Beginning of the third crusade	1189	DOMINIC (1170–1221)	INNOCENT			COEUR DE		(1188–1227)
The Latins take Constantinople (Fourth crusade)	1204		III			LION		
Albigensian crusade	1208	FRANCIS OF ASSISI	(1198–1216)			(1189–1199)		
Beginning of the Franciscans	1209	(1181–1226)						
Victory of Spanish Christians at Las Navas de Tolosa	1212							
Fourth Lateran Council	1215		HONORIUS					
Approval of Friars Preachers	1216		III		FREDERICK			
Origin of Papal Inquisition	1232	BONAVENTURE	(1216–1223)	ST LOUIS	II			
The Mongols invade Europe	1237	(1221–1274)		(1226–1270)	(1216–1250)			
The stake at Montségur	1244	THOMAS AQUINAS	INNOCENT IV					
First Council of Lyons	1245	(1227–1274)	(1243–1254)					
Restoration of Byzantine Empire	1261	JOHN OF PLANO CARPINI						
Death of St Louis at Tunis	1270	MARCO POLO (1254–1324)	GREGORY X				MICHAEL	
Second Council of Lyons	1245	ECKHART.(1260–1327)	(1271–1276)				PALAEO-	
Loss of the Holy Land/Helvetic Confederation	1291	JOHN OF MONTE	BONIFACE	PHILIP THE			LOGUS	
Bull Unam sanctam	1302	CORVINO (1247–1328)	VIII	FAIR			(1261–1282)	Mongol
Council of Vienne: suppression of the Templars	1311	WILLIAM OF OCKHAM	(1294–1303)	(1285–1314)				dynasty in
Beginning of Hundred Years' War	1337	(died 1350)	The popes of			EDWARD III		China
Black Death	1348	GREGORY PALAMAS	Avignon			(1327–1377)		(1279–1368)
Beginning of Great Schism	1378	(died 1359)	(1305–1377)					
The Poles defeat the Teutonic Knights	1410	NICHOLAS CABASILAS						
Beginning of Council of Constance	1414	(died 1371)						
John Huss burned at Constance	1415	CATHERINE OF SIENA	The Great	CHARLES V				TAMBERLAINE
Joan of Arc burned at Rouen/Council of Basle	1431	(1347–1380)	Schism	(1364–1380				(1363–1405)
Florence: reunion of Latins and Greeks	1439	ST SERGIUS (died 1392)	(1378–1417)		SIGISMUND		CONSTAN-	OTTOMAN
Russian church becomes autocephalous	1448	JOHN HUSS (1363–1429)	EUGENIUS IV		(1411–1437)		TINE	Turks
Constantinople taken by Turks/End of Hundred		JEAN GERSON	(1431–1447)	CHARLES VII			ORAGASES	MOHAMED II
Years' War	1453	(1363–1429)		(1422–1461)			(1429–1453)	(1451–1481)